The Remarkable Story of Fred Spiksley

In memory of
Martin Westby (1956-2020), football historian and author.
David Wheeler (1957-2017), teacher and publisher.

The Remarkable Story of Fred Spiksley

The First Working-Class Football Hero

Mark Metcalf
With research by Clive Nicholson &
Ralph Nicholson

AN IMPRINT OF PEN & SWORD BOOKS LTD.
YORKSHIRE – PHILADELPHIA

First published in Great Britain as *Flying Over an Olive Grove* in 2016
by Red Axe Books

First published in Paperback in 2021 by
Pen & Sword History
An imprint of
Pen & Sword Books Ltd
Yorkshire - Philadelphia

Copyright © Mark Metcalf, Clive Nicholson & Ralph Nicholson, 2021

ISBN 978 1 52677 531 3

The right of Mark Metcalf, Clive Nicholson & Ralph Nicholson to be identified as the Authors of this work has been asserted by them in accordance with the Copyright, Designs and Patents Act 1988.

A CIP catalogue record for this book is available from the British Library.

All rights reserved. No part of this book may be reproduced or transmitted in any form or by any means, electronic or mechanical, including photocopying, recording or by any information storage and retrieval system, without permission from the Publisher in writing.

Printed and bound in England
By CPI Group (UK) Ltd, Croydon, CR0 4YY

Pen & Sword Books Ltd. incorporates the Imprints of Pen & Sword Archaeology, Atlas, Aviation, Battleground, Discovery, Family History, History, Maritime, Military, Naval, Politics, Railways, Select, Transport, True Crime, Fiction, Frontline Books, Leo Cooper, Praetorian Press, Seaforth Publishing, Wharncliffe and White Owl.

For a complete list of Pen & Sword titles please contact

PEN & SWORD BOOKS LIMITED
47 Church Street, Barnsley, South Yorkshire, S70 2AS, England
E-mail: enquiries@pen-and-sword.co.uk
Website: www.pen-and-sword.co.uk

or

PEN AND SWORD BOOKS
1950 Lawrence Rd, Havertown, PA 19083, USA
E-mail: uspen-and-sword@casematepublishers.com
Website: www.penandswordbooks.com

Contents

Acknowledgements		vii
Chapter 1	Origins of Football and a Football Genius	1
Chapter 2	Sacked!	9
Chapter 3	Under Madden's Wing	18
Chapter 4	Birthday Disaster	26
Chapter 5	Trinity Triumph	34
Chapter 6	League Aspirations	42
Chapter 7	A New Hero Rises	49
Chapter 8	Back-To-Back England Hat Tricks	59
Chapter 9	Falling Short	74
Chapter 10	No Nets	85
Chapter 11	All The Way to The Palace	95
Chapter 12	1896 Hero	102
Chapter 13	Number One Footballer in The World	115
Chapter 14	Best of The Best	129
Chapter 15	End of an Era	136
Chapter 16	The Owlerton Gamble	142
Chapter 17	Champions of England	156
Chapter 18	The Bell Starts to Toll	164
Chapter 19	Lobbying at Elland Road	169
Chapter 20	London Calling	173

Chapter 21	Treading The Boards with Charlie Chaplin	181
Chapter 22	Bankrupt	186
Chapter 23	Germany 1914	195
Chapter 24	America's Missionary	201
Chapter 25	A Final Flirtation	208
Chapter 26	Return to Zabo	212
Chapter 27	The Club by The Coast	217
Chapter 28	A Focus on Youth	220
Chapter 29	Scientific Football	226
Chapter 30	One Final Bet	233
Fred Spiksley's Achievements		235
Bibliography		237
Index		241

Acknowledgements

Bengt Ågren, Alan Biggs, Michael Barrett, Paul Brown, Robert Boyling, Trevor Braithwait, John Brodie, James Callerdine, Shaun Campbell, Darron Childs, Denis Clareborough, Tom Crawshaw, J. Crowell, Mike Davage, Paul Days, Kal Singh Dhindsa, Jason Dickinson, Tim Downing, Susan Edlington, Keith Farnsworth, Jim Fox, Andy George, Richard Gibson, Steve Gordos, Mark Harvey, Eva-Kajsa Hedström, John Harvey, Stuart Hibberd, Brett Hudson, Peter Holme and Alex Jackson at the National Football Museum, Thomas Junglander, Richard Kane and Rob Hughes at Gainsborough Trinity FC, Steven Kay, Michael Knighton, John Lerwill, Colin Lobban and Richard McBrearty from the Scottish Football Museum, Krister Malmsten, Phil Martin, Adam Marseille, Roy Massey, Luis Javier Bravo Mayor, Andy Mitchell, Simon Mullock, Lynda Nicholson, Randall Northam, Jonas Nystedt, Tom O'Neill, George Orr, Pascal Bolder, Martin Peranrnau, Karen Shimmon, Bernd Siegler, Joyce Spicksley, Graham Spicksley, Richard Stonehouse, Andrew Stothard, Jen Sugden, Tom Sutcliffe, Gordon Taylor, Chris Waddle, R.D. Wells, Martin Westby, David Wheeler and Paul Whitaker. The staff at the following libraries: Sheffield, Gainsborough, Glossop, Manchester, Leeds, Fulham, Boston Spa and the British Library. The staff at Gainsborough Heritage Association, the National Archives and Lincolnshire FA. The Delvers of Gainsborough.

Chapter 1

Origins of Football and a Football Genius

The formative years of the modern game and Fred Spiksley

Frederick Spiksley was born at 1 Willoughby Street, Gainsborough, on 25 January 1870. His father, Edward, was a boilermaker at the nearby Britannia Ironworks. When informed that his third child was imminent he rushed home from work. He found Sarah, his wife of five years, being ably assisted by her mother, Lucy, and a midwife. The baby was born without complications and further boosted England's population, which rose from 7.75 million to 30 million during the nineteenth century. Fred's brothers, John Edward, who was always called 'Ted', and William, were aged 4 years and 23 months respectively. Their father had, rightly, celebrated their births lustily. Unfortunately, when he went to record their arrivals at the Register Office, his lack of formal education, strong countryside accent and alcoholic stupor combined to make him unintelligible to the registrar. Ted became a 'Picksley' and William a 'Spicksley'. Fred was correctly recorded as a Spiksley. He was baptised by Reverend R W Charteris on St Matthew's Day, 21 September 1870 at Gainsborough's Holy Trinity Church. Fred later joined his brothers as a pupil at Holy Trinity Church School.

Fred's parents came from Lincolnshire fenland families. Fred's paternal grandfather, another Edward, was an agricultural labourer for a local landowner on Metheringham Fen, where he occupied a tied cottage with his wife, Rebecca, and their five children. Metheringham Fen's main crops were wheat, barley, oats, turnips and potatoes. From an early age all four boys in the family helped till, sow and reap the soil. Fred's mother's parents, William, a carpenter, and Lucy Porter, an excellent seamstress who made dresses, lived on the Nocton Fen.

It is not known how much schooling Fred's parents had, as it wasn't until the Education Act of 1870 that universal education became enshrined in law. The driving force behind the act was Britain's need to remain internationally competitive at a time of rapid industrialisation that in its wake swept up people from the countryside and deposited them in urban locations. These included Sarah Porter, Fred's mother, who moved to Gainsborough in the early 1860s. In 1800 around 25 per cent of the UK's population was urban-based, compared with 77 per cent by 1900.

At 19, Edward Spiksley still had to share a bed with his brothers, William and Thomas. His farm labourer's pay was inadequate. Attempts to create a trade union for agricultural workers at Tolpuddle, Dorset, in 1833 had led to its organisers being deported under the 1797 Unlawful Oaths Act. As rural workers were unable to unite and organise, their wages consequently remained often pitifully low.

There were much higher pay rates within the expanding industrial and manufacturing sectors of the economy. In 1862, Edward's parents helped him load his basic furniture items on to a handcart for the 6-mile journey to nearby Lincoln. There he found suitable cheap lodgings before seeking work in the burgeoning engineering businesses. Messrs Ruston, Proctor and Company at the Sheaf Ironworks had a healthy order book that meant they needed good strong workers. The young man became a labourer in the boiler workshop and set out to save some money.

In the meantime, James and Henry Marshall, on inheriting their father William's ironworks business in Gainsborough, converted it into a joint stock company. From 1862 to 1864 they extended the existing Britannia Works by installing modern machinery on a 4.5 acre site on which 550 people were employed in various manufacturing workshops, including a plate furnace and facilities for rolling, grinding, drilling and riveting. Finished products included threshing machines for harvesting crops.

Marshall's would eventually employ 6,000 workers on a 40-acre site, and 16 million bricks were fired in the company's brick kilns, using the red clay excavated from the site when it was first levelled to expand the old ironworks. While the company dominated the small Lincolnshire town, there were also other smaller engineering employers such as J B Edlington, which began manufacturing hay-making machines in 1867 and still exists today, and Rose's, which manufactured tobacco and sweet-wrapping machinery.

In the spring of 1864 news reached Edward Spiksley that Marshall's was offering 2 shillings (10p) a week more than in his current post. This was a significant sum as the average craft weekly wage was four to 5 shillings (25p) with labourers on under 3 shillings (15p). As the new factory neared completion a steady stream of engineers, platemakers and boilermakers migrated to Gainsborough on the guarantee of better pay and conditions. Many new workers obtained accommodation from the company, the forward-thinking brothers building rows of terraced houses to provide accommodation for them. They later established the Gainsborough Building Society, which existed independently until it merged with the Yorkshire Building Society in 2001. This provided finance at reasonable mortgage rates for employees wanting to buy their own home.

Edward Spiksley moved to Gainsborough to work for Marshall's in 1864 with the added appeal that his childhood sweetheart, Sarah, now aged 17, lived in the town with her mother Lucy. Edward rented 3 Willoughby Street, a terraced house 50 yards from the free-flowing River Trent, and swiftly approached Lucy Porter requesting to marry her daughter. She agreed and the pair were married on 10 December 1864.

The couple's first child, Ted, was born on 23 December 1865 and William arrived on 30 December 1868. After Fred was born in 1870, their fourth child was born on 12 November 1875. To the Spiksleys' joy it was a girl, who was christened Florence Maud. However, tragedy struck when she died only thirty-six days later on 18 December 1875. She was buried in Gainsborough's Holy Trinity churchyard. The gravestone is still standing today.

Fred, began school at the age of 5 and although unaware of it at the time, many important things had happened in the world of football in the years surrounding his birth.

By the nineteenth century a very rough and ready form of mass rugby football had been played in Britain for centuries. Games that were played in towns lasted for many days and had goals many miles apart. The authorities had unsuccessfully attempted to prevent what were frequently little more than mass brawls. Now, with the countryside gradually emptying, restrictions could be imposed more easily. The 1829 Metropolitan Police Act heralded the advent of modern policing and in 1835, Parliament banned football on the highways. The annual ritual football matches – some of which still exist today, such as at Ashbourne, in Derbyshire – were successfully suppressed, often by violent methods.

Around the same time, major public schools were pushing ahead with playing football but with far fewer players. It seems reasonable to assume that the impetus must have, in part, derived from the earlier examples of mob football, although there is no concrete proof of this. However, with each school playing its own version of the game, which was generally dependent upon the surroundings in which it was staged, problems arose over which rules to use when the schools met. One of the key points of dispute was the use of hands, which was taboo at Eton but favoured at Rugby. The dispute would eventually be ended when two different games emerged: football and rugby.

The first time rules were put into written form was in 1845 for the game played at Rugby School. This undoubtedly acted as the impetus for those who favoured a game with the minimum use of hands to put into print their own versions, and Eton has a written set of rules dated October 1847. The following year the Cambridge (University) Rules were drawn up and although no written copy exists, they appear to have functioned quite well.

Following discussions between representatives from Cambridge University and the public schools of Harrow, Eton, Shrewsbury and Rugby, new Cambridge rules were compiled in 1856 and further refined in 1863. The opening game played under them took place on 20 November that year, when Cambridge Old Etonians and Cambridge Old Harrovians met under a set of rules – including eleven players per side – that remain recognisable over 150 years later.

It would be wrong to pretend this was a seamless transition to a universal playing code, as many schools continued to play their own versions of football. Consequently, there remained no single body able to command the authority of all those playing the game, even after the initiative by Ebenezer Cobb Morley from Barnes football club led to the formation of the Football Association (FA) on 26 October 1863. Such was the FA's lack of authority that by 1867, it had just ten members. Eton and Westminster stayed away. So while the public schools had saved football, it also needed some practical men to take it forward. Successive revolutions in play and organisation were ultimately to be imposed by teams of largely working-class men in Scotland and England.

Derived from the local cricket club, Sheffield Football Club had been established in 1857. Games took place between teams composed of members of the club which, along with the rules, were the culmination of matches between local players who had come together over the previous years or so to kick a ball about for pleasure. The games were crude but, unlike earlier forms of football, they rarely became riotous. Corners, free kicks and crossbars were pioneered, the use of hands died out quickly and a set of rules was being established making it possible for teams to face each other on a common front.

Crowds, too, were growing and in 1867 the first knockout cup competition outside the public schools was held, with Hallam beating local rivals Norfolk 2-1 in the final. A rival Cromwell Cup, open to clubs under two years old and donated by Theatre Royal manager Oliver Cromwell, came into existence the following year and was won by the newly-created Wednesday FC.

At the FA's 1867 AGM, William Chesterman, Sheffield's FA delegate and secretary of Sheffield FC, was one of six men present. He brought a letter describing the advances made in his locality and expressed strong support for the FA. The previous year, on 31 March, Sheffield had faced a representative London XI in Battersea Park, an event that signalled each region was keen to overcome the rules differences. Football was growing in the capital and on

26 January 1867, *The Field* magazine had identified many metropolitan sides that were playing similar games under rules used at Charterhouse and Westminster. These were not too different from the rules adopted in Sheffield.

By the start of 1868 there were twenty-nine clubs within the FA, making it possible to expand the FA committee to include the Old Etonian Arthur Kinnaird, aged just 21. As a player, he went on to appear in nine FA Cup finals from 1873–1883. However, he was just as remarkable off the pitch, serving the FA as treasurer for thirteen years and president for thirty-three years.

In 1871 match officials were incorporated into the rules so that an umpire was appointed for each half of the field, although only when a player appealed could they decide if there was an infringement. However, in situations where the umpires disagreed with one another, then a referee sitting on the touchline would make the final ruling.

The same year the match duration was set at 90 minutes and the unique position of the 'keeper was introduced as the only player who could handle the ball. In order to prevent abuse of this privilege, he could do so only in his own half. Each team was restricted to eleven players and the football size was standardised between 27 and 28 inches in circumference. Leather balls, with an internal bladder, were also refined by stitching pre-formed panels together. The corner, goal kick and free kick were formalised in 1872. Shinguards were invented in 1874 and in 1875 the 8ft-high crossbar was formally introduced.

It was just weeks after Fred Spiksley's birth in 1870 that England played Scotland for the first time ever at the Oval on 5 March 1870. The game's organiser was FA secretary Charlie Alcock. Although the 1870 game is not considered as a full international, the event, and four further games, acted as the precursor to modern international football, with the first full game taking place between Scotland and England in Glasgow on 30 November 1872. Interestingly, match reports contain no reference to any player passing the ball. The game was played under Scottish rules and follow-up games in England were under English rules. When the two FAs met with their Welsh and Irish counterparts in 1882 to regularise the rules – or laws, as they were known – it led to the standard two-handed throw-in from behind the head and the clear marking of the touchlines.

With children staying in the infants class until they were seven, Fred spent his first school year at Holy Trinity Church School alongside his brother, William. The class was a mixed one. The headmaster was Mr Charles Taylor, appointed to the post in 1875 after eleven years as a teacher there. Taylor was a keen advocate of football and at his instigation the local Holy Trinity Recreation Society members were persuaded in 1872 to establish a football section, which

Taylor later succeeded in turning into one of Lincolnshire's finest clubs, Gainsborough Trinity.

From early on, one of Taylor's pupils had a mania for dribbling a ball. Fred Spiksley could rarely be seen without an India-rubber ball as he went between home and school. He tried to keep it under control as he kicked the ball against house walls, dodged pedestrians and trapped the ball just as it seemed certain to enter the road. The path from 3 Willoughby Street to Fred's school was a thoroughfare that consisted of an uneven earthen road in a poor condition. When it rained, streets became a morass of clinging mud. There were no paved walkways or gas lamps on Willoughby Street and workers on early shifts needed to tread carefully. Bridge Street, near the Trinity School, was cobbled and did have gas lamps, but it lacked a pavement. The school closed in 1939.

Fred's enthusiasm undoubtedly helped him develop the skills that later earned him great fame, although by then dribbling had become less important in football. In the 1870s and into the 1880s football was dominated by the individual approach, whereby each forward, of which there were eight with only two backs, ran or dribbled with the ball as far as he could before either losing it to a defender or having it taken from him by a frustrated colleague. However, as players and coaches scientifically sought to refine the sport, it didn't take too long to realise that by combining (passing) it was possible to create greater goalscoring opportunities.

Fred Spiksley and his friends must have been extremely disappointed when Charles Taylor retired in 1877, as his successor, John Walker, was more interested in academic exercise than athleticism and sport. Walker banned football on the basis that it was a danger to the windows. Instead, pupils were encouraged to join the school choir and participate in church services. It would not be until Fred reached the end of his compulsory education at aged 10 and moved to Gainsborough Free Grammar School, where would compete his formal education, that he would be able to enjoy playing school football again.

On Fred's twelfth birthday, in January 1882, his father gave him an extra-special expensive gift. He had left Britannia Ironworks in 1878 and had successfully applied for the tenant landlord licence for his local pub, the Crown and Anchor Inn, in Bridge Street, which was owned by the rapidly-expanding Hewitt Brothers business. In addition to selling beer, the inn had adjoining lodgings that served as a temporary resting place for travellers. It was a very competitive trade as there were eight pubs in Bridge Street. Even so, the regular ships entering Gainsborough's prosperous, thriving inland port with its own custom house meant there was never any shortage of thirsty customers for strong ale among the seamen, who also took advantage of the piano and music hall within the pub, referred to in newspaper adverts as 'Spiksley's Varieties'. Edward Spiksley advertised for a good pianist and vocalist in the *Stamford Mercury* of 24 September 1880.

The music hall scene obviously rubbed off on a young Fred Spiksley and it wasn't long before he was learning to play the piano with some aplomb. He joined the Gainsborough Music Society at 13 and even became the team pianist during his time at Sheffield Wednesday. Fred wasn't the only footballer of his generation to be musically talented. John Southworth twice finished Division One's top scorer, but after retiring early due to injury, he later became a professional violinist and played with the Halle Orchestra.

Despite being unable to read or write Edward Spiksley was, though, fully aware of the importance of profit and bought his son that extra-special birthday present: a Horncastle football. This was every young footballer's dream as it was the ball the emerging stars played with. These included E. Rhodes, who earlier that month had become the first Sheffield Wednesday player to notch four goals in an FA Cup tie as Staveley were beaten 5-1 in front of 2,000 spectators.

Wednesday eventually lost to Blackburn Rovers 5-1 in a replayed semi-final. The losing side included Scotsman James Lang. After impressing in the Clydesdale side that finished runners up in the 1874 Scottish FA Cup, he went south in 1876 to become the first ever professional footballer, an illegal occupation under the FA rules at the time. Amazingly, Lang was blind in his left eye.

In the 1882–83 competition, Blackburn Olympic, bankrolled heavily by local foundry owner Sydney Yates, swept to success in the FA Cup final by beating Old Etonians 2-1. After six final appearances the losing amateur side never returned and their defeat caused apoplexy among football's upper and middle class administrators, with the FA immediately threatening to expel any clubs found to be paying their players 'over and above legitimate out-of-pocket expenses'. Clubs who did so attempted to keep it hidden until, eventually, over forty major clubs, including most of the big North West ones, threatened to form their own 'British Football Association' in 1885. With that, the FA, after losing a few snobbish moralists, capitulated and professionalism became permitted. Working class lads could now view football as a paid occupation.

Delighted by his present, Fred dashed to school to show the other boys. He kicked the ball out of his hands as high as he could and, with very little space to work in, he instantly brought the ball under control when it re-entered planet earth. The youngster's ball control was such that as he developed as a footballer, he maintained he was better with the ball when he was a kid! He delighted in juggling with the ball, a feature he maintained in his professional career to the pleasure of the watching crowd, but to the occasional despair of his playing colleagues and coaches who wanted him to cut out 'the fancy skills'.

With their new ball Fred and his mates were now doubly determined to play football. They met in the playground and plotted how to raise funds to start a football club. The youngsters' enthusiasm was mirrored at higher levels, in 1882 and 1883, by the founding of clubs which are still in existence today, such as Burnley and Tottenham Hotspur.

The children's elders were generous and, armed with the necessary funds, the youngsters were soon up and kicking, with Fred appointed as the captain – after all it was his ball! His power extended to him naming the team: Eclipse, an undefeated eighteenth-century thoroughbred racehorse who won eighteen races, including eleven King's Plates. Although the new football team quickly faded, the horse remains revered in the racing world with the Eclipse Awards for American thoroughbreds named in his honour. The Sheffield-based Eclipse Tools, named after the horse, is now part of Spear and Jackson.

On Easter Monday 1883, the football club in the small Lincolnshire market town of Horncastle, around 38 miles from Gainsborough, had arranged to play Notts Rangers. At the time, the match was Horncastle's biggest and, fearing humiliation, they approached Gainsborough for help. After agreeing to play, Charlie Booth from Gainsborough Working Men's Club (WMC) recruited Charlie Howlett, the Gainsborough Victoria 'keeper, who must have known he was in for a busy afternoon.

The WMC had allowed Fred to watch their training sessions and as he became a regular spectator, he was gradually allowed to participate in the kickabouts, where his flicks and tricks impressed the older players. After having less luck finding any outfield players, Booth considered asking Fred to play at Horncastle. A calculated risk was taken and answered in the affirmative. With the two Charlies, the softly-spoken Booth and the banjo-playing livewire Howlett, Fred Spiksley took the train to Horncastle, where schoolboy met them. Fifteen-year-old left full back Ambrose Langley, who was already a big raw lad, could hardly hide his disgust on seeing Fred. However, thirteen years later the pair were to share a room on the eve of the biggest game in English football. Despite his stature, Fred played impressively against Notts Rangers.

On 26 February 1884, the 14-year-old Fred attended school for the final time. It is impossible to say exactly how beneficial his schooling was, but it clearly didn't do him any harm because as he toured the world in the first four decades of the twentieth century he, unlike many footballers who later followed him, quickly learnt a series of languages including Swedish, German and Spanish.

Chapter 2

Sacked!

Early gambling exploits

If Fred Spiksley was 14 today he would have been signed up by a top football club and his diet, daily routine, education, training and match routine would be well established. Most major clubs have a huge network in place as they seek to snatch the best talent from their rivals. They liaise with schools and managers of county or district teams. Community schemes help maintain contact with people who organise football at grassroots level. Clubs are looking for talent and attitude from a very early age and most run sides – often through their football academies, which have 9,000 players nationally in their ranks – consisting of players from 8 years up to 18.

Theo Walcott cost Arsenal £5 million when he moved from Southampton in 2006 at the age of 16. Fred Spiksley was certainly as good. However, in 1884 there were – openly – no such things as professional footballers. Fred Spiksley needed to find work. Billy Meredith, one of football's earliest superstars, was a coal miner for many years before reluctantly signing for Manchester City.

Fred's burning ambition was to become a jockey like George Fordham, who was champion jockey from 1855 to 1863. In Fred's formative years the only regular mode of transport was horse-drawn, and Willoughby Street was the primary horse quarter locally. William Robinson, farrier and blacksmith, established his forge at the top of the street, while local ship owners had fine carriages and quality horse stables. Surrounded by horses, Fred Spiksley delighted in their sights, sounds and smells. His fascination meant he would help muck out stables, put fresh water in troughs and fill the hayrick with fresh sweet fodder. He mastered the art of being able to control horses because they knew he cared deeply for them.

Fred delighted in visiting the White Hart coaching inn in Lord Street to watch the midday arrival of the mail coach from Barton-on-Humber. Railways had replaced mail coaches in most locations, but the arrival of these magnificent carriages and four beautiful glossy black stallions still created a stir as the horses were changed before setting out to complete the journey to Lincoln.

The Gainsborough Trent Port Steeplechase was on the opposite bank of the River Trent. Everyone wanted to see the action, including Fred Spiksley.

Spectators assembled at key leaping points and the joint start and finish line. Booths selling beer and food enjoyed a lively trade and the race was spectacular, with horses jumping hedges and ditches in thrilling style. Fred was captivated and wanted to become a jockey when he grew up. On leaving school, Fred begged his parents for help to become an apprentice jockey. Although they knew nothing about horse racing, the couple were willing to enquire about what sort of life their son would have if he attempted to become a professional jockey. Meanwhile, they found Fred a temporary stable boy's job with Pellinger's Livery Stables at the White Hart Inn.

Sarah Spiksley bought the *Sporting Life*, a newspaper that was published from 1859 to 1998 and was best known for its horse racing coverage. The paper listed the leading horserace trainers and, according to Fred, his parents wrote to the 'leading horserace trainer of the day to enquire about an apprenticeship'. This may have been Matthew Dawson of Heath House Stables, Newmarket, who was one of the first trainers to run his own stable rather than rely on a wealthy patron. No doubt Fred's size, weight, height, commitment and enthusiasm, together with his close affinity with horses, would have been positives that compensated for not having the strength in his forearms and upper body, which are essential for controlling the horse. The major problem would have been Fred's lack of riding experience. According to Fred, any plans were scuppered when 'as generally happens, friends of the family butted in with their advice and jolly well put the tin lid on it'.

Fred was left in despair. It must have been no consolation that his mother then read a *Gainsborough News* (GN) notice for an 'office boy and messenger'. Instead of featuring within the paper, Fred would be helping fill its pages.

Accompanied by his father, Fred met Charles Caldicott, owner of a weekly Friday newspaper that was first published on 12 May 1855. Charles's father, William, had purchased a general printing business in 1846 and had produced a modest newspaper that he gave away free to avoid newspaper taxes. In the nineteenth century, funding for Britain's protracted overseas wars had meant high taxation on newspapers, with paper, stamp and advertising duties. This boosted government coffers but also raised the price of papers so that their circulation was restricted to reliable society members.

However, in the 1830s all duties were considerably reduced and in 1853 advertising duty was scrapped. Then, on 1 July 1855, stamp duty was abolished with duty on papers finally dropped in 1861. These changes helped establish many more newspapers including the GN covering Retford, Workshop, Isle of Axholme and Gainsborough. With no significant regional competitors, William Caldicott made a very tidy profit, allowing him to buy out the *Doncaster and Pontefract News* and papers in Retford and Epworth. The installation in 1856 of a steam-powered printing press speeded up print runs. The paper was politically neutral, non-religious and allowed freedom of expression with support for good causes such as charities. William died in 1877 and the business passed to his son, who during his subsequent 27-year period in charge, expanded it by publishing the *Gainsborough Evening News* to coincide with Tuesday's market day.

Broad-shouldered, full bearded and with bushy eyebrows, Charles Caldicott looked very severe as he examined Fred's school certificate and asked the youngster some questions. The good academic achievements, plus Fred's good manners, were sufficiently impressive for him to be offered a weekly wage of 2 shillings (10p) for the office boy post, with the promise that on his sixteenth birthday he would start as a compositor's apprentice if his father could meet the financial requirements. Edward Spiksley accepted the offer and Fred started work in the newspaper industry on St David's Day, 1 March 1884.

When Fred had worked almost two years in the office, his father paid an unknown sum for his indentures – an agreement binding an apprentice to a master – and on 25 January 1886, Fred began a five-year apprenticeship as a compositor, a practice which involved a person inserting each metal letter of a word into frames for printing. Fred's wages rose to 3 shillings (15p) with a guarantee of 10 shillings (50p) a week if he successfully completed the five years.

From Monday to Friday, Fred worked from 8am to 6.30pm with an hour for lunch. On Saturdays he worked from 8am to 1pm. No talking was permitted except on work-related business and any worker arriving late could expect to be sent home with a commensurate pay deduction. If Fred could apply himself to the work in front of him over the following five years and obtain a qualified skill, then his future prospects would be much brighter compared to anyone else who remained as an unskilled labourer. For males, completion of an apprenticeship was a major rite of passage comparable to marriage.

However, being an apprentice could be dangerous. In the nineteenth century, employers and workplaces were subject to few safety regulations. Catching limbs in complex machinery was frequent and a fellow apprentice, Albert Tune, got the toe of his boot caught in the gear and cogs of the printing press mechanism. Tune's left toe had to be amputated and in order to walk he required a specially made boot.

By tradition, the season's first flat race meeting was held in March at Lincoln racecourse. The main attraction was the one-mile Lincoln Handicap, but when Fred asked his employer in 1887 if he could be excused work for half a day to go, he was met with a blank refusal. With the passing of the Bank Holiday Act

1871 a number of religious festivals had become legally paid holidays, but it wasn't until the 1936 Annual Holiday Bill that an annual paid holiday became a statutory right. The 17-year-old young man was on thin ice if he skipped work to watch the horse racing. But, consumed by his passion for the sport of kings, that is just what he did. Leaving work after lunch he bought a rail ticket to Lincoln and thoroughly enjoyed himself. He considered it well worth losing a day's pay.

Coming home, however, he began to have some reservations, which proved to be well founded. The following day he was confronted by his employer and, with no trade union to represent him, Fred was sacked for gross misconduct. Fred's apprenticeship and the money his dad had paid for it were gone and despite Edward Spiksley's plea for leniency, a pompous Charles Caldicott was unmoved. Edward Spiksley was naturally very angry at his son's stupidity, which threatened his work prospects and caused great family concern.

Sadly, the incident also failed to curb Fred's enthusiasm for horse racing, as well as the gambling which goes with it, and was merely the beginning of what became a life-long addiction. In the late 1940s Fred was in his seventies when Joyce Spicksley, whose husband, Alan, was his nephew, met him in the kitchen at a family shop in Gainsborough: 'He was ironing the old big white £5 notes and he had a large suitcase stuffed with them that he had won at Doncaster Races. Yet when he died a few years later he owed money. He was known as a big gambling man and was always betting. It meant he had a lot of money on occasions and nothing on others. I never thought very highly of him, he was consumed by gambling on the horses and he would go all over the country betting.'

Out of work, Fred Spiksley, at least, could indulge in his football. In mid-June 1887 an under 18s football tournament was organised by Lincolnshire FA as part of Queen Victoria's Golden Jubilee celebrations. When a Gainsborough side called the Jubilee Swifts was entered, Fred happily accepted the invitation to play, with his first match on Saturday, 9 April 1887.

While working at the print works, Fred had played in some local club matches. On 17 October 1885 he assisted Trinity Institute (TI) to beat Saint John's 2-1. TI were widely known as the reserves of Trinity Recreationists, Gainsborough's premier football club.

Football was becoming popular. Its simplicity and little need for equipment meant many more young boys were playing the game. B. Spooner, a Holy Trinity churchwarden, had overseen the Recreationists' aspiring footballers for many years. He ensured that only physically strong boys with football skills were given trial matches against the senior XI.

Fred Spiksley played at right wing in the TI winning side that lined up in a 2-3-5 formation as follows: Hyde, Spindler, Watson, Musgrave, Scaithe, Leaning, Spiksley, Bingham, Atkinson, Baker, Martin. There are no match reports and while his selection was recognition of his abilities, he wasn't chosen again for some time. Possibly his light build counted against him.

In the early evening of 17 December 1885, the then office junior performed with distinction for Gainsborough Working Men's Club, whose secretary Charles Taylor, Fred's former head teacher, selected him at right wing against Wesleyans FC. A 2-1 success was noted in the GN: 'The two Working Men's goals were scored by their centre forward, Mee, who was brilliantly supported by the teenager Fred Spiksley'.

In April 1886, while playing for Gainsborough Wednesday second XI, Fred scored in a 3-1 defeat of Morton Saint Paul's second XI. He then played in three drawn matches for Wednesday, scored in a 4-3 defeat against Gainsborough Victoria, hit two in a 5-1 defeat of Haxey and netted three goals in three consecutive victories.

When football resumed after the 1886 summer break, the youngster scored for Wednesday (named because of the day when they played their games), as Ferry and District was defeated 4-1. On 30 October 1886, Fred was again playing for the Working Men's Club in an important Lincolnshire County Cup-tie with Lincoln Rangers. The match finished 0-0, but there was controversy when Fred narrowly had a goal disallowed for offside.

On 19 March 1887, Fred, recently sacked by Charles Caldicott, was present to watch Gainsborough Trinity first team play Notts Jardines. The home team faced a crisis with three right-sided team members missing due to illness and injury. Youngster David Brelsford had potential and was asked to play as he was already stripped as the nominated reserve, a role which, once the game started, was superfluous as substitutes only became an accepted part of football in the 1960s. Reserve full back David Deitz lived close enough to the ground to be summoned to replace George Vamplew at right half.

Faced with playing with ten men, a gamble was taken to allow Fred Spiksley to make his competitive debut at inside right at 17 years and 54 days. Today we are familiar with players graduating to first team football at the age of 16, but in 1877, football was a much rougher and dangerous game and opportunities for youngsters such as Fred would have been limited. Fred was only 190 days older than Wayne Rooney was when he made his Everton debut against Tottenham Hotspur in 2002.

The Jardines were a good side with real strength down the left, where the May brothers, Teddy and Billy, were a powerful combination. They quickly exerted control over the young novices and Jardines led 2-0 at the interval. The home side had taken 30 minutes to mount a serious effort on goal, when Fred Spiksley hit a fine low shot that skimmed off the muddy surface forcing the Jardine 'keeper to make a smart save.

Having snowed in the morning, the heavy pitch cut up badly as the game progressed. Spiksley switched with Brelsford to take up the outside role in the second half. His pace and trickery quickly began to cause problems, only for the away side to score a third goal against the run of play.

From the restart the ball was played out to the Trinity outside right. He skipped past Robertson, cut back inside the experienced Jardine captain, full back William 'Wiggy' McLeod, named because he wore a wig, before rounding Grundy the 'keeper and then crossing to his unmarked captain Brown who found the net to make it 1-3. This led to a breathless finale but with no further goals the away side were victors.

In 1921, Fred Spiksley recalled: 'Much to my surprise, McLeod found marking me a constant source of worry. I was constantly swooping down on him, and at the end of each encounter he was at great pains to carefully adjust his wig. The local supporters thought this was hilarious, and doubled up with laughter by his performance, they shouted out: "Eh up, Wiggy, keep your hair on!"' Before moving south to become a professional footballer, McLeod, capped by Scotland in 1886, had played for Cowlairs, one of the original members of the Scottish League when it started in 1890. He was a very good player and so for a youngster to make his afternoon so uncomfortable was some feat.

Afterwards, the GN match report by Charles Jennings noted: 'Spiksley, considering his young age and light weight, played an excellent game with his shots and screws being very good. His passing was well timed, and the measure of his performance is enhanced when you consider that he was up against two excellent backs in McLeod, the Jardines captain, and Robertson. Spiksley would be a great addition for the team.'

Nevertheless, when Trinity beat Brigg Town 4-0 in the Charity Cup final, Vamplew, Tom Smith and Abe Watkin returned to the side in place of the youngsters, leaving Fred to concentrate on guiding Jubilee Swifts towards cup success. Jubilee Swifts had been the brainchild of successful businessman, Mr Cooke, a football enthusiast who owned a Boston jewellery, watch and clockmakers shop. The knockout competition attracted eighty-two entries and Cooke donated a prize of a 'Waterbury Pocket Watch' for every boy in the winning team.

Fred Spiksley's side thrashed Lindum Avenue 13-0 in the first round, as he used his blistering pace to score eleven. Swifts then crushed Lincoln Mayfield

12-0, with Fred Spiksley hitting nine goals. The Swifts' right winger was a pale youth who was much faster than anyone else. Having spent hours practising with his India-rubber ball, his brilliance with a football made him simply unplayable for those of a similar age. Fred then scored six as Gainsborough Wanderers lost 10-0.

The following round was a much tighter contest and at the interval it was 0-0 with Lincoln Park Avenue. The two Park full backs, Rawlinson and Collingwood, played very well to restrict Spiksley's opportunities. After the five-minute interval, Park Avenue took the lead, Duce's effort being the first the Swifts had conceded in the tournament. Within a minute the score was 1-1 when Spiksley scored from a free kick. Then Pinning made it 2-1 before Spiksley completed the scoring in a 3-1 victory. The fifth round was comfortably negotiated as the Swifts notched six without reply against Lincoln Wanderers, thanks to goals from Spiksley (3), Winn (2) and Pinning.

A special thrill awaited the youngsters as the prestigious location for the semi-final was Grimsby Town's ground at Lee Park, Cleethorpes, where Gainsborough Swifts would meet Grimsby Humber Rovers. The Grimsby side were much bigger and stronger than their opponents, who were accompanied to Cleethorpes by a large following and who were surprised when it was announced that the Swifts' line-up was radically different from the earlier games, with just four players in their settled roles. Confused by the changes, the Swifts were heavily beaten 7-0, all the goals coming when they kicked into a strong wind in the second half.

Humber Rovers beat Horncastle Gridirons 3-2 in the final. The crowd included Fred Spiksley, who was delighted when his name was shouted out at the presentation ceremony afterwards. For finishing as the cup's top scorer with 31 goals, he was awarded a watch made by Waterbury, the American company established in 1880. It was a proud moment. The competition had been widely reported in the GN, whose readers included growing numbers of football fans who delighted in reading an impressive number of local match reports. Spiksley's talent meant that Gainsborough Trinity Football Club could not overlook him.

Trinity had their roots in the year after Fred Spiksley was born. Canon George Langton Hodgkinson was sent back to Gainsborough in 1867 after a three-year curacy at the Holy Trinity Church from 1861 to 1864. On his departure, the church had massively overspent on a new organ and Hodgkinson was charged with repairing the damage. Along with his wife, Fanny, a linguist in many languages, the 'new' man quickly revived spirituality among his former parishioners, allowing him to pursue his belief in the Muscular Christianity Movement that was promoted by Thomas Hughes, author of *Tom Brown's Schooldays*.

In 1871 the Holy Trinity Recreation Society was established. Having played first class cricket for Middlesex, the canon at first prioritised the summer sport. Then at the first AGM in May 1872 it was announced that a football team was to be established under the direction of Holy Trinity Church School teacher Charles Taylor and churchwarden James Donson.

Early games were played at the top of Pingle Hill overlooking Marshall's Britannia Ironworks. The Recreationists were first mentioned in the GN when, in a fifteen-a-side game, they beat Trent Football Club 2-0 on Boxing Day 1874. Wearing blue stockinette caps helped the team recognise their own players in muddy conditions. In a period when it wasn't compulsory for sides to wear different coloured shirts, such a change wasn't formally introduced until after the formation of the Football League in 1888. The colour of the caps meant Trinity became forever known as The Blues.

In 1876 the Recreationists were challenged to a football match by Gainsborough Town Sports Club, which was formed in May 1874 when the cricket and rugby clubs combined. The game was played at the Northolme sports ground, which had been a cricket ground from at least 1840 and probably earlier. The Recreationists won the match 6-0.

In September 1881, Lincolnshire football clubs came together to form the Lincolnshire FA. In addition to membership fees, the clubs agreed to make their players available for county matches that were becoming an increasing part of the football calendar. Trinity played their first Lincolnshire County Cup-tie on 4 February 1882 and after drawing 2-2 they beat Grantham Victoria 3-1 in the replay at Pingle Hill.

Over the following years, Trinity began asserting their superiority as Gainsborough's finest side. Charles Caldicott found that when they won, his newspapers sold in larger numbers, as followers were keen to read about the success of their local team in what was starting to become an engaging pastime for the working classes across northern England. Realising that his finances might help Trinity to continue to win, Caldicott had himself co-opted on to the club committee. Trinity could now be sure of fielding a competitive side each week.

On 24 October 1885, Trinity Recreationists played their first FA cup-tie when they met Grantham Town at Northolme. Trinity won 4-1, but there was controversy when the defeated club objected to Sammy Pearson appearing for the victors as he had been signed by Lincoln City as a professional. The appeal was disallowed but Trinity were informed that Pearson could not play for them again without Lincoln City's permission. Gainsborough lost in the following round 2-1 against Middlesbrough.

During the summer of 1885 Trinity Recreationist Football Club joined forces with Gainsborough Town Football and Cricket Club on the Northolme sports field, and Gainsborough Trinity was born. Combining forces meant there was finance to build a new grandstand and erect a wire fence around the pitch to keep spectators off it. The construction of a 6ft 6in-high wooden perimeter fence that incorporated a substantial pair of entrance gates allowed for an entry fee to be charged for fans. This general move towards professionalism wasn't welcomed by everyone. Feeling it betrayed his Christian principles, Canon Hodgkinson resigned as club president.

The Trinity committee recognised that Fred Spiksley was a special talent and knew this hadn't gone unnoticed elsewhere. If they intended retaining his services then they needed to act quickly. Charles Caldicott organised a committee meeting at which it was agreed to offer the 17-year-old a professional football contract. Fearing the youngster's dad would not allow him to sign it unless he was also offered back his apprenticeship, the businessman invited Edward Spiksley to meet him. The apprenticeship was reinstated on the agreement that Edward consented to his son signing a two-year contract to become a professional footballer.

Despite this, Fred's passion remained horse racing and in September 1887 he paid another apprentice to rush over shouting that his mother had been taken seriously ill. It was a lie and he skipped work to go to Doncaster and watch the St Leger. On his return only his footballing exploits prevented him from being dismissed for a second time.

Chapter 3

Under Madden's Wing

Spiksley's first season as a Trinity professional

The summer of 1887 was marked by riotous celebrations for Queen Victoria's Golden Jubilee. On Wednesday, 22 June Gainsborough shopkeepers decorated their frontages, with an undeclared competition breaking out to see who could find the most imaginative, decorative designs. Large crowds admired the displays. The following morning church bells rang out. There was a children's procession and then a massive party for youngsters, after which there was a six-a-side football competition, bicycle races, hot air balloons, games and dancing.

John (Jack) Madden, the new Trinity coach from Dumbarton, captained one of the football sides. The son of Irish immigrants, John Madden, was born on 11 June 1865, the youngest of nine. Money was tight and he received little formal education. At 15 his brother-in-law, Bill Burgess, secured him a job as a 'catch boy' in a riveters' gang in Denny's shipyard on the River Clyde. The job meant catching red-hot rivets in a metal bucket as part of a team effort that involved precisely inserting rivets in steel plates on a ship's hull so that it was water tight. This hard, noisy and dangerous work was combined with periods when work was scarce.

Football was sweeping across Scotland and, after practising with a tin can at an early age, Madden had developed a real talent for dribbling, winning many 'dribbling with the ball' races. After playing junior football he joined Dumbarton in 1886–87, sparking controversy by becoming the first Roman Catholic to play for 'The Sons of the Rock'. Scoring a debut goal in a victory over Third Lanark dispelled any problems. Dumbarton reached the Scottish FA Cup final and Jack played in the 2-1 defeat against Hibernian at Hampden Park.

Unlike in England, the Scottish FA was determined to retain the amateur tradition and it wasn't until 1893 that professionalism was permitted. Between 1872 and 1887 England beat Scotland just twice and it was little wonder that English professional clubs sought to recruit good Scottish players by paying them more than they could earn in engineering workshops, mines, mills, shipyards and factories.

Scots gladly moved south and from the 1887–88 season onwards, English clubs competed frantically to recruit the best from north o' the border. Losing such talent weakened the domestic Scottish game, leading to angry scenes and violence when anyone with an English accent arrived unexpectedly on a scouting mission.

Gainsborough Trinity had a progressive, ambitious committee. Determined to keep up with their Lincolnshire rivals, they recruited Glasgow football agent Mr Wilson to find them a top class centre forward and a full back. John Madden's father had died three years earlier and his income sustained a large family. As a fast, dangerous forward he had the attributes Gainsborough required. Preventing him signing professionally, however, were the new FA rules that any professional not local to a team had to live no more than 6 miles away over a two-year period if they were to play in FA competitions.

More than anything, Madden was going to be needed for important cup matches. So Gainsborough asked if he minded registering as an amateur, for whom the residential qualification period didn't apply, and instead be paid as their football coach. Madden keenly accepted the offer, unaware that the coaching role was a sham.

Meanwhile, the Dumbarton full back Bobby Ferguson also signed for Gainsborough. Madden asked the Gainsborough committee to arrange a competitive pre-season friendly and when both new men turned up it became apparent that the new coach genuinely wanted to be one!

Fearing losing him, Madden was allowed free rein. It was an inspired decision. Madden impressed on his new charges the need to pass the football along the ground and retain possession. He was an expert in coaching the art of movement off the ball and creating space, tailoring skill sessions to suit each player's role within the team. Madden could shoot with great power and a back heel manoeuvre he perfected was pure genius. In addition to being a fine masseur and fitness trainer, he impressed on players the need to prepare mentally for a game, to eat properly and restrict their alcohol consumption. Madden was way ahead of his time.

He continued working part of the week on the Clyde – earning between £1 and £1 10s (£1.50) – before travelling on the Friday overnight train to Lincolnshire. Gainsborough beat local rivals Lincoln City 1-0 in Madden's first game. As always, before departing north he discussed with the players what had and hadn't worked well. Madden earned £2 10s (£2.50) a week plus his travelling expenses.

On his return south, Madden participated in the Gainsborough Working Men's Club third annual sports day. In the 440 yards handicap race, a young

Fred Spiksley won easily despite a 32-yard handicap. Spiksley then entered the 440 yards race in the Worksop Athletics and Sports meeting. Sheffield's Tom Kinman was one of England's fastest quarter-milers and yet he was given a 15-yard head start on his Gainsborough rival, who thrashed him by 8 yards. Weeks later Kinman won the Amateur Athletics Association (AAA) Northern Counties Championship. Having become a professional sportsman, Fred was barred from AAA events and he never raced again until his football days were over when, despite a serious knee injury, he won regularly.

As a youngster, Fred had been fortunate to meet Charlie Booth, fifteen months his senior, who had got him to play for Horncastle. Booth's mother, Keziah, was just 12 or 13 when he was born and he never knew his father. He was left with his grandparents and, after his grandfather died, Charlie at aged eight began working at Marshall's clay-pits. The money earned kept his grandmother out of the workhouse.

Charlie loved the outdoors and his own company. He and Fred were chalk and cheese, but when they were both out one evening honing their football skills, they struck up an unlikely friendship. When they ran dribbling the ball the younger man won every race, but without the ball the power and stride pattern of the bigger man won any sprint race. Fred was unaware that Charlie competed in professional sprint races for money. Spotting that Fred was becoming taller, Charlie asked whether, in return for paying him a fee, he would like some sprinting lessons.

Without an income, Fred agreed that in return for lessons he would bring his new trainer some fresh eggs. He began sneaking into his parents' hen coop and taking half a dozen eggs. One morning he was surprised to find no eggs. He soon discovered why when his parents accused him of stealing. He was grounded for a week. When he did escape he found Charlie had entered him for a quarter mile race. When Fred duly won the competition his presentation to his parents of the £6 winnings helped change their attitude. From then on Fred collected half a dozen eggs for the Booth family each week.

Fred maintained throughout his life that he would have won the AAA 440 yards race. 'From 17 to 22 I experienced a phenomenal increase in my strength, speed and acceleration. It is difficult to compare my pace on the football field with the speed of the amateur quarter milers on the running track, but what is certain is that whenever I got past a defender even when keeping the ball under control at my feet I was never ever caught by anyone when I was at my best.'

The start of the new competitive football season saw the introduction of pitch markings, including the corner, half way line and centre circle. Two semi-circles, each with a radius of 6 yards from the posts, were now compulsory and marked the area from where goal kicks could be taken.

Fred Spiksley played at inside right for the Trinity opening game against Notts Rangers, which was played at Morton Lane as Northolme was being used for cricket.

Trinity lined up as follows: Hoodless, Ferguson, Jubb, Smith, Billy Brown (captain), Cater, Vamplew, Spiksley, Madden, Chambers, Robinson.

The home side won 3-1 with the third coming when Cater's fine pass was fired powerfully home by the inside right. Victory was achieved despite the first-half loss of Madden after a nasty tackle left him with a severe ankle injury. To add further insult, when the subsequent free kick was fired home the 'goal' was chalked off as there were no direct free kicks in 1887. The GN match reporter praised Fred Spiksley but expressed some doubts, stating 'on several occasions his light weight told against him'. Such concerns appeared to be shared by the Trinity selection committee and, against Madden's wishes, they rested their youngest professional in the following games.

However, the match on 15 October 1887 was the biggest of the season so far: the FA Cup first qualifying round against Boston Town.

The FA Cup was the invention of Charles Alcock when on 20 July 1871 he proposed in his role as FA secretary 'a competition for the prize of a silver challenge cup and the prestige of becoming the best football team in England'.

Sitting in a small, oak-panelled room in the offices of the *Sportsman* newspaper just off Ludgate Hill in London, Alcock's fellow FA committee members realised the brilliance and simplicity of the proposal, which Alcock had taken from the annual football tournament at Harrow Public School, where he had been a pupil. The knockout element would add extra excitement to matches and the prize would give clubs an incentive to join the FA and play in the competition. It would ensure the Association's position as the game's guardian. The proposal was voted upon, passed, and recorded in the FA minute book. The first national football tournament, the best known in the world for many years afterwards, was born.

Silversmiths Martin Hall designed a silver cup to be presented to the annual winners. It was heavily embossed, 18 inches high with a capacity of 4 pints and mounted on an ebony plinth. Two handles curved from its sides and on the top was the figure of a footballer. The engraving on the cup's body read: 'The Football Association Challenge Cup'. It may have been a humble £20 trophy, but it was to become a national treasure known throughout the country as 'The Little Tin Idol', but generally referred to as the 'English Cup'.

The first game in the tournament, which attracted fifteen clubs in its first season, took place on 11 November 1871 and saw Barnes beat the Civil Service, who only managed to raise eight players, 2-0.

The first northern side to take the trophy were Blackburn Olympic in 1883. Then, as professionalism seeped into the game, Blackburn Rovers completed a hat-trick of successes.

In 1887, John Madden wanted Fred Spiksley at inside right and the Trinity selection committee were content to let the coach have his own way.

At half-time the game was effectively over as Trinity raced into a 4-0 lead. Then, on the hour mark, the home inside right justified his selection by scoring a great goal when he put spin and swerve on the ball so that it curved well away from the 'keeper and into the goal. It was, for its era, a truly remarkable goal and stunned the 2,000 inside Northolme who had never seen anything like it.

In time, a crucial part of Fred Spiksley's game was his skill in moving the ball in the air. This was virtually impossible in wet conditions when the leather football would become heavy and misshapen. However, on dry days Fred could spin and swerve the ball to score goals, cut out opponents, reach better-placed colleagues and generally confuse the opposition. At corners he could use the outside of his right foot to swerve the ball away and conversely he used the outside of his left to spin and swerve the ball so it could dip and bend into the goalmouth under the crossbar.

Defenders and 'keepers were unnerved. This time the GN reporter had to admit: 'If Spiksley maintains the form he showed on Saturday in a 7-0 victory he is well worthy of a permanent place. He is certainly light, but I have not the slightest doubt that Spiksley will live long in the memory of the footballing public, with his speed, agility, and his deadly shooting.'

However, on 5 November 1887, the second qualifying round FA cup tie between Lincoln City and Gainsborough Trinity again saw the team selection committee unwilling to risk Fred Spiksley in a fixture with a violent record. Lincoln, passionately backed, won 2-1. Fred Spiksley returned to the Trinity side for the next few games and scored regularly, including another curling effort in the 5-1 defeat of Sheffield Heeley.

Over the winter months of the 1887–88 season, Gainsborough were able to maintain a good level of success, with Madden regularly scoring including three against Kiveton Colliery in a 10-3 win in which Fred Spiksley notched his first senior hat-trick. Keen to ensure the emerging star remained grounded, Madden later told him off for failing to pass to better-placed teammates after he scored a real beauty against Small Heath Alliance. The scorer was initially hurt, but when he considered things more deeply he realised Madden was correct and resolved not to repeat his mistake. Spiksley would go on to score many goals in his career, but he also became famous for creating chances for those playing inside him. In his 1901 book, *Association Football*, the great England half back Ernest Needham wrote the following, which proved that Spiksley had learned a valuable lesson from Madden and had developed to become a greater player: 'When he finds himself in difficulty he will always pass the ball to someone better placed – a form of unselfishness that a good many well-known players might do well to copy.'

When Trinity played Lincoln City away in the Lincolnshire County Challenge Cup, there was no chance that Fred Spiksley would not be selected. Confident of success the 5,000 crowd included 1,700 from Gainsborough, who saw their heroes win for the first time at their local rivals' steeply-sloping John O'Gaunt's ground. Concerned beforehand that they might lose, the City committee had sent their players away for special training, thus ensuring they also stayed away from heavy drinking before the game. Afterwards, a single John Madden goal was likely to have provoked just such bouts among losers and winners alike. It was some goal! Penned in and surrounded, the Trinity centre forward spun round to place the ball accurately just inside the posts.

The second half was a fierce affair and Fred Spiksley came in for some close attention. By emerging unscathed he showed he was more than ready for such encounters. Having played brilliantly, the visiting 'keeper Charlie Howlett, who wore spectacles when playing, was carried shoulder high from the pitch by the delighted visiting fans. The victorious side were met by a cheering crowd when they returned to Gainsborough. With the Britannia Ironworks band belting out some fine tunes, the team were chaired shoulder high to the club's Sun Inn headquarters.

Over the following weeks, Trinity continued to play with aplomb. In the Lincolnshire Cup semi-final, Trinity won 4-1 at Grantham Town. There was then revenge for the 4-0 early season thrashing when Trinity defeated Grimsby Town 1-0, courtesy of a Dick Sharman effort. Of their last twenty-two games, Trinity had won nineteen and lost two.

In the GN Charity Cup semi-final game there was a 10-0 destruction of Grantham Rovers with Spiksley hitting four. Sheffield Heeley were then beaten 4-2 in a thrilling final. Spiksley got one goal and also collected his first senior winner's medal. Charles Caldicott was delighted that Gainsborough Trinity had won the trophy. All eyes now turned towards the Lincolnshire Charity Challenge Cup final, which Trinity had reached only once before.

In its infancy, football was marked by constant appeals over a whole series of infringements, real and imaginary. Many FA Cup ties were replayed and sides thrown out. Gainsborough's final opponents were Grimsby, who in early April wrote to the local FA resigning in protest that the final game would take place at the home of Lincoln City, a club with whom, for a multitude of reasons, they were in dispute.

There then followed farce upon farce. Grimsby and Gainsborough played each other in friendlies with Grimsby winning 6-1 and losing 1-0, before claiming that they should be awarded the cup! Gainsborough wrote to the FA saying they would turn up in Lincoln on 14 April and kick off the game before claiming the cup. The FA responded by moving the final until the following weekend. In the event Gainsborough didn't carry out their threat and on 5 May the FA instructed the clubs to play the game in Boston on 12 May. Gainsborough refused and there the matter lay until the AGM of the Lincolnshire FA in July, when a motion was passed that the trophy and medals be withheld.

Angered by the perceived injustice, Gainsborough Trinity wrote to Lincolnshire FA stating they would resign if the Challenge Cup and medals were not handed over to them. When the FA ignored this request, Trinity quit, thus absenting themselves from future Lincolnshire Cup competitions. In the event, the absence was only for twelve months.

Worse was to follow for Gainsborough Trinity in the summer of 1888. The club had pursued their Challenge Cup grievance to the detriment of all other affairs and thus forgot to renew John Madden's contract. When they finally got in touch he had re-signed for Dumbarton.

It was a big blow for Gainsborough and a young Fred Spiksley, who fully appreciated everything the Scot did for him, stating years later:

> I owe a great debt to Madden as I was placed under his guiding influence, and he became my coach, mentor and friend. On being introduced to senior football there is no doubt that for their future success and welfare young players greatly need the steadying influence of an experienced and talented player close at hand. His advice, if followed, will go a long way towards bringing out any ability that young players may possess. Of course, if the ability is not there in the first place, you cannot bring it out, but if the innate ability is present, there is no doubt that a good coach will develop all that he has to work upon. Then the player's improvement will depend entirely upon himself. When I started in the Gainsborough Trinity first team, I was positioned as an inside forward to Jack Madden our centre forward. Now Madden was already a player with a great deal of experience, and his tremendous ability was clear for all to see. The wonder to me was how a player of such exceptional skill came to play football for Gainsborough Trinity.

After leaving Trinity, John Madden would go on to have a successful playing career with Celtic, who had just played their first match in May 1888, the first ever Old Firm Derby. At Celtic, Madden won three Scottish League titles and represented Scotland twice, scoring five goals. However, it would have been little surprise to Fred Spiksley that it would be Madden's coaching career which was to gain him legendary status. In 1905 he became Slavia Prague coach and manager, a position he retained for twenty-five years, collecting countless trophies. Amazingly, Madden was still coaching teams from his wheelchair at the age of 73 and he remains a Slavia legend.

Chapter 4

Birthday Disaster

A career-threatening injury at Olive Grove

A revolutionary move that changed forever the face of football and many other sports marked the beginning of the 1888–89 football season. It was the development of a league system and Scotsman William McGregor was the man responsible. Following the introduction of professionalism, the Aston Villa committee man recognised that clubs needed a guaranteed source of income if they were to have the funds to pay players.

With support from fellow Villa committee members, McGregor searched for other clubs keen to back his new idea. By early March 1888, McGregor was confident enough to send a formal letter to five clubs: Blackburn Rovers, Bolton Wanderers, Preston North End, West Bromwich Albion and Aston Villa. He suggested clubs might overcome their current problems by proposing that 'ten or twelve of the most prominent clubs in England combine to arrange home and away fixtures each season.' The five clubs were then asked to propose other teams who should be invited to become involved.

On the eve of the 1888 FA Cup final, representatives of Aston Villa, Notts County, Blackburn Rovers, Wolverhampton Wanderers, Burnley, Stoke and West Brom held a successful meeting and invited Preston, Everton, Accrington, Bolton Wanderers and Derby County to join them at the Royal Hotel, Manchester, on Tuesday, 17 April 1888, in formalising affairs and arranging fixtures for the 1888–89 season.

This meeting marks the birth of competitive league football, though its historic nature didn't stop clubs beginning an ongoing tradition of squabbling among themselves! Even the name proved problematic, with McGregor's suggestion of Football Union overruled in favour of William Sudell's Football League. McGregor, who became chairman of the new organization, wanted clubs to divide gate money, but delegates, who felt that a guaranteed sum of £15 for visiting clubs was more preferable, rejected that. Egalitarianism had been swiftly abandoned. The clubs were, though, open to change and adopted rules requiring the bottom four clubs to face a re-election battle, with non-League clubs seeking entry.

So good was McGregor's idea that it was immediately imitated as clubs, left disappointed at not being invited, rushed to form a parallel Football Combination. Twenty clubs, including Gainsborough Trinity, joined up. However, there were too few weekends for the number of clubs involved, midweek games being almost impossible to arrange due to many players' work commitments and – in an era lacking electric floodlights – dark winter nights. Some teams didn't even realise they were members and by the end the league had largely collapsed.

The first Combination games took place on 8 September 1888. Fred joined his team mates on the 7.45am train from Lincoln to the Potteries to play Port Vale. His elder brother, William, had started up his own pork butcher's business and had already left to begin work before Fred was washed and dressed.

Fred was always very particular about his playing kit. As he always changed into a fresh shirt at half time he made sure he placed both of his blue tops in a battered portmanteau. Long knickerbockers (shorts) and blue football stockings, tie-ups and shin guards were also packed with a towel, toilet bag and a bar of carbolic soap. Fred's boots were typical of the time, being largely adapted workmen's boots that were designed for strength, with an indestructible block toe and studs hammered into the soles. Even after he became an established footballer and ordered his boots made to measure, he believed that workmen's boots were better than those that were increasingly advertised for sale for young players stating they 'kept their shape, were much lighter, and were not an encumbrance in wet weather'.

Joining the team in their private saloon, Fred was in a good mood and looking to build on his successful first season with Trinity. He had enjoyed every minute and after being capped for Lincolnshire had even been presented with a top hat by a wealthy patron. However, the loss of Madden and his Scottish counterpart, Ferguson, was bound to have an impact, and Gainsborough were further weakened by the loss of 21-year-old Harry Chamberlain, the darling of the Northolme crowd. Scorer of nineteen goals the previous season he had now moved to Lincoln.

Fred's partner on the left, Harry Robinson, had developed diabetes and his absence was another blow. Sadly, he died on 16 September 1888. To compound matters, no pre-season matches had been organised and the away side were heavily beaten, 6-1.

The rush was now on to find new players. William Croft was sent back to Scotland and two new Scots were recruited for the match away to Long Eaton Rangers where, on their arrival, the home stadium and its world famous cycle track impressed the Gainsborough players. Having travelled through the night, debutants Pollock and Watts were shattered and it was no surprise that their side lost 3-2, with Spiksley scoring once.

The defeated side's poor start continued with a 3-1 defeat at Rotherham Town and there was a growing sense of panic that Trinity may be heading towards a disastrous season. However, William Croft had had some success in recruiting new players and after employing football agent John McCabe from Leith, Edinburgh, Gainsborough were able to sign four new players: Shamrock Coyne, an Irishman from Hibernian, and three Scots, William McKay from Hearts, Alec Brady from Sunderland and John 'Jack' Angus from Newcastle West End. Each new man would earn double the match fee paid to local players. Only Coyne was available for the first Gainsborough home league fixture, which Newton Heath won 5-1 before a crowd of 2,000.

The gate for the second home fixture fell to 600, who witnessed an improved performance. Coyne scored and Trinity beat Leeds Association 5-0. The following weekend the Scot was joined by McKay and Angus in the team and, with both newcomers playing on the left of the attack, Spiksley was moved to centre forward with instant success. He scored five times in an 8-0 thrashing of Lincoln Ramblers. Angus then scored three times as Lincoln City was beaten 4-1. Angus and McKay were ineligible for FA matches as they hadn't completed the required residential period. Trinity overcame a similar problem for Coyne by registering him as an amateur while secretly paying him a wage.

One player who wasn't receiving a wage was Fred Spiksley who, along with his father, had no idea that when he signed his two-year football contract with Trinity he was becoming a professional footballer. As such, Fred had never asked for the money he was supposed to be paid and was well into his second season when Dick Sharman asked why he wasn't collecting his 2s 6d (12.5p) for home games and 5 shillings (25p) for away games to compensate for loss of earnings. Fred calculated that he was owed £6 10s (£6.50). He had, of course, been receiving his apprenticeship wages, but he was rightly upset that no-one from the club had informed him about collecting his match fees. Now aware of his value to Trinity, when he finally went to get what he was owed Fred asked for his contract to be amended to a weekly wage of 7s 6d (37.5p), which was agreed.

Trinity beat Notts Jardines 4-0 in the FA Cup second qualifying round, Spiksley netting twice. He then scored three in a 4-4 draw with Grantham Town. The following weekend the four new signings, all forwards, played together for the first time. When Fred Spiksley, again switched to centre-forward, was starved of the ball he was encouraged to leave the field early by some of the Trinity supporters already angry at seeing captain Tom Smith lose his place to the newcomers.

Fred believed the new players were playing for themselves, but he was persuaded to play in the FA Cup tie against Boston Town and scored twice in a 5-3 win. The game was Coyne's last for Trinity after he received a letter from Everton inviting him for a trial and he departed hastily. His leaving angered local players, including Spiksley, who refused to play against Notts Rangers and Long Eaton Rangers. However, having failed to secure a contract with Everton, Coyne returned to Gainsborough in the hope of once again playing for the local club.

On Monday, 3 December, three strangers with suitcases alighted from the Manchester train on platform 1 at Gainsborough's Great Northern Station. Burnley had started their first season in the Football League very badly and were bottom of the table. Aware that Gainsborough had done well after signing four new players, the East Lancs club's directors sought to boost their hopes of avoiding a re-election battle by obtaining the signatures of some of the four men. Angus had let slip what was going on and declared he wasn't involved. The station porter was warned to listen out for Lancashire accents, the news of the poachers' arrival immediately sweeping through Gainsborough as they made their way to hide out in the lodging houses of the three players set to transfer their allegiance to the Turf Moor club.

The Britannia Ironworks closed for an hour at dinner time and so when all six men finally emerged to make a dash for the Manchester midday train, they were pelted with eggs and tomatoes then punched and had their clothes torn before finally reaching the sanctuary of their railway carriage. As the train departed, disgruntled Gainsborough fans threw more eggs. Angus's loyalty pledge to the club later disappeared when he left without warning to go to Everton. He was later converted into a 'keeper during a short spell with Sunderland and returned to play eleven League games in the 1890–91 season when Everton captured the Division One title. He died of typhoid fever in the summer of 1891.

With only nine players to call on, Trinity withdrew from their FA Cup game against Grimsby. Letter writers to the local paper wanted Trinity not to sign any more Scots! Arthur Elliott was offered a contract to play at centre forward and this allowed Fred Spiksley to play outside left.

On 22 December a full-strength Sheffield Wednesday side – all Sheffield born and bred – played a friendly at Northolme and Gainsborough acquitted themselves extremely well in a 1-1 draw. The home goal saw Spiksley hit a 40-yard crossfield ball to Tom Smith on the right wing. He combined with George Vamplew to create space for a cross which found the unmarked Spiksley, who had run 80 yards to score easily. Everyone was impressed.

In the GN Charity Cup, Gainsborough drew Wednesday away in the third round. A special chartered train took 500 supporters to Sheffield. A 6,100 crowd saw Wednesday immediately swarm all over the away defence in which full backs Fred Palmer and Charlie Jubb performed heroically. It was 0-0 when tragedy struck as Spiksley, celebrating his nineteenth birthday that day, made a powerful run. Wednesday full back Teddy Brayshaw was far too late with his reckless sliding tackle and left his opponent lying on the ground, having snapped his leg between the knee and ankle. Brayshaw had received the ball just at the moment Spiksley had put the outside of his right foot to it and the shockwave created by the collision fractured his shinbone. Attempts to stand up were agony and the Gainsborough physician Doctor Wright confirmed it was a broken leg. The injured player was taken to the Arundel and Surrey Hotel where his leg was set. Without a key player the away side lost 4-0.

Spiksley's absence was a big blow personally and for his side. Over the following weeks, Trinity enjoyed mixed fortunes including defeats at home to Lincoln City (1-0) and Grimsby Town (7-1). The injured youngster, who must have feared his career might already be over, missed Trinity's final nine matches of the season and was confined to his bed for eight weeks with splints. He required crutches when he got up and with his muscles in his right leg having wasted considerably, he needed to build them back up with a programme of exercises during a period when he also restarted his apprenticeship. Plenty of walks and lots of swimming were a boost and over the summer of 1889 he was able to start practising his ball skills once more.

By the start of the 1889–90 campaign, Fred hadn't played competitively for almost eight months. The season saw the introduction of a new law which allowed a referee to rule a player 'out of the game' (send him off) for dangerous play or poor conduct.

With twenty teams, the Football Combination had proven unmanageable. The Football League, however, with just twelve teams, had proven an unqualified success. It was imitated in 1889–90 with the formation of the Football Alliance, the Northern League and the eleven-team Midland Counties League. The last of these was the brainchild of Jack Strawson, the Lincoln City secretary. Trinity joined it along with Burton Wanderers, Derby Midland, Derby Junction, Leek Town, Lincoln City, Notts Rangers, Rotherham Town, the Sheffield Club, Staveley and Warwick County. This guaranteed twenty competitive games.

Trinity's first game at home to Lincoln City saw them include new 'keeper William Gresham, recruited from Boston, and he was beaten twice in a 2-1 defeat, with the winner coming from his brother who was playing for Lincoln. There was some relief when Trinity won 5-4 at the Sheffield Football Club and although the pitch was a quagmire, the conditions didn't prevent a real thriller taking place before 1,250 spectators.

As his form started to return, Spiksley notched an early equaliser in a friendly match with Blackburn Rovers, only for the Football League side to show their superiority by roaring to a 5-1 success. Earlier in the decade Rovers had won the FA Cup in three successive seasons. The fact that the East Lancs side had been willing to play in Gainsborough, nevertheless made it a special day.

On 28 December 1889, Trinity faced Rotherham Town at home in a Midland League match and in the visitors' goal was Arthur Wharton, the first black professional footballer.

Wharton was frequently referred to as a 'darkie' in match reports and he suffered racial hostility on many occasions. His bravery was to pave the way for other black footballers and sports stars to follow in his footsteps.

He had travelled to England from Ghana to study in Darlington and soon discovered he had a special sporting talent. In 1885 he won the AAA 100 yards championship at Stamford Bridge, London. He retained the title the following year and became the first man to run the distance in 10 seconds exactly.

At football, he took to goalkeeping and was especially noted for his ability to punch the ball long distances. He was persuaded to play for Preston but, being a free spirit, he argued with manager William Sudell. Instead, Arthur joined Rotherham as a professional for the 1889–90 season and played at centre forward where he could use his blistering speed and keep his sprint trainer happy by avoiding the extra risk of injury that went with playing in goal, violence against 'keepers being fair game in 1889. Yet when the Rotherham 'keeper De Ville was injured against Burton Wanderers there was no other option but to put Arthur between the sticks. He thrilled the crowd with his special tricks including catching the ball between his knees, picking up opposing forwards and dumping them in the goal and pulling down the crossbar to prevent shots entering the net. Arthur's actions naturally infuriated opposition fans and players and led to a number of incidents, many of quite a violent nature in which he gave as good as he got.

Playing in goal against Gainsborough Trinity, Wharton, who was commemorated in 2014 with a 16ft permanent memorial at the National Football Centre at St George's Park, was brilliant and as shot after shot rained down on him he performed heroically. Only once was he beaten when Spiksley feinted one way and sent him the other. As the game entered the final minutes the away side led 2-1 when the Trinity scorer broke clear and, as he moved to equalise, Wharton dashed forward and literally jumped on his right leg.

The 'keeper's actions prevented a goal and ensured his side won the game, but left the recipient fearful that he had suffered another serious injury. The home support, aware that Fred had recently returned from a broken leg, roundly booed the 'keeper. When the match ended a number of fans invaded the pitch and after surrounding the 'keeper, an unseemly scuffle broke out which was only ended when the police arrived quickly to restore law and order. Thankfully, the Trinity outside left was saved by his shin pad and departed with just a sore leg.

Over the following weeks Gainsborough progressed through to the FA Cup fourth qualifying round and were drawn away to Lincoln City who, despite kicking up the hill, took an early two-goal lead. Trinity's 'Tuppenny (2d) Gods' – so called because they paid a 2d entry fee and were the most fanatical – were taunted by City's most vociferous supporter 'Leather Lungs', who offered odds of 3 to 1 on City. Fred Spiksley was a gambling man and must have fancied the odds, as soon after he scored with an unstoppable cross shot. The match proved a thrilling one that City won 5-3.

Trinity had more success in the Lincolnshire County Cup. Initially, Grimsby Humber Rovers proved stubborn semi-final opponents, but four second half goals took Gainsborough into the final. On 5 April 1890 when Trinity played their final home Midland League game of the season, the match with Leek Town was delayed by 20 minutes so that the GN could take a special team photo which was printed in the paper on 2 May 1890. The game attracted a 1,500 crowd and saw Gainsborough win 9-2, with Spiksley and Willcocks both hitting three.

However, what everyone was talking of was when Elliott, standing on the half way line, flicked the ball up and aimed a low volley that just kept on going and going and going right past a transfixed Critchlow in the away goal to make it 8-2. Was it a fluke or pure genius? We will never know as no-one asked the scorer afterwards, but it split the crowd with half laughing and half applauding enthusiastically.

Elliott notched another goal as Grantham Rovers were beaten 6-0 in the final of the Lincolnshire County Challenge Cup at Lincoln's ground. The trophy was presented when the team returned home to Gainsborough for a celebratory tea at the Sun Inn. When Walter Forrest accepted the trophy on behalf of Gainsborough Trinity, he reminded everyone what had occurred in 1888 before stating: 'The committee have always been determined not to rest until the County Cup has been won.'

The Midland Counties League's first season ended for seventh place Gainsborough with a 3-2 defeat at Lincoln City, who were crowned champions. Gainsborough had scored forty-seven goals, the second highest, and conceded thirty-two. With twenty-three, Fred scored almost half of Trinity's league goals. During the 1889–90 season he scored thirty-six goals, twenty more than Arthur Elliott and Taffy Thomas, who finished in equal second place in the Gainsborough score chart.

Fred had played particularly impressively in the second half of the season, notching twenty-five goals in eighteen games. His achievements were chronicled in the *Athletic News*, regarded as the leading sports paper of the time. As the season came to a close letters began arriving for him at his parents' pub. One in particular couldn't be ignored, as Blackburn Rovers were prepared to offer him £2 10s (£2.50) per week to play for them. If he accepted, it meant he would be playing for the FA Cup holders as on 29 March 1890, Rovers had thrashed The Wednesday 6-1 in the final, with William Townley hitting the final's first ever hat-trick.

Football, however, was a precarious business and hadn't Fred broken his leg not so long back? He also had his apprenticeship to complete and with nine months to go he couldn't let his father down again, especially as it would give him a trade to fall back on if football failed to bring any future financial rewards.

Fred let everyone know he would be playing for Trinity in the 1890–91 season and he ended the current campaign on 30 May by creating one of the goals as his side beat Notts Olympic 4-1 in the Gainsborough News Charity Cup final at the John O'Gaunt's ground. However, Charles Caldicott's great pleasure was extremely brief as just two days later the defeated side correctly pointed out that Trinity 'keeper David Brelsford had earlier played for the club's reserve side in the competition. The outcome was that while the Trinity players were allowed to keep their medals, Notts Olympic were awarded the cup.

Chapter 5

Trinity Triumph

Gainsborough Trinity win the Midland League and Wednesday are lucky to get their man

The 1890–91 season was to be Fred's last with his local club and it would be a roaring success. Unlike the previous summer, the Trinity outside left was healthy enough in 1890 to participate in the local rowing club's regatta. Elitism had been ended at the club's AGM when high entrance and membership fees were replaced by cheaper ones. As a result, membership numbers multiplied and the additional income helped to purchase new boats and improve the boathouse. Rowing with Roy Goodall, Fred Spiksley snatched the novice coxed pairs title in a titanic final in which the pair beat Joy and Schofield. Then, in the scratch coxed pairs' event, Spiksley and J.R. Rawlings won their heat and semi-final before beating Woodhouse and Longmire by 4.5 lengths to take the title and collect a silver cup.

A week later, Gainsborough Trinity played their first practice match and thankfully, the club committee hadn't repeated the previous summer's mistakes and had strengthened the team. The injured William Gresham was fit to resume in goal while Harry Walkerdine from Notts County would play centre forward. John Clements had also previously represented Notts County and had been recruited to play at full back, while Scotsman Harry Swinton, previously with Bury, was another new signing for a side whose half back line was to be Steve Carlin, Billy Brown and Fred Palmer. Billy Cooke and Taffy Thomas would form the right attacking flank. Arthur Elliott had been courted by a number of clubs, but in the end he also re-signed for the Blues. Hopes were high for a successful season.

The League campaign began with a 5-1 success at Long Eaton Rangers, but in the second game there was a shock. After taking the lead through Elliott, Trinity conceded a 'goal' when a Gummer shot that missed by some distance was awarded by the referee who, sitting on the half way line, was asked to adjudicate after the Gainsborough and Rotherham umpires failed to agree. Rotherham won 3-2. The growing number of occasions when the umpires failed to agree was creating increasing demands for the referee to assume full control of games – after all, it would undoubtedly produce improved decision making, as has proven the case ever since!

On 4 October 1890 the Gainsborough FA Cup game against Lincoln City became a landmark match when the referee was given complete control of events. If the experiment and those that followed were successful then there was every chance it would be permanently introduced for the start of the 1891–92 season, and also be combined with the introduction of neutral referees and linesmen to end accusations of favouritism against match officials. For this important occasion, the FA decided to appoint the experienced referee Arthur Kingscott, known as 'The Knight of the Whistle'.

The match clashed with the Nottingham Goose Fair, which was considered to be the 'Carnival of the Midlands' and meant that many potential spectators were unable to attend. Nevertheless, football specials conveyed 1,270 travellers from across Lincolnshire, who poured into the pubs before the match.

A crowd of 3,200 created a great atmosphere and as the players dressed beforehand the referee entered both dressing rooms, warning them against rough and dangerous play. The match started punctually at 3pm. The result was a 3-1 victory for the away side who clearly benefited from some inconsistent decisions by the referee. At 2-1 he failed to spot that Elliott's shot had gone over the line before 'keeper Jack Robinson, who was the man of the match, palmed it away. Minutes later, Gresham unsuccessfully disputed whether a Lincoln shot had crossed the line and then, almost from the restart, Joe Duckworth got away with hacking down Harry Walkerdine as he raced towards the Lincoln goal.

There were also other rough challenges by Lincoln players with the *Athletic News* report stating: 'Lincoln City's persistent infringement of the "laws of the game" should have been penalised with at least two sendings-off.' Robinson became a big football star. He was one of the first 'keepers willing and able enough to make diving saves and wasn't afraid to dive at the feet of an attacker and take the ball from him. He went on to play eleven times internationally and must be regarded as one of England's greatest 'keepers.

Trinity played their first home League game on 18 October 1890 and it came after the club committee decided to up admission prices from 4d to 6d (2p to 2.5p), with the only concession being that advanced tickets could be purchased for 4d. Having massively improved the ground and invested heavily in new players, the committee needed to increase revenues. Just 550 people turned up to witness a 4-0 success in which Cooke netted three. A letter in the GN by 'A Working Man' blamed the price increase for the small crowd as 'the majority are working class and most earn less than 18 shillings [90p] a week out of which they pay 6 shillings [30p] rent. This leaves very little to keep a wife and family going.'

Gainsborough had been invited to play a club match against Woolwich Arsenal on the Invicta playing field, a great amphitheatre that could accommodate 15,000 fans. An 8,500 crowd saw Arsenal go ahead when Arthur Christmas scored. Spectators had been left thrilled by the speed and ball control of Spiksley and as he sprinted away from the home full back Peter Connolly and half back David Howat, someone in the crowd bawled out 'Oh, my goodness! He runs like the wind!'

On 75 minutes the youngster escaped from Howat and met a cross to spectacularly volley the equaliser. Arsenal quickly re-took the lead and then survived fierce pressure to win the match, after which cries of 'Brave Trinity!' went up from the crowd. Rough working hands were employed by two men to hoist Fred onto their shoulders and carry him back to the pavilion, where he was heartily cheered. Despite the defeat Gainsborough were absolutely delighted with the £150 they received as their share of the gate receipts.

On Boxing Day, Port Vale returned home punch-drunk from Lincolnshire as they were thrashed 11-0 at Northolme, with Elliott and Spiksley both netting three. In twenty games so far in the season, the latter had scored twenty times.

In the New Year another letter was posted through Fred's door by a local unidentified man who had been asked by Accrington to observe his performances and who had the previous season written to him stating that the East Lancs Football League club sought his signature. With his apprenticeship shortly to be completed on his twenty-first birthday, Fred this time wrote to the small, unfashionable but friendly club indicating that their offer was something he would like to take up. Fred agreed to visit Accrington and discuss terms.

Accrington, known as 'the Owd Reds', were battling to avoid having to apply for re-election. Fred couldn't prevent that happening this season, but Accrington's charismatic secretary Joe Hartley wanted to steal a march on his rivals by recruiting some of the best players around in order to demonstrate that his club should remain in the League and subsequently be a force to be reckoned with. In 1891 it was perfectly legal for clubs to approach players before their contracts expired, but secrecy was important as once news leaked out a deal had been agreed then the player and his family might experience resentment and even violence by fans of his current club.

Although violence at football was never organised, it wasn't unusual. When Trinity beat Derby Junction 1-0 on 3 January 1891, the referee, Mr West, needed protection by the Gainsborough players. Home fans had attempted to assault West after he blew the final whistle on 80 minutes. They were unaware that it had been agreed to cut the game by 10 minutes because of bad light and thought he had abandoned the match.

Eight days later, Fred, with his overcoat collar turned up as he left Gainsborough by train, travelled to Accrington where he enjoyed lunch with Hartley, club president D.W. Spark and chairman, Mr Hargreaves. They outlined how they could find Fred a good job as a compositor with a local printer and also pay him £2 10s (£2.50) a week throughout the year as a professional footballer. The contract was ready to sign, but Fred asked if he could take it home to discuss this with his parents before putting pen to paper. Hartley was happy enough with this and Fred departed believing he would soon be returning.

However, when he arrived back in Sheffield he had missed the final train home. He was directed to the Maunche Hotel by the stationmaster, where he bumped into Fred Thompson, the Wednesday captain. During the ensuing conversation, Fred let slip why he was in Sheffield and the Wednesday full back urged him to not to sign the contract in his pocket and wait until he had heard from the Olive Grove club. Thompson departed hastily.

Fred returned home on the early hours train and went to work on a day when the North played the South in an England trial match in Nottingham that saw the first official use of goal nets. They were invented by a Liverpool civil engineer, John Brodie, who had taken out a patent for his 'net pocket'. As they were made on Merseyside, it was appropriate that a player from there was the first to put a ball into them: Everton's Fred Geary scoring for the North after quarter of an hour. By the start of the following season, every major team was using them. Yet goal nets are still not compulsory and despite being mentioned as a necessity in all competition rules, a game could go ahead without them: 'Nets may be attached to the goals and the ground behind the goal, provided that they are properly supported and do not interfere with the goalkeeper.' (*Laws of the Game 2008–09 FIFA*).

After he had finished work on 12 January 1891, Fred was handed a telegram by his mother from Henry Pearson, the Wednesday club secretary, inviting Fred to meet him, John Holmes and Arthur Dickinson, the Sheffield club's president and financial secretary respectively. Dickinson's title was slightly confusing as he effectively picked the side at Wednesday for many years, and in 1899 oversaw the club's conversion to a limited company and actually became the first shareholder. Dickinson's duties included scouting for players in Scotland, and he joined the Wednesday committee in 1876 and stayed until 18 May 1920.

Two days after the telegram a return ticket to Sheffield arrived. At the meeting the following Sunday, Fred was offered £3 a week for forty weeks of the year and the promise of a compositor's job in Sheffield for a further 10 shillings

(50p) a week after he had completed his apprenticeship. As with Accrington, Fred asked for time to discuss the offer with his parents. When he did so they were happy with Wednesday's terms and their son agreed to join a non-League side rather than one from the Football League.

Fred Spiksley had arrived in Sheffield to discuss terms the day after he and Gainsborough had played one of their finest matches, against Staveley. A close-knit community in North Derbyshire, Staveley was steeped in sporting tradition and boasted a very good football team. They included two men who later became England internationals: full back Harry Lilley and Ernest Needham, the latter nicknamed 'Nudger' by his teammates because of his ability to nudge opponents off the ball. Needham became a footballing legend at Sheffield United, joining them when he was 18 after working on the pit bank in the local colliery since he was 13.

Due to heavy rain, the match was played at Pingle Hill as Northolme was only good for water polo. In the event it was Staveley who were all at sea as the local side beat them 10-0 in a match that was played in a second half snowstorm. The final goal was the best of the afternoon, when Gainsborough's outside left dribbled at lightning-fast pace through the bewildered Staveley defence. Needham never forgot the game and years later wrote:

> In this game we had to rely on football science ... our skill and speed simply bewildered our opponents so that we kept them guessing from start to finish.
>
> Our captain told me to shift from left to right half to stop the outside left. I might as well have tried to stop the wind. The outside left was Fred Spiksley ... the finest outside left I have ever met and whose dribbling was a treat to watch. He could either combine with the others and make openings by lively centres, or cut past the back on the inside to go for goal himself. He could also shoot with either foot.
>
> Being such a dangerous man, he got a lot of knocking about, but he took it as a rule with very good grace. I shall never forget Freddy's dazzling wing play with Wheldon of the Villa, as the left wing in 1898, when England beat Scotland 3-1.

Having agreed to join Wednesday, Fred wrote to Accrington thanking them for their offer but declining it. Within 48 hours, Accrington replied by telegram upping their offer to £182 a year, the equivalent of £3.50 a week and more than

Wednesday's offer. A few hours later there was a knock on his parents' door. They answered it and found Joe Hartley standing there. He was quickly ushered into the parlour. His character soon won over Fred's parents, who also saw a strong business case for their son to play for Accrington.

Hartley stressed to Fred that his club were in the Football League while Wednesday were struggling in the Football Alliance. He then confided that Arthur Elliott, Fred's partner out left for Gainsborough, had agreed to sign for Accrington. As Fred agreed, the offer was a strong one that couldn't be refused. The decision seemed almost straightforward, but he turned Accrington down. Fred explained his reason in an article published on 8 May 1920, 'I could only blurt out that I preferred Sheffield to Accrington because it was much closer to my home and family.' This was very similar to what he had said in an earlier article in 1907.

However, in 1920 he added the following: 'You may wonder why I was so keen on this point when Accrington's offer was so superior, and want to know my reasons. I do not care to answer this question, but if you cared to ask Mrs Spiksley I have no doubt that she would suggest that there must have been a woman in this case, and I have been married for too long to enter into any argument with a lady.'

Spiksley was obviously deliberately cryptic in his justification for signing for Wednesday. What is clear is that some part of his decision-making was based upon his relationships with women. He seems to be suggesting that if you were to ask Ellen in 1920, the person who knows him best, she would have confirmed that the only factor in Fred's life that would overrule money and gambling would be a woman. Therefore, because Accrington were offering more money than Wednesday and a chance to play League Football, then there must have been a woman in his life at this time.

Knowing that he was set to play for Wednesday in 1891–92 made Fred determined to end his time with Gainsborough by winning the Midland League and he helped his side beat Lincoln City 3-0, with Walkerdine scoring three in 5 minutes. The following day Fred came of age and he travelled to Sheffield to sign his new contract.

On the next day, Fred came out of his time as an apprentice at the GN. Charles Caldicott presented him with his certificate as a qualified compositor and Fred tendered his resignation to take up a job in the composing room with the *Sheffield Telegraph*. Wednesday had arranged lodgings at 19 Talbot Street, where he shared rooms and rent with accountant Thomas McCabe. Over the following two and a half seasons he worked Monday to Friday at the paper. While he continued playing for Gainsborough in 1891 he travelled there each weekend.

Moving to Sheffield was essential as it was feared that once Gainsborough fans heard Fred was leaving some would see the move as a betrayal. Fred wasn't keen to face the same treatment as the players poached by Burnley.

Gainsborough's good form continued as Grimsby Town were beaten 2-1 in the Lincolnshire Challenge Cup semi-final. Afterwards a Grimsby fishmonger delivered half a ton of fish to the Hickman Arms in Gainsborough, with instructions to distribute it to the winning team and the deserving poor of the town. Eating the fish clearly didn't do the Trinity players much good as the following weekend they lost their third League game of the season when beaten 3-1 at Derby Junction. The losers were now a point behind leaders Derby Midland. But when the sides met at Northolme, Trinity moved into first place with a fine display that saw them win 3-0.

Hitting the top was a real pleasure, unlike Fred's journey with his eldest brother, Ted, who was intent on building a new life overseas and had successfully applied for a job in the iron and steel industry in Pittsburgh, USA. Since moving to Sheffield, Fred had visited his brother most nights but on the evening of Friday, 6 March 1891, the pair journeyed to Liverpool and booked into a local lodging house.

The following morning, Fred helped Ted to stow away his sea chest and after the final farewells the ship cast off for America at 8am. The pair didn't know when they might see each other again and must have sorrowfully departed in opposite directions, with Fred off to face Sheffield United at Bramall Lane. The venue had first opened as a cricket ground on 30 April 1855 and first class cricket was to continue being played there until 1973. This was long after the Bramall Lane committee had been forced to drop its hostility to football during the late Victorian era in order to generate the income they required to keep it open.

With Wednesday playing away the gate was boosted by fans keen to see their new signing, and the 500 Gainsborough fans present were shocked to learn that Fred Spiksley was departing. The away side took an early lead, but ended up defeated 2-1. Gainsborough had lost a vital match and their supporters departed doubly disappointed after the news that their outside left was leaving. Wednesday fans were also upset as their new man had played poorly. With hindsight, Fred shouldn't have played as he was exhausted and emotionally drained from a tiring journey to Liverpool and back.

More disappointment followed as Trinity lost 1-0 to Lincoln City in the Lincolnshire County Challenge Cup final. However, the following weekend, Gainsborough beat Port Vale 3-1 to capture two valuable points. Two days later, on Easter Monday, Warwick County took a two-goal interval lead when they played Gainsborough at home. Defeat would have ended the away side's title chances, but with Spiksley providing a succession of beautifully weighted crosses and corners the home side were under constant second-half pressure. When County did try to break away they were pushed back by the Gainsborough half back line of Murrell, Carlin and Henrys. Arthur Elliott scored two and after Billy Cooke put his side ahead, Fred Spiksley wrapped up the scoring for a 4-2 win.

This was a vital victory. It meant that in the final game of the season Gainsborough knew as long as they avoided being beaten 11-0 at home by second-placed Long Eaton Rangers, then they were certain to finish in top spot as the Lincolnshire club enjoyed a two-point advantage and a far superior goal average. The title was in the bag and it may have been that complacency had set in as Rangers took a 3-1 lead, only for the champions-elect to hit back when Spiksley ghosted in to net from a fine Murrell cross. Taffy Thomas then did some splendid work and Walkerdine sent hats up in the air as he made it 3-3.

So it was that on 17 July 1891, Gainsborough Trinity received twelve Midland Counties League championship-winning medals for presentation by the Trinity executive to the players. The medals were designed in silver with a 'gold shield' in the centre and a 'gold scroll' below.

Along with the medals, Gainsborough were presented with the Midland Counties League championship pennant. Gainsborough's great success in a league where they competed with much bigger sides had nevertheless come at a cost, as they were losing some of their top players with Fred Spiksley going to The Wednesday, Arthur Elliott to Accrington, John 'Taffy' Thomas to Sheffield United, Arthur Henrys to Newton Heath, George Murrell rejoining Grimsby Town and Harry Walkerdine rejoining Notts County. The team had been decimated, but they had won the title and every man jack of them had earned it.

Chapter 6

League Aspirations

An impressive first season playing for Wednesday in the Football Alliance

Fred's new club, The Wednesday, who became Sheffield Wednesday in 1929, had attracted their record crowd of 16,871 when they lost 2-0 to West Bromwich Albion in the FA Cup on Valentine's Day 1891. In 1890, Wednesday had reached the final against Blackburn Rovers but lost 6-1 against a side from the Football League – a league which the losers had designs on joining. At the end of the 1889–90 season, Sunderland had become the first change to the original League line-up, when they were elected to replace Stoke.

The numbers passing through the turnstiles indicated Wednesday would be a healthy addition to the Football League. One problem was the Sheffield club's form: they had slumped from top spot in 1889–90 to the bottom of the Alliance in 1890–91. Out of twenty-two games, just four were won.

Wednesday Football Club had developed out of Wednesday Cricket Club, which was formed in 1820. Three of the then twelve league clubs were also developed from local cricket clubs in Burnley, Accrington and Derby County. Similar to the Gainsborough club for which Fred played a handful of games, Wednesday took this name because matches were played on Wednesdays. Four years after its inauguration the club opened Darnall cricket ground, considered to be one of England's finest, and within a few years it had seats for 8,000 spectators.

On Wednesday, 4 September 1867, John Pashley's proposal to form a football club was accepted by members and a committee was established by the sixty or so who joined the new club that night. In their first game, the Mechanics Club were beaten by three goals and four rouges to one rouge in a game played at Norfolk Park. A rouge was the outer part of the then 12 feet wide and 9 feet high goal, and was separated from the middle part – the goal – by posts on either side. One goal was worth any amount of rouges. Rouges were abolished in 1868 when the goal width became 8 yards.

In 1877, Wednesday won the first Sheffield Challenge Cup competition, beating Heeley 4-3 in a thrilling final that attracted 8,000 to Bramall Lane, with most of these spectators working in either the steel or cutlery industry. Sheffield has a long industrial history; coal was burned at Templeborough by Roman soldiers, and the Sheffield manorial accounts of 1442–43 refer to coal-pits and charcoal-making; they also say that there were a number of water mills on the rivers. The list of Sheffield taxpayers in 1297 records a Robertus le Cotelar (Robert the Cutler), although the cutlery trade is probably even older. Sheffield had thus acquired a distinctive character early in the second millennium. By 1851, Sheffield was a borough with 135,310 people and the numbers continued to rise as it was transformed dramatically by the building of great steelworks that gobbled up labour.

Benjamin Huntsman, a Doncaster clockmaker, invented 'cast steel' in the mid eighteenth century. Key to this was the understanding that coke fuel could reach higher temperatures than charcoal. Coal mined from the Barnsley seam was excellent coke and Huntsman became a full-time steel maker on the east side of Attercliffe Green in 1751. Over the following century the Sheffield–Rotherham region became the world's number one steel-producing centre. As industry developed more workers were needed and as their wages increased, partly as a result of trade union agitation, and when Saturday early closing became the norm the way was open for emerging football clubs to seek support.

Capturing the first Wharncliffe Charity Cup in 1879 cemented Wednesday's place among the local giants of football. By then, Wednesday had begun to embrace professionalism with the signing of James Lang, but the greatest Wednesday player in the pre-league period was left-winger Billy Mosforth, an engraver who played nine times for England. Mosforth was lightning quick, possessed great dribbling ability and could hit accurate screw or spin shots that would change direction as they came in from the corner flag. In an era where individualism was king, Mosforth, known as 'The Little Wonder' had a valid claim to the throne. Future Wednesday left wingers would be judged against this marvellous player.

Confusion following the death of secretary William Littlehales in January 1886 saw Wednesday fail to send in their 1886–87 FA Cup entry. Most of the club's best players joined local side Lockwood Brothers and did very well by reaching the fourth round. Without their stars, Wednesday even lost 16-0 against Halliwell, which remains their record defeat.

In April 1887, Mosforth and Cawley, both of whom had previously been banned by Sheffield FA over payment allegations, helped form Sheffield Rovers with the intention of assembling all of Sheffield's best players to fight for the FA Cup the following season. It was felt that if the players needed expenses to play they should have them and it was agreed these would be 5s (25p) and 7s 6d

(37.5p) for home and away games respectively. Such payments, much less than at many other professional clubs, really only covered a player's loss of wages when he was absent from work playing football.

Rovers only ever played three games, but their formation forced Wednesday to hold what proved to be an historic meeting in June 1887 at the Garrick Hotel, Sycamore Street. At the meeting it was agreed the players would from then on be paid expenses – the amounts quickly rose to around £2 a week in 1888.

If Wednesday had remained an amateur club they would have been overtaken by other clubs prepared to pay the best players to play for them. Professionalism meant Wednesday required a ground where they could be assured of a larger financial return. Bramall Lane was ruled out because the committee there insisted on taking a massive slice of the gate receipts. Instead, Wednesday secured a seven year lease on a field off Queen's Road and adjacent to the Midland railway line, which often meant the match ball needed rescuing during games. Bill Russell was paid to fulfil the task. The new facilities cost £5,000: the stream which ran through the field was covered over, the ground was enclosed and subsequently named Olive Grove. The adoption of professionalism allied to a new ground helped ensure that Wednesday became Sheffield's premier club.

In 1888, Wednesday applied unsuccessfully to join the Football League and a year later, after another unsuccessful application, the club helped form the Football Alliance. Wednesday won their first league match 2-1 at home against Bootle on 7 September 1889. The game was watched by 2,000 people and despite a poor season, 6,000 through the gates was common throughout the 1890–91 season.

However, if Wednesday were going to become a Football League member, then the 1891–92 season required a major on-field improvement. Hoping to recapture the fine form of the 1889–90 season, the Wednesday committee chose to augment the squad with just three new players in Fred Spiksley, Third Lanark's Gavin Thomson and the experienced Scotsman Tom Brandon from Blackburn Rovers, who became club captain.

In a most unusual move for the times, Brandon, who had a reputation for head-butting opponents, was given a two-year contract that also included the summer months. To Blackburn's disgust, Wednesday lured him across the Pennines with what ultimately proved to be a false offer of a public house. A deeply homesick Brandon returned to Blackburn in December 1893.

Brandon's younger brother, Bob, had signed for Wednesday in October 1890, but was released at the end of the season. Another younger brother, James, signed from Preston North End and played briefly for Wednesday in the 1891–92 season. Cousin Harry Brandon did much better after he arrived in December

1890 from Clyde and the utility player made over 200 competitive Wednesday appearances, including the 1896 FA Cup final.

In Fred Spiksley, Wednesday had signed a rare talent. He had four seasons of professional football under his belt, had survived a broken leg and was now stronger than ever. Wednesday would have been excited by the prospect of signing a player who had played 126 times for Trinity and had netted 131 goals. Fred first wore a Wednesday shirt on 18 August 1891 in a public trial match – the whites versus stripes at the Sheaf House Ground close to Bramall Lane, which was now being used regularly for football after United were formed in March 1889. He was very roughly treated by opposing right half Ernest Bartlett, who used his considerable weight advantage in a series of heavy charges.

One Bartlett challenge had his opponent's head scraping along the cinder running track surrounding the pitch. Fred years later commented, 'This was the worst game I had to contend with'. Bartlett never made a first team appearance but, having been overpowered, Fred Spiksley's name wasn't on the team sheet for the first friendly match of the season away to Sunderland Albion.

Fred hadn't turned down League football to play reserve football and immediately sought out John Holmes to request to be released from his contract. When the Wednesday chairman was joined by Arthur Nixon, the pair couldn't persuade the impetuous young man to bide his time and he continued to demand his cards in order to seek another club. A desperate Nixon told the new Wednesday winger that the side wasn't yet officially confirmed, bringing to an end an increasingly acrimonious meeting. A few days later Fred was informed he would play at Sunderland. No reason for the change was given, but the move proved a wise one as although Wednesday lost 2-1, their goal was scored by debutant Fred Spiksley, who thereafter never had to worry about his place in the Wednesday team when he was fit.

Fred made his competitive debut for Wednesday at home to Grimsby Town in the Football Alliance on 19 September 1891. The Wednesday line up was as follows: Smith, McConnachie, Mumford, Brandon, Betts, Cawley, Gemmell, (James) Brandon, Thompson, Woolhouse, Spiksley

Five of the side had played in the 1890 FA Cup final. Goalkeeper Jim Smith helped Wednesday to two Sheffield Challenge Cups and two Wharncliffe Charity Cups. A steel smelter, Smith was a real character who smoked a clay pipe during games, throwing it away when the ball came towards him.

Billy Betts, who was also a fine cricketer, was one of Wednesday's early greats and during the three years in the Alliance missed just a handful of games. Despite becoming one of Wednesday's first professional footballers, Betts continued working as a stoker at Neepsend Gas Works. He had a reputation for being made of solid steel and played for England against Wales in February 1889. His grandson, Dennis Woodhead, later played over 200 games for Wednesday. Betts sat next to Fred Spiksley and Tom Crawshaw when Wednesday last won the FA Cup at Wembley in 1935.

Henry Woolhouse was a versatile forward who scored five in Wednesday's club record 12-0 FA Cup win against Halliwell in January 1891. His place was threatened by the arrival of Fred Spiksley, although he did play in Wednesday's losing semi-finals in 1894 and 1895.

Tom Cawley debuted for Wednesday on 5 November 1881 in an FA Cup-tie at Providence. He made his final appearance in the FA Cup over a decade later and rightly earned a reputation for fairness and superb ball control that in an era of 'kick and rush' meant he stood out on a football pitch. Off it, his decision to speak up in support of professionalism was vital in ensuring Wednesday survived. In 1889, Cawley netted four times in an international trial match, but still wasn't selected to play for England.

Albert Mumford signed professionally for Wednesday in 1887 and it was his two goals against Bolton Wanderers on 8 March 1890 that helped his club win their FA Cup semi-final 2-1. Incredibly versatile, Mumford later helped the reserves to two league titles before his loyalty was rewarded with an 1896 benefit match against Sheffield United.

The home side beat Grimsby 4-2 with Woolhouse, scoring three times, repeating his feat from an earlier game against the Canadian touring side. Woolhouse still bore the scars from the tourists' match in which he and James Dalton tangled in a bout of wrestling during which the Canadian sank his teeth so hard into his opponent's cheek that blood poured from his mouth. The pair were separated with great difficulty, but neither was dismissed from the field. Dalton, who was Irish, later played for Sunderland. He's a very early example of the soccer cosmopolitanism common today.

On 17 October 1891, Fred Spiksley created two goals and opened the scoring with his first Alliance goal as Burton Swifts lost 5-2 at Olive Grove. Wednesday then lost 3-2 at Bootle. Following the introduction of the penalty kick, Tom Brandon's goal was the club's first from 'the spot'. The penalty taker was allowed to place the ball anywhere along the twelve-yard penalty line that ran the full width of the pitch and within which any offence meant a penalty.

In late October, Fred played in his first Sheffield derby match against a United side from the Northern League. It was a friendly, but there was nothing welcoming about Bob Cain's early heavy charge that left him with double vision. Wednesday lost 5-0 before a crowd approaching 23,000. For days afterwards, Fred feared venturing out and when he did he hid himself away. The result did, however, prove positive. Wednesday directors hadn't previously considered the virtues of regular formal training and practice. Thereafter it was agreed that any player not employed elsewhere would train for a minimum of two hours each morning.

Wednesday won five and drew one of the six games after the heavy derby defeat. They also took revenge by beating United 4-1 with the newspapers stating that Spiksley scored twice when he argued he had, in fact, scored all of Wednesday's goals! Journalists covering the game would have experienced difficulties identifying the players after heavy rain resulted in the unnumbered players' shirts and hair being completely soaked and covered in mud.

The Wednesday outside left did, though, enjoy some fortune, because after enjoying a hot bath he felt a shooting pain in his knee and discovered a large piece of flesh hanging loose. The player decided to cut it off, but was prevented from doing this by one of his teammates who sought out Dr Lockwood. The doctor stitched up the wound but the pain was excruciating and the injured man was given brandy to prevent him passing out. The injury stopped Fred Spiksley from playing over the next four weeks as his knee kept breaking out in abscesses, the result of foreign substances in the wound. The treatment had worked, though, preventing the potentially fatal tetanus infection from developing.

As 1892 dawned, Wednesday lay in second place and on 9 January they beat Small Heath 6-3 with Spiksley scoring two and Brown three. The winning side had a new goalkeeper in Bill Allan, whose enormous feet meant a cobbler needed to work overnight to make a good pair of football boots big enough for him to play. Allan became a regular over the next four seasons, earning the nickname 'William the Silent' for his quiet demeanour.

On 23 January 1892 a 16,500 crowd crammed inside Olive Grove to see Wednesday face Bolton Wanderers in the FA Cup first round. Playing his final game of a long career for the Lancashire side was Kenny Davenport. At 3.47pm on Saturday, 8 September 1888, Davenport, an England international, had become the scorer of the first ever League goal as he put his side ahead at Pike's Lane in a game that Bolton eventually lost 6-3 to Derby County.

Wednesday won 4-1 and their outside left scored twice – both from close in – but he was left needing to visit the hospital when Sandy Paton's boot inflicted a wound that required ten stitches. Dai Jones scored the single Bolton goal. In 1902 the Welsh international died of tetanus after he suffered a similar knee injury to Fred Spiksley's in the 1891–92 season.

In the FA Cup second round Wednesday overcame Small Heath 2-0 in a rough game that led to Olive Grove being closed for a fortnight by the FA. Then, in the last eight of the competition, they came up against West Bromwich Albion and were outplayed, losing 2-1. With six league games remaining, the Sheffield club needed a strong finish to have any chance of again winning the Football Alliance. In the event they won twice and ended in fourth place, five points behind champions Nottingham Forest. Wednesday, however, had shown they were a force to be reckoned with. In addition to their respectable fourth place they had beaten League side Bolton in the FA Cup and Accrington (6-0), Preston (6-1) and Notts County (5-2) in club games. They now hoped to be accepted into the Football League.

And what of Fred Spiksley's first season at Olive Grove? It hadn't been easy, as in many games he had faced 'big bruisers', all keen to knock the lightweight youngster into the crowd. Yet the Gainsborough lad ended the season having played sixteen of twenty-two league games and scoring nine goals. He also scored two in the FA Cup as well as many other goals in the numerous club games that were played throughout the 1891–92 season, in which Wednesday played over seventy games in total. Fred's form was so good that he had even been selected as England's first non-playing reserve for the international match in Wales that was won by the away side 2-0.

It had clearly been a good first campaign for Fred Spiksley in Sheffield Wednesday colours and he later commented: 'My workload was a heavy one and to come through it was a tremendous achievement in itself. Having survived my first season, I was extremely proud of myself, and insofar as Wednesday was concerned then my selection as first reserve for England was evidence that Wednesday had little to complain of as to the bargain they had made.'

On 22 April 1892 the Football League agreed to form a Second Division. The League had been expanded to fourteen clubs in 1891–92 and two clubs would now be added to form a First Division of sixteen. These would then vote for twelve new members to form the second tier. However, the matter was largely predetermined with the League minutes stating: 'It was felt that the Alliance as a body (except St George's) should be admitted to the League'. The Alliance, born three years earlier, was to be absorbed.

With twelfth-placed West Bromwich Albion excused from applying for re-election in recognition of having won the 1892 FA Cup, there were five Division One places up for grabs. Applications from Liverpool, Newcastle East End and an amalgamated Middlesbrough side were rejected. This meant the three re-election applicants from Division One in Accrington, Stoke and Darwen competed with Nottingham Forest, Newton Heath and Wednesday from the Alliance in the contest for Division One places in 1892–93. Wednesday won the most votes and Darwen the least. The latter thus dropped down into Division Two, where the vast majority of Alliance teams joined them, plus Burslem Port Vale, Northwich Victoria and Sheffield United. The Football League had expanded to Manchester, Lincolnshire, Cheshire and South Yorkshire.

Chapter 7

A New Hero Rises

Wednesday's first season in the Football League

Having achieved entry to the Football League, Wednesday sought to improve their team and facilities. Newcomers for the 1892–93 season were Alec Brady, Harry Davis and Alex Rowan. Scotsman Brady had started at Partick Thistle and, after playing for Sunderland, had moved to Gainsborough Trinity before swiftly departing to Burnley. In February 1889 he re-signed for Sunderland. At the start of the 1889–90 season, a registration dispute between Burnley and Everton delayed his debut for the Toffees until November 1889. He thereafter played for eighteen months at Everton where, as the first of many inside forwards who could bring others into play with deft, accurate passing, he helped the Toffees capture the newly-minted League trophy in 1890–91. He then sensationally quit England to return home to play for Celtic, before joining Wednesday a year later, coming south with Fred Spiksley's former coach, John Madden.

This was the second time that Wednesday had tried to sign Madden in a twelve-month period. With Wednesday turning their attentions north of the border to pay for first class talent, the club had to resort to their own poaching missions similar to that of Burnley in 1888. The man who 'ran the gauntlet' was Arthur Dickinson, the club secretary. In 1899, Dickinson was to recall his adventures in Scotland in the *Lancashire Evening News*:

> In September 1891 I had a rare adventure. I went up to get Towie, who afterwards came to North End. He was playing then with Geordie Dewar's old team – Dumbarton. In the same club was a full back named Spiers, whom I also wanted. John Wilson's agent met me and at Partick we picked up Jack Madden, of the Celtic. Wilson and I got off at Bowling and Jack went straight on to Dumbarton to bring up the two players. We arrived at the appointed rendezvous – Sinclair's Restaurant, a noted football house, and one that every Scotch player is acquainted with – and presently in came Madden, accompanied by Towie and Spiers. We had to use a great deal of persuasive eloquence

to effect our purpose and at last seemed to have succeeded. Towie took up a pen to sign the professional form and it was all but done when the door opened and in walked the Dumbarton club secretary, the trainer and two or three gentlemen with opinions and muscle. We were squarely trapped.

Wilson bolted and got clear beautifully. Jack and I were left to face the music and without any preliminaries we prepared to depart. We scrimmaged our way down the stairs and there found a crowd – hundreds of them – waiting for us. The entry of the club officials, and our reception by the multitude were partly of the same plan. The crowd yelled like savages and made for us. Madden hadn't any interest in me, except that he had seen me landed in a hole. And that was good enough excuse for him, so he stuck to me like a brick. We got our backs against the wall and, by Jove, Jack did fight!

He was real pluck. Sheer weight of numbers separated us and it was a case of making a bee line for the station. I don't know how he got along, for the crowd followed, letting go at me at every possible chance. Several times they tried to trip me up and had I gone down it might have proven awkward. I was thoroughly mauled. Finally I struggled into the station and rushed into a standing train. Luckily it was about to start for Glasgow – my destination. In the same train the agent was seated, spick and span and comfortable without a scratch.

I was bleeding from my mouth and nose. When my face 'developed' I had two blackened eyes and was generally cut and bruised. With such a face I dare not appear in public, and for two days after stayed in my hotel in Glasgow. Then I had to send for a chemist to paint away the discolouration around my eyes before I dared venture forth as a respectable man. I never heard how Madden fared after we parted for I did not see him again for another year.

One year on and it looked as though Dickinson had finally got his man.
No-one knew it, but a Roman Catholic priest, acting as a detective, was hot on the two players' trail and had followed them from Glasgow. Two hefty bodyguards accompanied God's man when he located Madden and persuaded him to return to Scotland. Madden was spirited away on the night mail train. To prevent Brady being whisked back north, Arthur Dickinson had him smuggled

by train to Boston and locked away in a safe house for two weeks until it was clear that the priest had tired of looking for him. Brady arrived back in Sheffield the day before Wednesday's first Football League match.

Wednesday also signed Harry Davis from Birmingham Saint George's. Davis had done well in fixtures against Wednesday and was seen as the ideal replacement on the right wing for the released Duncan Gemmell.

Having lost Gavin Thomson with a broken ankle at the end of the previous campaign, Madden's loss left Wednesday short of someone to lead their front line. Dickinson left for Scottish side Albion Rovers, where his target was Alex Rowan, who two seasons earlier had struggled at Nottingham Forest. Dickinson hoped the homesick teenager with raw talent had matured since returning to Scotland. The change was remarkable; Rowan, who had netted six goals against Clydebank in October 1891, was now 6 feet tall and 12 stones. He had the physique to deal with the heavy kicking, charging and elbowing prevalent in the Football League. Rowan gladly signed for Wednesday.

The Wednesday first team pool for the start of 1892–93 was:

Keepers – Bill Allan, Jim Smith

Backs – Tom Brandon, Albert Corbett Mumford, John Darroch, James Brown

Half backs – Harry Brandon, Billy Betts, Alex 'Sandy' Hall, Bob McConachie

Forwards – Harry Davis, Bob Brown, Alex Rowan, Thomas McIntosh, Harry Woolhouse, Alec Brady, Walter Dunlop and Fred Spiksley

Wednesday's first ever Football League game was at Notts County. With Trent Bridge occupied for cricket, the game was at the Nottingham Castle Ground on 3 September 1892. The 13,000 crowd included 2,000 from Sheffield, but as kick-off approached, many fans remained locked out. There was then a rush to gain entry and once inside fans spilled on to the pitch, resulting in a 25-minute delay while they were relocated to a less-crowded part of the ground.

With Tom Brandon superbly marshalling his defence, Wednesday soon got the upper hand in a fast-flowing game played on hard ground. The surface suited Fred Spiksley well and he hit a shot that flicked off the crossbar. On 11 minutes, Notts conceded the opening goal when, from a Spiksley corner, either Harry Davis or the captain, Tom Brandon, scored (most records give the goal to Brandon). At the interval two mounted policemen came into the ground to ensure the crowd didn't encroach on the pitch. When the match resumed, Brady missed narrowly and with both sides failing to net the match finished Notts County 0 Wednesday 1.

The following Saturday, Wednesday played their first home game in the Football League. Ironically, it was against Accrington, the club for whom Fred had come so close to signing. The match was played in a refurbished Olive Grove: the major ground improvements made there during the summer of 1892 turning the Wednesday ground into one of the finest enclosures in the country. The pitch had been re-turfed and levelled, thus ending visiting teams' complaints that Wednesday gained an unfair advantage by the peculiarity of their ground. The playing field measured 125 × 86 yards, easily accommodating the pitch measurements required for cup-ties, although Wednesday, in fact, adopted a medium-sized layout of 115 × 76 yards.

The purchase of an additional piece of land at the 'Heeley End' allowed the stand there to be enlarged and improved. An old wooden stand running down the side of the pitch had been replaced by a brand new brick-built one capable of hosting 1,000 people at 1 shilling (5p) each on comfortable seating. Underneath were the dressing rooms and bathrooms that contained a tiny gas stove for the comfort of the players and one slipper bath large enough to accommodate eleven men. Two Wednesday players, Harry Davis and Fred Spiksley, were known for being exceptionally clever in getting stripped after the match and getting into the bath first. In front of the stand an enclosure costing 6d (2.5p) to enter was to prove popular. The uncovered 'Sheffield End' stand had been taken back and raised.

Despite the changes, the pitch's proximity to the terracing and seating remained so close that the intimacy and personal bonds between players and spectators remained strong. Wednesday supporters felt they were part of the team. This bond was strengthened because Wednesday never trained behind closed doors and fans watched the training sessions for free. Afterwards, it wasn't unusual for the players to have a beer with fans at the Earl of Arundel and Surrey Hotel.

The ground improvements cost Wednesday around £2,000, a hefty sum, but the club committee were confident that the impressive new facilities could be paid for as they were convinced they had assembled a top quality team the public would want to watch, especially with the guaranteed regularity of top class teams such as Aston Villa, Everton and League champions Sunderland visiting. Despite the massive improvements there was still the need for Bill Russell to be regularly despatched on to the nearby railway tracks to fetch balls that had been kicked there. As a result, Wednesday kept half-a-dozen spare balls handy on match days.

Against Accrington, Rowan replaced Walter Dunlop, with Davis moving out to the wing to accommodate the new player. The home side were three up by half-time and ran off to great cheers after winning 5-2, with Brown scoring twice and Davis, Rowan and Spiksley one each. The return match two weeks later at Accrington's Thorneyholme Ground, which at the time was used for both football and cricket and is still a cricket ground today, saw the East Lancs side win 4-2.

Victory over Burnley was followed by a draw at Nottingham Forest and then four straight victories, including a 3-2 success against Sunderland that was watched by 20,000, the largest home crowd of the season. The Wearsiders had thrashed Aston Villa at Perry Barr on 17 September 1892 and afterwards William McGregor dubbed them the 'Team of all the Talents'. The week before the game with Wednesday, Sunderland had beaten West Bromwich Albion 8-1, with Johnny Campbell scoring twice. The Scot finished as Division One top scorer in 1891–92, 1892–93 and 1894–95.

Campbell opened the scoring against Wednesday. Gaining possession on the halfway line, he raced away before beating Allan with a surprise snapshot. Sunderland 'keeper Ted Doig, who always wore a cap to hide his baldness, also had no chance when Hall equalised with a long dropping shot. Jock Scott restored Sunderland's lead but after Brady equalised, Hall scored the winner from a free kick that saw the ground erupt. Sunderland's defeat failed to prevent them racing to the title.

The week after beating Sunderland, Wednesday beat Bolton Wanderers 4-2 in a game in which Spiksley scored his first League double. A fortnight later, Jack Southworth notched two as Wednesday lost 3-0 at home to Blackburn Rovers.

The weekend between the two League games marked Fred Spiksley's debut in the annual inter-association match between Sheffield & Hallamshire and Glasgow. Such matches between city teams were a popular feature in football's early years. The first Sheffield v Glasgow game took place at Bramall Lane on 14 March 1874. It ended 2-2, but in the next sixteen times the sides met, Sheffield won only once, in 1891, when the Glaswegians were beaten 4-3 at Bramall Lane.

During his time at Trinity, Fred had made three appearances for the Lincolnshire Association team across four seasons. Although he was to go on and achieve much greater accomplishments, it's known that Fred was deeply proud of representing Lincolnshire and cherished the caps he was awarded.

Fred had made his debut for Sheffield & Hallamshire against the London FA in February 1892 before a crowd of 10,000 at Bramall Lane.

Sheffield & Hallamshire: W.J. Lilley, Mumford, Lilley, Howell, Betts, Whitham, Needham, Dobson, Hammond, Woodhouse, Spiksley.

Playing in white jerseys, Sheffield scored on 30 minutes when Spiksley's perfect ball presented Harry Hammond (Sheffield United) with an unmissable chance. Hammond and Spiksley continued to combine superbly and the home side won 4-1, with Hammond scoring three. The victors had now won twelve against the London FA's thirteen in the series of matches.

In 1895 Fred and Harry Davis scored in a 2-0 victory in London and the following season the Wednesday outside left scored two as London were beaten 7-4 in a thrilling Monday afternoon game at Olive Grove. Both sides' forwards were in superb form and failed to be hampered by the torrential rain and muddy pitch. However, London had their revenge in 1897 when an over-confident Sheffield side lost 4-1 in the capital with the only consolation goal coming from Fred Spiksley. In 1898 and 1899, Sheffield won 3-2 at Olive Grove and 7-0 at Owlerton.

In October 1892, Fred lined up at outside left against Glasgow in the following XI:

Massey (Doncaster Rovers), Whitham, Lilley, Howell, Betts (captain), Needham, Davis, Leatherbarrow (Rotherham), Hammond, Woolhouse, Spiksley.

The game ended 3-3 with Davis scoring twice for the home side and Fred once. Fred made many other appearances against Glasgow and in 1893 was part of the Sheffield side that thrashed their opponents 7-2. In the next game, played in Glasgow in 1895, the away side lost 3-1 as the Scots took advantage of 'keeper Billy Foulke's inability to reach down to fast low ground shots. Foulke showed his class, though, when the teams, without Spiksley, met in Glasgow in 1897 when he played brilliantly in a 0-0 match. Fred Spiksley was later part of the successful Sheffield sides in 1896 (5-1) and 1898 (2-1), as well as playing in the losing games in 1899 (4-0) and 1902 (2-0 at Owlerton). Games between Glasgow and Sheffield continued annually until 1938 and were briefly revived between 1949 and 1957.

In late November 1892, Goodison Park witnessed a brilliant match in which Everton were beaten 5-3. According to the *Liverpool Mercury*, Fred Spiksley scored the third and fourth Wednesday goals and assisted his inside partner, Brady, a former Evertonian, to two. The Wednesday attacking-left pairing were becoming a potent force.

In early 1893 attention turned to the FA Cup tie with a Derby County side containing John 'the Good' Goodall and youngster Steve Bloomer. Olive Grove was packed with 18,000 inside and with just 7 minutes remaining the away side led 2-0.

As disappointed Wednesday fans began making for the exit gates one who was determined to stay till the end was George Ulyett, who had played once for Wednesday against Notts County in the FA Cup in 1882–83, but was best known as a Yorkshire and England cricketer. Ulyett was a Spiksley and Wednesday fan and when one of his fellow supporters said the odds against Wednesday were 50-1, he quickly struck a bet with him. Within seconds it was 1-2 as Davis scored. On the restart the scorer made space for a fine centre that Rowan pounced on to level. When the referee sounded his whistle after 90 minutes, the home side now had an extra 30 minutes in which to win the tie.

A New Hero Rises

Ernest Hickinbottom had kicked Fred Spiksley black and blue throughout and continued to do so until the 120th minute. But when Betts swung the ball over him, the Derby half back was left helpless when Fred Spiksley raced away before drawing Jimmy Methven out of position, cutting inside at speed and then rounding 'keeper Jack Robinson to score a dramatic winner. Spiksley had won the game and the Wednesday fans now had a hero they could adore.

This was to be a defining event in Fred Spiksley's professional football. Against top quality opposition in an FA Cup tie where Wednesday were dead and buried, Spiksley had delivered the winning goal. From then on, with Fred Spiksley on the field, the Wednesday players and supporters alike knew that no match was ever lost. Spiksley became 'The Olive Grove Flyer'.

However, if the victorious side thought they were through, they were quickly disillusioned. It was an era when many clubs, for a variety of reasons, protested after losing an important cup-tie, which is exactly what Derby did. A replay was ordered by an FA sub-committee when they realised that Brady, signed in the summer, hadn't completed his residential qualification period in Sheffield and was thus ineligible for FA and county cup matches.

The replay was to take place at Derby's Racecourse Ground. Sheffield papers accused Derby of poor sportsmanship and in return, the *Derby Telegraph* noted that after Wednesday had thrashed Notts County 5-0 in 1890, and the latter subsequently had their protest upheld and won the second game 3-2, then Wednesday had themselves made their own successful appeal. Wednesday went through 2-1 after winning the third match.

The replay on a Monday afternoon attracted 14,000 spectators, including many away fans who took advantage of football specials laid on by the Midland Railway Company. So tightly packed was the crowd that there were frequent interruptions as spectators spilled on to the pitch.

Derby's Hickinbottom was determined to ensure his opponent didn't score and Spiksley required treatment several times, with one ridiculously high tackle leaving him poleaxed. Fred could see Bloomer was disgusted by the tactics of his own side and the Derby man afterwards said to Fred: 'If this is first class football I don't think much of it'.

The game was won in extra time when John Goodall scored a great goal that was out of place with the previous poor fare. Derby were through, or were they? It transpired that Bloomer had unknowingly broken the rules by signing two professional contracts – with Derby and Burton Wanderers. A third game was ordered and on 2 February 1893, Wednesday and Derby played again. On a working day a crowd of 10,000 was inside Olive Grove to witness a thrilling encounter.

Goodall scored early before Betts hit a scorcher on 8 minutes to level. Within a minute of the restart the ball was sent out to Spiksley. In a repeat of the first tie he destroyed his marker and left Robinson helpless as his powerful shot rocketed home to make it 2-1. Woolhouse made it 3-1 and the contest was over when Spiksley made it 4-1 and even though Tom Little reduced the arrears, it was the Sheffield side that progressed to the next round. Or had they? Derby protested that Allan had broken FA rules by playing in a summer six-a-side match in Scotland. With no evidence the claim was worthless but, just in case, Arthur Dickinson had prepared his own appeal based on the fact that Derby had played a charity match in Grantham in October 1892 without seeking the FA's approval. By now the FA were utterly fed up with this farcical state of affairs and consequently changed the rules. In future, all clubs competing in the FA Cup had to send in a full list of players two weeks prior to each match and any appeals had to be made seven days prior to kick-off.

Wednesday overcame Burnley (known as the 'Burnley Butchers' for their robust style) next in the FA Cup, courtesy of a Fred Spiksley goal. From one corner the Clarets centre half Tom Nicol ignored the ball and, with the referee's attention elsewhere, planted his knee into Spiksley's ribs. The injured player needed smelling salts to be revived before being carried off and strapped up with swathes of tape and bandages. The pain in his side was excruciating and a wiser man would have ignored captain Tom Brandon's half-time pleas to return to the field. When he did return, he was virtually a passenger and his opponents ignored him. Burnley pressed strongly for a winner, but led by Brandon, Wednesday stood strong.

One boisterous fan taunted Fred about how he wasn't going to score. The man was a milkman but swore like a trooper. With minutes remaining the ball was mistakenly kicked Fred's way and, ignoring the pain, the unmarked Wednesday player took a shot before Tom McLintock could reach him and the ball swerved past Jack Hillman for the winning goal. Years later, the Wednesday hero recalled three men had won the game: 'Tom Brandon, myself and the milkman'. Fred endured severe pain over the following weeks as Nicol's 'tackle' had broken two of his ribs. It was a minor miracle that he had played on with such a serious injury, let alone score the winning goal. An injured Fred missed his side's following two League games. However, he did play against Everton in the FA Cup, but his presence, and it was no more than that, had little effect as Everton won 3-0.

On 11 March 1893, Wednesday lost 1-0 at home to Wolves. Two days later Fred debuted for England against Wales. The following Saturday, a poor Wednesday side were beaten 3-0 at West Bromwich Albion and fell to eleventh in the table: just one place outside the bottom three. A 2-2 draw with Derby provided some relief, but with Fred Spiksley away with England over Easter, Wednesday lost 4-0 at Burnley and 1-0 at home to Stoke.

With one match remaining the new boys knew that defeat at home to Notts County would see their opponents leapfrog them in the table. This would put Wednesday into the bottom three, forcing them to play in a test match series against one of the top three sides in Division Two, with the winners playing in Division One in 1893–94 and the losers playing in Division Two.

The final League game was played on Easter Monday 1893. Wednesday were buoyed by the return of Fred Spiksley, fresh from his triumph against the Scots just two days earlier and the England international was greeted with a two-minute standing ovation prior to kick-off.

The game started frantically but after 4 minutes, Jimmy Oswald scored for County. The scorer was then booked for two rough challenges on Allan in the Sheffield goal. There were no yellow or red cards at this time and spectators could only tell if a player had been booked when they witnessed the referee take out his notebook and record the offender's name. Just before the interval, the away centre half Jack Hendry, a robust character, was also booked. Then on 41 minutes, Harry Brandon rolled the ball to his cousin Tom and his shot levelled the scores when it beat England 'keeper George Toone. Just 5ft 7in tall, Toone relied on his great agility to confound attackers, but it was to no avail on this occasion.

After the interval the pace failed to slacken, but with 75 minutes gone the score remained 1-1. County were then denied when Allan made three great saves before Harry Brandon hit one of his trademark long ground shots that put his side ahead. Within 30 seconds County captain Jack Oswald, a boilermaker by trade, hit a low fast shot into the Wednesday net. County's hopes were dashed within a minute, when Harry Brandon hit home a free kick from 12 yards to ensure that Wednesday had survived by finishing in tenth place.

County finished twelfth, while below them were Accrington and Newton Heath. When Sheffield United, who finished second in Division Two, beat Accrington 1-0 in the test match series it proved to be the defeated club's last ever Football League match. Heavy debts meant that on some occasions they had been unable to raise a team. Consequently, the club tendered their resignation to the League and soon went out of business. Fred Spiksley had been fortunate when he opted not to sign for the East Lancs side in 1891.

After a fine start, Wednesday had faded. Good crowds, though, meant that the money invested in Olive Grove was being repaid. In the League, Wednesday had scored fifty-five goals. Equal top scorers with thirteen each were Spiksley and Rowan. The outside left had, however, outscored the Scot in the FA Cup to end up as the season's top scorer – not bad for a player who should have been dead!

During the winter of his first season in Sheffield, Fred had contracted a terrible choking cough, often finding himself waking up during the night in pain. When it failed to clear in the spring, he approached Arthur Dickinson who took him to the doctor. The medic paid particular attention to his chest and lungs and after the examination he spoke to Dickinson alone. When he emerged, Dickinson handed the player a prescription before dashing away.

From then on, Dickinson always appeared busy whenever Fred tried to speak to him and when the player then asked Harry Pearson and Arthur Nixon about a contract for the 1892–93 season, he found them evasive. A confused Spiksley started considering moving on and when Alf Shelton, an England international and his friend at Notts County, heard about his predicament he arranged for him to see Mr Brown, the Notts County secretary. When Dickinson discovered Fred's intentions he was presented with a major dilemma: the doctor's diagnosis was that his patient had galloping consumption with a life expectancy of just twelve months! Should he tell Fred Spiksley he had tuberculosis? After much soul searching he decided to keep quiet and then gambled by offering the seriously sick player a twelve-month contract.

One year on and Fred Spiksley looked in great condition. Dickinson was confused. He took the player to see Sheffield's top consultant, Mr Pye-Smith. At the end of comprehensive medical examination the patient was asked to wait outside. Within minutes a delighted Arthur Dickinson danced out of the doctor's consulting room to tell Fred the good news and let him know why he hadn't been able to look him in the eye the previous year when they had visited the doctor together.

Fred's lungs were now as clear as a bell, with no trace of consumption or chest weakness. According to Pye-Smith, Fred Spiksley wasn't dying, although he was suffering from exhaustion and overwork. The remedy was plenty of fresh air and relaxation.

'Well, well, well; and here you are, an England international, and you're supposed to be dead!' cried Arthur Dickinson. On hearing the news the Wednesday directors were equally jubilant. They offered Fred Spiksley a three-year contract, the first ever in football. The increased terms were £4 a week for all year round and it was further agreed that the player could again enjoy the benefits of clean Lincolnshire air by living in Gainsborough during the week. The only proviso was that Fred would pay his own travel costs. Of course, by living in Gainsborough it gave the player an opportunity to frequent the race tracks he so enjoyed, but it also meant Fred would be away from the serious pollution for which Sheffield was well known.

Chapter 8

Back-To-Back England Hat Tricks

A blue cap England debut and a special day at Richmond

Each season since 1884 England had contested matches against Ireland, Scotland and Wales for the Home International Football Championship. Ireland, where organised football started in the late 1870s and the Football Association was formed on 18 November 1880, and Wales didn't have the quality enjoyed by England and Scotland and, consequently, what every English footballer desired was the blue cap awarded for matches against Scotland.

While playing for Wednesday in the Football Alliance, Fred Spiksley was chosen as England's first non-playing reserve for the 1892 international against Wales. The England side were chosen by an FA Council sub-committee of seven, drawn from every region of the country where the organisation were represented.

Before the championship started, a North v South trial match was held with the teams composed of amateur and professional players. All seven selectors would then dine together to select sides for the Wales and Ireland games. These matches might even be played on the same day and, until 1895, it was tradition to select one England side consisting of all amateur players to play either Wales or Ireland, and a second consisting of ten professional players and one amateur, who would captain the side, in the other game. Not surprisingly, the team for the big game against Scotland was strongly influenced by the performances against Wales and Ireland. With Wednesday now in Division One for the 1892–93 season, the England selectors were aware of Fred's good form against better opposition, his healthy goal tally and his ability to create numerous goal-scoring opportunities for his teammates.

When the teams were chosen for the Ireland and Wales games (played on 25 February and 13 March respectively), the former consisted largely of players with Corinthians FC connections. Gilbert Oswald Smith, from Oxford University, was selected for his debut. He would go on to play twenty times for England, sixteen as captain, and was considered by many to be the best player of the late nineteenth century. He scored once as Ireland lost 6-1.

For the Wales game the England team were a fully professional one:

John Sutcliffe (Bolton Wanderers), Tom Clare (Stoke), Bob Holmes (Preston) (captain), John Reynolds (West Bromwich Albion), Charles Perry (West Bromwich Albion), Jimmy Turner (Bolton Wanderers), Billy Bassett (West Bromwich Albion), John Goodall (Derby County), John Southworth (Blackburn Rovers), Edgar Chadwick (Everton), Alf Milward (Everton).

Today, club versus country remains a contentious subject, but back in 1893 there was never any argument: England came first! It was, therefore, an historic moment when Everton refused to release players to represent England. The Toffees were facing an FA Cup semi-final replay against Preston three days after the international match. England captain Bob Holmes was a Preston player and his club were happy to release him, but Everton were concerned that if Chadwick or Milward were injured playing for their country, then their Cup chances would be jeopardised. In the event, the selectors refused to make a fuss and elevated Stoke's Joe Schofield and Wednesday's Fred Spiksley to the starting line-up. This especially delighted followers of Schofield as the match was at the Victoria Ground, Stoke.

Spiksley's selection meant he became the first Gainsborough man to play for England. He was followed by Alf Spouncer who received his only cap in 1900, and Arthur Brown who played twice, scoring once, between 1904 and 1906. All three men were pupils at Gainsborough Free Grammar School and started their careers at Gainsborough Trinity.

A third change was forced on the selectors on the morning of the game when star forward John Southworth was forced to withdraw with a troublesome leg injury. John Whitehead, of Accrington, was called up as his replacement. Spiksley's selection elevated him to playing alongside the finest English players, such as John Goodall and Billy Bassett.

Bassett charged down the wing like a whippet. He was clever on the ball, possessed a powerful right-foot shot and served his club for a grand total of fifty-one years: thirteen as a player (1886–99), six as a coach (1899–1905), three as a director (1905–08) and twenty-nine as chairman (1908 until his death in West Bromwich in 1937). He scored 77 goals in 311 first class matches, played in the 1888 and 1892 FA Cup-winning sides and in the losing side of 1895 and made sixteen appearances for England.

Wales lined up in the usual 2-3-5 formation as follows:

James Trainer (Preston), Dai Jones (Chirk and Bolton Wanderers), Charles Parry (Llansilin), Joseph Davies I (Druids and Wolves), Edwin Hugh Williams (Flint and Crewe), Edward Morris (Chirk), Edward Jones (Middlesbrough), James Vaughan (Chirk), John Butler (Druids), Benjamin Lewis (Wrexham and Chirk), Robert Roberts IV (Crewe).

The England professionals received a £1 appearance fee for home matches. Players stayed overnight before the game at a hotel near to the ground and shared a room with a teammate. Lunch consisted of roast mutton with dry toast, and after the meal one small cigarette was allowed! The trainer took charge when the players arrived at the ground and after the game, the players returned to the hotel, completed their expenses forms and had their heads measured for their England caps before returning home.

The FA moved England matches around the country to give as many supporters as possible the chance to see the national side. The game was Stoke's second international match, the first in 1889 had seen England beat Wales 4-1. England had won eleven and lost two out of the fourteen matches between the countries.

A 12,000 capacity crowd cheered the sides' emergence from the dressing rooms. Butler kicked off 7 minutes after the advertised time of 3.30pm, before Fred Spiksley had his first touch of the ball at 3.41pm. He immediately darted past the Welsh right back Dai Jones, before sending a perfect cross over to Billy Bassett, who shocked everybody by missing badly. Spiksley and Schofield then combined and when the former pushed the ball across to John Goodall, he also missed a great chance.

Wales responded on 15 minutes and Sutcliffe made a fine save from Butler. A Goodall scorcher then sizzled by and with the England forwards now combining superbly, Wales were hanging on. On 30 minutes, the England outside left dribbled with pace past the Welsh defenders before hitting the ball round Trainer to make it 1-0. It was a fine individual goal combining speed, skill and composure. The England side now fed the scorer, who didn't disappoint as he notched up his second with a blistering left-footed shot. England led 2-0 at half-time.

However, Wales were not going to go down without a fight and Sutcliffe was forced to make three fine saves. Nevertheless, the game as a contest was over when, from a Spiksley through ball, Bassett banged home England's third. The two then combined superbly to set up Goodall for the fourth goal.

Goodall made fourteen appearances for his country and scored twelve times, including two marvellous efforts when England beat Scotland 4-1 in April 1892, which might not have pleased his Scottish father! His combination of great speed and clever footwork, with a willingness to shoot from distance and accuracy in front of the goal made Goodall one of the best marksmen the game has ever seen. He had finished as top scorer for Preston in the inaugural Football League season, after which he quit the League and FA Cup winners, moving to Derby County and accepting the tenancy of a local pub.

As the match continued, England scored again when Bassett found Reynolds and as the final whistle loomed, Schofield was unfortunate when Trainer made a diving save with his right hand. When the ball ran loose it was Fred Spiksley who was first to it and drove it home to make it 6-0 and complete his hat-trick. Years later, Fred was to say of his England debut that it seemed as if he could do no wrong. Everything he touched turned to gold and the Welsh defenders were unable contain him. Indeed, Trainer had prevented an even more comprehensive defeat. The keeper was capped twenty times but fell on hard times when he retired and any football team visiting London, where he was experiencing the seamy side of life, used to expect him as a caller in search of some cash.

For many years England's final goal was recorded as Schofield's, mainly because *The Times* credited the sixth goal to him. Several other papers, all of whom must have relied on a single source, reported that Spiksley and Schofield had broken through to score England's sixth goal. Schofield was seen as the latter player and this served to back up the *Times* match report.

Fred Spiksley laid claim to scoring a hat-trick on his England debut several times in writing, including his biographical pieces in 1907 and 1920. In 1929 Schofield's own reminiscences in the *Athletic News* included the Wales game in 1893 where he doesn't mention scoring in the match.

A much larger number of newspaper reports credited Spiksley with scoring a hat-trick, including those listed below. Modern day statisticians and historians largely agree that Spiksley did indeed score the hat-trick, including the England Online database, which is the most authoritative voice on statistics for the England international team. The papers at the time included the following praise for Spiksley:

'Trainer saved a grand attempt from Schofield, but Spiksley caught the leather on the rebound and scored an easy goal.' *Manchester Courier, Lancashire General Advertiser* and *York Herald*, 14 March 1893.

'Trainer managed to save, but Spiksley quickly clinched matters by adding the sixth point.' *Wrexham Advertiser*, 18 March 1893.

'Fred scored three against Wales and had a hand in a fourth.' *Lincolnshire Echo*, 27 March 1893.

For clubs of the 1890s, the ultimate accolade was to win the FA Cup, but this was very much seen as a team effort. So for an individual player the biggest recognition was to play against Scotland, effectively meaning that you were considered the best Englishman in your position. At the time, players received a red cap for playing against Wales, white against Ireland and blue against Scotland.

In the early hours of Sunday 26 March 1893, an anxious Fred Spiksley was lying awake fretting over whether he had been selected for the following Saturday's game in London between England and Scotland. The England selectors would have selected the side after the previous day's FA Cup final between Everton and Wolves.

The signs were mixed: the Wednesday man had notched three against Wales, but was omitted for the final trial match at Derby. The selectors were expected to select eight professionals, including Sheffield United's Ernest Needham. In the end, however, a good FA Cup final display by amateur George Kinsey for Wolves saw him preferred to Needham.

In his autobiography, Spiksley recalls overhearing a paperboy outside his Talbot Street window drumming up custom. He was up like a shot when he heard 'Read all about it – Spiksley picked for England'. He was down the stairs, out the door and running barefoot into the street to grab a paper. It was true, at 23 he was going to earn his first blue cap. Neighbours congratulated the player as a lump came to his throat.

The England team lined up as follows:-

Lewis Hewitt Gay (Old Brightonians), Alban Hugh Harrison (Old Westminsters), Bob Holmes (Preston), John Reynolds (Aston Villa), John Holt (Everton), George Kinsey (Wolves), Billy Bassett (West Bromwich Albion), Robert Cunliffe Gosling (Old Etonians), John Goodall (Derby), Edgar Chadwick (Everton), Spiksley (Wednesday).

With the Scottish FA refusing to select Scots who played their football in England, their team were all home-based, not to mention all amateurs, as professionalism had yet to be accepted in Scotland.

Scotland:

John Lindsay (Renton), Walter Arnott, Bob Smellie (both Queen's Park), David Mitchell (Rangers), James Kelly (Celtic) (captain), William Maley (Celtic), William Sellar (Queen's Park), Tom Waddell (Queen's Park), James Hamilton I (Queen's Park), Alex McMahon (Celtic) and Johnny Campbell (Celtic).

The sixty-strong Scottish FA party that travelled to London did so in two groups. With rumours that Nottingham football scouts were intending to shadow their star players – and make them offers they couldn't refuse to play permanently in England – the SFA officials kept a keen eye on the squad. As they travelled from Euston by wagonette to their hotel, the advance party witnessed a spectacular blazing fire on Ludgate Hill close to St Paul's Cathedral.

Fred Spiksley came south on the afternoon of Thursday, 30 March and met with the England team at the Third Avenue Hotel ahead of the game at the Richmond Athletic Ground. He was naturally excited. Aware that he would miss two League games over Easter, he was also concerned about what might happen to Wednesday, struggling close to the bottom of Division One. Like the Scots, he saw the flickering flames that lit up the cathedral dome.

By Friday morning, only eight of the England side had arrived – Goodall, Gosling and Harrison were missing – for a light training session at Richmond. The temperature was the highest on record for this time of year and Richmond Athletic Ground was a hive of activity as workmen struggled to get it ready for the big match. A temporary stand was being constructed and a grand marquee erected. The previous evening a message had been relayed from the Duke of Teck, Queen Victoria's cousin by marriage, saying that he would be attending the match with his family and friends. The duke's butler was set to arrive at 2pm to approve the arrangements for his visit, including hamper deliveries from Fortnum and Mason. It would be the first time that royalty had attended an international football match.

The England players were informed they needed to finish training by 2.30pm so that the local fire brigade could water the bone-dry pitch. Fred was impressed with the playing surface: the ground was completely level and the turf was holding up well. Bob Holmes and Billy Bassett organised the training session, which concentrated on high intensity cardio activity and a team exercise focusing on quick passing. A four-a-side game completed the team session before the players began working with colleagues from their section of the pitch. Spiksley and Bassett practised meticulously together, hitting over crosses and corner kicks.

Meanwhile, the Scots spent a leisurely day taking in the London sights. Back at their hotel the England players did some light skipping exercises after which games were played by all except Bassett. He was a practising Christian and it was Good Friday, so he read for the rest of the day. The Football League founder and Aston Villa director William McGregor was among the England party and he later reported how Kinsey, whom he described as 'a rough diamond', looked round the hotel before saying, 'Mac, if I brought my friends in here and told them I had dined here then what do you think they might say?' When the Villa man admitted he didn't know, Kinsey told him, 'They would say I was a ******* liar.'

Fred was up early on Easter Saturday and his newspaper brought bad news: Burnley had beaten Wednesday 4-0. This may also have been the morning when Fred, who was still very much a junior international who had risen up from a working-class terraced street in Gainsborough, found the rest of the players laughing at him. Footballers are, of course, known for playing practical jokes on one another and they see it as part of team bonding, but on this occasion it appears that on one of the mornings prior to the Scotland game in 1893, the team were being driven though Hyde Park when the Wednesday player saw gardeners bedding out young plants and asked what they were doing. One of his companions gave the rest a big wink before telling Fred that they really did take care of the flowers, so much so that they took in all of the geraniums every night and put them out fresh again the following morning. Fred was convinced and the rest of the players were delighted!

Following a light breakfast, the England team travelled to the ground where they arrived at 11.00am. The sun was already beating down, but bad news soon arrived: John Goodall's slight knee strain hadn't recovered from injury and the Derby man was only on his way in order to support the team. Charles Alcock was in a sweat. He was rescued by Leslie Gay, who suggested the FA secretary should contact George Cotterill, his Old Brightonians colleague and England international. He was nowhere near as good as Goodall, but he did live locally. Cotterill was also on the phone. He had been capped for England in the international against Ireland and was quickly summoned to appear.

The Scots greeted news of Goodall's absence enthusiastically as he had been the architect of their downfall in four out of five of the last internationals between the countries, scoring no fewer than five goals in total. Being the son of Scottish parents meant the Scots could never accept Goodall was really English.

The Scottish side, chosen by seven selectors, weren't without their critics in a nation now desperate to reassert its earlier supremacy over the Auld Enemy. Professionalism had seen England improve their playing standards and when Scotland were thrashed 5-0 in 1888, this first victory in nine years was achieved with seven professional players in the team. Since then England had won twice and drawn and lost once.

The Scots had triumphed 8-0 and 6-1 in their respective matches against Wales and Ireland in 1893. Two completely separate sides had been selected, but the selectors chose the one that beat Ireland with the exception of the captain, John Adams of Hearts, replacing him with Queen's Park veteran, Wattie Arnott. This was to be his tenth game against England and many Scots felt it was one game too many.

William Sellar had previously played six times against England and his record of just one victory wouldn't be improved upon. James Hamilton was asked to lead the forward line, but many Scots were dismayed that Celtic's Jack Madden, Spiksley's former Gainsborough Trinity colleague, had been overlooked, especially after scoring four against Wales. Not one of Scotland's team had previously netted against their opponents! The Scots consoled themselves with the fact that England's XI consisted of players from nine different clubs, but in reality, England had a nucleus of five experienced professionals in their ranks: Holmes, Reynolds, Holt, Bassett and Chadwick.

Goodall's absence wasn't Alcock's only concern. Journalists were unimpressed by the facilities as the press accommodation consisted of an open-sided marquee on level ground several yards behind the perimeter rope. Although the gates weren't due to open until 1pm, as spectators began to arrive at 10am, the combination of the hot sun and the crush outside meant that by midday a decision was taken to allow the crowd into the ground. As more spectators arrived the demand for water grew and it became difficult to direct people into areas where they could see the match. Rather than send fans away disappointed, the ground authorities permitted people to enter and the area in front of the press accommodation was soon six rows deep, making it impossible for reporters to see the game. Some fans then began scaling trees to get a bird's eye view. The ground capacity was 12,000, but up to 20,000 people were thought to be present, paying record receipts for an England international of £811.

The royal party and the Scotland team arrived just after 1pm (over two hours behind schedule) and struggled to gain entry. It was unheard of in 1893 for royalty to extend their patronage to football, so the attendance of the duke and his wife Princess Mary Adelaide of Cambridge was seen as a sign of the growing importance of the game nationally. The duchess was famous for her extravagant lifestyle and partying and was known as 'Fat Mary' on account of her extremely wide girth. She was wearing a blue dress with matching hat and peacock feathers, which delighted the Scottish supporters. FA president and Scot Lord Kinnaird and his predecessor, Major Sir Francis Marindin, who were intent on explaining the finer points of the game to the duke and his guests, accompanied the royal couple.

Occupying the second carriage were the 24-year-old Princess Mary of Teck, better known as Princess May (after the month of her birth) and the youngest of her three brothers, Prince Alexander. The princess wore a beautiful white dress and looked resplendent. Sixteen months earlier she had been betrothed to Queen Victoria's grandson, Prince Albert, the Duke of Clarence, who was second in line to the throne. However, tragedy struck six weeks later when Prince Albert caught pneumonia and died at Sandringham House in Norfolk. The appearance of royalty had encouraged the ladies to grace the grandstand seats and after halting at the royal enclosure, Charles Alcock offered his official greetings, the national anthem was played and the Union flag and the duke's standard were raised.

Both teams were presented to the royal party at 2.30pm, one hour before kick-off. Earlier, the England team were all handed their white shirts, complete with embroidered badge bearing the traditional three crowned lions worked in purple and red. The players would be allowed to retain the badge.

Forty-five minutes before kick-off, the teams, with England now captained by Cotterill, had their photographs taken behind the grandstand by Gunn and Stuart, a local firm of professional photographers. Goodall was included in the photograph, as was match referee Charles Clegg, who later called the two captains together in the pavilion for the toss. Cotterill won and chose to defend the River Thames end of the ground, giving England the advantage of the sun behind them in the first period.

When their team emerged from the pavilion first, the Scottish supporters (who far outnumbered their English counterparts) burst into prolonged cheering as the skirl of the bagpipes broke out. The sight of millionaire Gosling performing his usual pre-match routine of making sure his limbs were relaxed by shaking himself down like a dog caused great hilarity.

The bright sky and glorious sunshine were more suited to cricket than football. The game was set to be played on the maximum size pitch permitted under international rules: 130 yards long by 100 yards wide. With the field in immaculate condition the game was certain to be fast and there was no one quicker than the England outside left! At precisely 3.30pm, Hamilton kicked the match off.

Great combination play on the England left saw Chadwick and Spiksley force Lindsay in the Scots goal to save in quick succession from Gosling and Chadwick. There were claims that the latter's shot had crossed the goal line, but Charles Clegg waved away the protests. Hamilton then missed a good opportunity after Sandy McMahon and John Campbell combined.

The Scots fans urged the ball to be fed out to the celebrated Queen's Park right wing duo of Tom Waddell and William Sellar. Johnny Holt, whom Fred described in his autobiography as only 'a hop-o'-my-thumb five feet three inches', immediately set about scotching the tricks of the duo known as the 'Scottish spiders'. Intercepting the ball he knocked it back to Gay, who promptly picked it up and took five steps forward before hearing the referee's whistle. In 1893, picking up the ball from a back pass was allowed, but carrying it for more than two paces meant an indirect free kick for an offence committed just eight yards out. Fortunately, when Hamilton had the kick knocked to him he shot high over the crossbar.

England took a fifteenth minute lead when Chadwick drew Davie Mitchell before finding Spiksley, who then forced Arnott to retreat before his perfectly weighted cross picked out Gosling, who netted with a powerful header. England fans roared with delight. Lindsay did brilliantly to prevent the scorer doubling the advantage. Arnott's experience helped his fellow defenders retain a measure of control and the Scot then made a fine goal line clearance from a Bassett shot. The pace of the England forward line was simply too much for the Scots – but for some poor misses, the match would have been over in the first half hour.

When England relaxed the Scots broke out of their defence and stunned their opponents by equalising. McMahon and Campbell combined and when the ball was crossed into England's goalmouth, Gay was charged over by Sellar to allow Tom Waddell a free header to make it 1-1. Charging like this was allowed, and Sellar had utilised the rules to Scotland's advantage. Sellar then hit a shot against the post. Hamilton shot narrowly wide and a Willie Maley shot dipped just over the bar as England held on to ensure the game remained level at the interval. There was now the prospect of a really thrilling second half.

Not everyone was happy. Telegraphic arrangements hadn't been put in place and with insufficient telephones, journalists were unable to send reports back to London or Glasgow. The Scottish press were particularly angry at being unable to send the half-time score to Ibrox.

In the first aid tent the St John Ambulance were doing a roaring "trade" as spectators, collapsing from dehydration and sunstroke, were hauled away by overworked stretcher-bearers. Fortunately, Charles Alcock had arranged for water carts and the needy were soon back on their feet. However, no thought had been given to the provision of water for the press and they sweated pints in the 'press oven'.

On the restart, Scotland's James Hamilton failed to shoot and when he tried to round Gay, the 'keeper grabbed the ball. Jimmy Kelly was then unlucky with a dipping shot and on 55 minutes, Scotland scored their second after Sandy McMahon began a brilliant passing movement that was continued by Tom Waddell and finished with aplomb by William Sellar; his first goal in seven internationals against England. The Scottish fans danced deliriously, including linesman Archibald Sliman, the SFA president.

Bassett was fuming. In 1889 he had scored England's two first-half goals before Scotland struck three, including a last-minute effort, to win 3-2. Following the final whistle the winners had gloated so much that the West Brom winger, well known as a bad loser, vowed he would never again lose to what he considered were the arrogant Scots. He wasn't the only Englishman to become agitated. Sitting in the players' pavilion, Rupert Sandilands, a prominent England international, jumped up and after removing his jacket, collar and tie declared, 'For heaven's sake get me some boots!'

England were dumfounded and Gay was forced to make several fine saves as the Scots sought to extend their lead. Holt, the experienced Holmes and the athletic Alban Harrison were, however, slowly developing an understanding and began to anticipate the Scottish forwards' intentions. In midfield, John Reynolds, in later years known as 'Baldy' started to rediscover his form. The Villa man, who by now had started to show signs of his future baldness, was encouraged when he realised how heavily Willie Maley was breathing. Chadwick raised hopes of a comeback with a delightful crossfield ball to the unmarked Bassett, who left Maley struggling in his wake and as three defenders converged, he fed the ball through to Cotterill for a clear run on goal.

For the first time, Cotterill was able to show his athleticism and as Arnott and Kelly strained every sinew, the England captain shrugged off their desperate tackles before sliding the ball beyond Lindsay to make it 2-2. For a brief second there was silence before an almighty roar reverberated around Richmond Park. England had looked beaten, could they now win the game?

As the players regrouped for the kick-off, Fred Spiksley noticed a bare-footed young woman dressed in white emerge from the royal enclosure. She began running up and down the touchline and Fred recognised her as Princess May. She was clearly enjoying the game and, as Fred confided in his autobiography, he was, for one fleeting moment, completely distracted by the sight of this beautiful princess and lost his concentration.

Driven on by Holmes, Holt, Reynolds, Chadwick and Bassett, England pressed forward. When Bassett collected the ball, Fred signalled with his left arm and in an instant the outside right sent over a brilliantly accurate 60-yard pass that Fred, leaving in his wake a struggling princess, met 9 yards out. Instantly controlling the ball with his right foot, and with Arnott, Smellie and Lindsay in front of him, the outside left hammered it home with his left foot past all three Scottish players to make it England 3 Scotland 2 on 78 minutes.

The execution was so brilliant that it looked as if the whole task had been one single movement. The control of the ball, the changing of the feet, the speed of execution and the power of the shot were completed with such audacity and panache that all three defenders had no chance. None of them moved.

The Scots appealed vigorously for offside, but referee Charles Clegg, aware of Fred's lightning pace, had no doubt that it was a goal. After the game, the Scottish press continued to dispute England's third but, as Bassett pointed out, it was amazing that they had such a good view of the 'offside goal' when they complained throughout the match that they couldn't see. Bassett pointed out 'Spiksley is the fastest man in football and has no need to wander offside as he can beat your boys in a foot race every time'.

England were back in control. In Spiksley and Bassett they had players who were now unstoppable. On 80 minutes, Bassett hit another long ball out to the

England left, where Chadwick and Spiksley combined to send the latter towards goal with only Arnott to beat. An ageing Wattie knew he was out of his depth and at the risk of conceding a penalty, he tried to hack down his opponent, who leaped over his flailing boot before beating Smellie to make it 4-2. Arnott appealed that he had fouled the England man and argued it should be a penalty. It was a desperate plea that the referee consequently ignored.

Bassett then left Maley yards behind and delivered a cross-field pass to Cotterill. Running in at pace, Cotterill linked with Spiksley to beat the last line of the Scottish defence. Spiksley took aim from distance and Lindsay could only parry his shot out to Cotterill. Cotterill again set up Spiksley, who from 15 yards out volleyed home with his left foot to make it 5-2 on 84 minutes. It was as spectacular a goal as you are likely to see and completed Spiksley's hat-trick, the first ever by an English player against Scotland. The England winger also noticed Princess May waving a white handkerchief in appreciation of his achievement. 'And didn't the Duchess of Teck enjoy the game!' said William McGregor in 1902, quoted in the *Sunderland Daily Echo* and *Shipping Gazette*.

Throughout the game the English had been upstaged by the Scottish singing, led by Mr Hay of Dumfries in the Scrimp Stand. When the home crowd now called for the Scots to sing another song, there was no encore. At Ibrox Park the half time score was only just going up and was met with general satisfaction. When the final result eventually arrived in Glasgow many hours later, several considered it to be an April Fools' joke.

Home fans made a guard of honour for their heroes and there was great cheering and clapping. 'Three cheers for Fred' was the shout and the crowd responded heartily. As the England player was lowered to the ground, he noticed that McMahon had tears streaming down his face. The Scots captain had constantly urged his side to keep the ball away from England's left wing during the game, but it had proven impossible. Lord Kinnaird then awarded each England player his blue cap, as the police cordoned off the area in an effort to hold back the spectators who were keen to get a view of royalty and the players.

Fred was bombarded by a horde of Scottish reporters once he left the sanctuary of the pavilion. Much of the questioning was about the third England goal and whether he was offside. The scorer explained how he had met the ball with three players in front of him and that as they were off balance he shot the ball through. 'I suggest you speak to Mr Clegg. All I know is that I did my best for England and it is beyond all doubt that the Scottish team was licked by superior play.'

The game was won and lost by the speed of the England wingmen and the stamina shown by their professional players in the heat. In contrast, the Scottish backs and half backs had nothing left in their legs in the final quarter of the match, with goals conceded in the 78th, 80th and 84th minutes. England had run their opponents off their feet and for many years afterwards, the shrewdest football experts proclaimed that the Richmond international was the fastest ever played. England's victory gave them the Home International Championship title for 1893, with three victories and seventeen goals for, three against.

Fred Spiksley had scored a hat-trick in each of his first two internationals, becoming the first player to achieve such a feat. Only two other English players have followed into the record books: Steve Bloomer in 1896 and Vivian Woodward in 1908. In recognition of his achievement the FA presented him with a gold fob watch chain, detailed with a small metal plate bearing an inscription that credited the hat-trick. (Sadly, a family burglary means there is no knowledge of the chain's whereabouts today, but its existence was reported in the centenary issue of the *Gainsborough News* in May 1955.)

Two other players have scored three against Scotland: Dennis Wilshaw, of Wolves, in 1955 and Jimmy Greaves, then of Chelsea, in 1961. By scoring three times in 6 minutes, Fred Spiksley also became the scorer of England's fastest hat-trick, a feat beaten by Middlesbrough's George Camsell, (three in 5 minutes) in 1929, and then Spurs' Willie Hall (three in 4 minutes) in 1938.

According to many record books, Fred Spiksley only scored two goals against Scotland in 1893. This is because that with one exception – which credited the goal to Holt – the contemporary match reports awarded England's fifth goal to Reynolds. Why this should be the case is uncertain, but it is known that throughout the game journalists complained they were unable to see the action clearly. By the time the final goal was scored the game was impossible to see, particularly as it was scored some 80 yards away from where the press tent was positioned.

The following is a small selection of quotes by journalists on this issue.

'It was hardly possible to follow the game with any accuracy owing to the crowd.' *Dundee Courier*

'The arrangements proved wretchedly inadequate, and the reporters saw even less of the game than at Fallowfield for the FA Cup final last week.' *Derby Daily Telegraph*

'The reporters had to thank the FA for their inability to see the game properly…Some hundreds of people were placed in front of and on a level with the press seats, the arrangements being a disgrace to the Association, and an insult to the press.' *Aberdeen Journal*

Doubts about who did score England's last goal in 1893 began to emerge when high profile characters later began writing their own memoirs. Firstly, Fred's exploits featured in two lengthy series of newspaper articles he wrote.

They appeared in 1907, when all of the England team that featured in 1893 were alive, and also in 1920. In both accounts he recalls how he scored three goals against Scotland on his England debut.

Bassett had no doubt that his teammate had scored three, writing in the *Shrewsbury Chronicle* on Friday, 18 October 1907, 'I kept swinging the ball across, and either Edgar Chadwick or Fred Spiksley met it perfectly, Spiksley took three centres in hand and scored each time, and amid a scene of tremendous excitement England won by five goals to two'.

Sir Frederick Wall was the FA secretary from 1895 to 1934 and was present at the match against Scotland in 1893. In 1934, Wall's book, *Fifty Years in Football*, was published and contains considerable coverage of the game. He also states that Spiksley scored three.

Like Wall, J.A.H. Catton had no special friendship with Spiksley. Catton wrote under the pen name of 'Tityrus' and was a popular sports journalist who, after starting out as an apprentice journalist to the *Preston Herald*, later became editor of *Athletic News*. As stated by Paul Brown in his book *The Victorian Football Miscellany*, 'Catton was famous for his impartiality'. In his book *Wickets and Goals*, published in 1926, Catton credits Spiksley with the last three goals, scored in the space of ten second-half minutes. He also describes the kind of player that Spiksley was.

There are several other eye witness accounts of the match, including from J.A. Brierley, a highly-respected sports journalist who worked for the *Lancashire Evening Post* from late 1898 through to the early 1940s. There are also numerous newspaper articles, some of which were written on the centenary of Spiksley's birth in 1970, in which it is stated that Fred Spiksley scored three. These include one in the *Sunday Express* of 19 March 1933, which is headed 'When Queen Mary ran up and down a football pitch' and describes what it contends was the 'greatest international match ever'.

There appear to be no articles written following the game in 1893 in which Reynolds, or any eye witness, claims it was he who scored against Scotland. As stated earlier, Reynolds was famously nicknamed 'Baldy' and, during the research for this book, it was suggested that his bald head made it possible for journalists at the game to be sure that he did, in fact, score the last goal. However, the England team photograph, included within this book, shows that Reynolds wasn't bald by 1893.

Unfortunately, there is no one at the FA to turn to for an official review on the information collected during our research, which can be viewed online at www.spiksley.com. Meanwhile, the England Online database has ruled that Spiksley *did* score three.

Such was the level of the defeat that the Scottish FA called an emergency evening meeting after the match, with many of those present pushing the case for the Scottish League to fully embrace professionalism. The following month, the SFA agreed that Scottish clubs could pay players. Three years later it was agreed that Scottish players playing in England could play for their country, and five were chosen in the 1896 Scotland side who beat England 2-1.

On the night following the match, many of the England players were back in bed early, the pace of the game having taken its toll. Those who did manage to stay up enjoyed a few drinks in Reynolds's room where, according to McGregor, the Villa man showed the other players how to charge the brandies and sodas they were enjoying to the FA. McGregor commented later how such future bills became so large that the FA eventually had to concede and allow the players an allowance for expenses above the match fee.

On the Sunday morning, the Spiksley was disappointed to hear that his club had been beaten in the penultimate game of the season and would now need to win their final match the following day to avoid the test match series. Fred then joined his England colleagues on a pleasure trip to Kew Gardens before taking the train home for a do-or-die match in Sheffield that saw Wednesday beat Notts County 3-2 to ensure First Division survival.

Chapter 9

Falling Short

Wednesday's FA Cup exploits, 1894 & 1895

Wednesday strengthened their squad for the second League season and brought in several new players. Inside forward Jock Smith had won a League championship medal with Sunderland in 1892 before moving to Liverpool, while Jim Jamieson joined from Everton and proved an outstanding left half with great heading ability and a never-say-die attitude. Centre forward John Miller had been part of a fine Dumbarton side who won the Scottish League title in 1891–92 and, having previously played for Corinthians FC and Nottingham Forrest, Jack Earp arrived, initially as an amateur, in late September 1893. An outstanding full back, he became a firm Olive Grove favourite following Tom Brandon's departure. Completely reliant on his right foot, Earp was very fast, highly competitive and a leader of men. He became team captain and forged a fine partnership with Ambrose 'Mick' Langley, whom Fred Spiksley had played alongside for Horncastle Town in 1883. After representing Grimsby, Langley, then playing for Middlesbrough Ironopolis, was signed by Everton. However, soon afterwards a letter arrived from Merseyside saying he was being granted a free transfer as, having watched him again, Everton believed a knee injury had left him too slow.

This injury would trouble Langley throughout his career. But it helped him choose Wednesday over Aston Villa in 1893, with the former content to sign him without the necessity of a medical, whereas the Birmingham club were insisting on one before confirming their contract offer. Langley's strength, coupled with his tactical knowhow, tackling, heading ability and long clearance kicks, made him the perfect defender. He finally left Sheffield to sign for Hull City as player-manager in 1905.

Wednesday began the season impressively; recovering from a 2-1 half-time deficit to draw with champions Sunderland after Miller netted his second goal. Wolves and Blackburn Rovers then beat Wednesday 3-1 and 5-1 respectively. These defeats marked the end of the Wednesday players taking their own food to away games as the club now began providing them with a round of sandwiches and a bottle of ginger beer for the train journey. A further uplift in catering arrived in 1896 when Wednesday won the FA Cup and the players were served with cold ham and chicken.

If the catering in 1893 had improved for Wednesday's players, the same couldn't be said for the kit provision. Each player had to wash his own shirt and knickerbockers. Spiksley was lucky as his mother did his, although he always insisted he did the ironing. Players also had to buy their own boots, stockings and shin guards, which helps explain why, in the Olive Grove era, the Wednesday players wore multi-coloured stockings.

Wednesday's poor start to the season continued with a home defeat by Newton Heath, a draw at Sunderland and a 4-2 loss at West Bromwich Albion, where Spiksley opened his scoring account for the League's bottom-placed club.

Fortunately, Wednesday's form picked up with victory at home to Blackburn Rovers and a 4-0 thrashing of Derby County, in which Alec Brady scored three. There was also a first Football League derby match against Sheffield United, who had been promoted at the end of the previous season, which ended 1-1. Spiksley scored the Wednesday equaliser in front of a highly enthusiastic crowd of 27,000 packed inside Bramall Lane. The attendance was even more remarkable considering local miners were in the sixteenth week of a national strike over a living wage.

The game was so rough that the referee Mr Fitzroy Norris was forced to halt proceedings before half-time to speak to the teams. With the injured Davis unable to play after the interval the away side struggled, but would have won the game if Fred, escaping the clutches of a tight-marking Rab 'Gypsy' Howell, hadn't snatched at a late chance when left with only Hewlett to beat. During Fred's career, Howell was arguably his most difficult opponent and United's outstanding record against their near neighbours in the late Victorian era – they lost just once between 1893 and 1900 – can partly be credited to this.

Fred said of Howell: 'He followed me like a shadow and stuck closer to me than a brother. The crowd would shout "Keep yer 'ands out of 'is pocket, Rab" at which he would just grin and move closer to me. If I ever looked like I might outwit him the bounder would grab either my shirt or my shorts and pull me back. If he could not reach me he would scythe me down.' United had started their first season in League One in great form and on 13 November they won 2-1 at Olive Grove.

There was also no cheer for the Wednesday fans who travelled to Goodison Park. The game started well as on 5 minutes 'Spiksley went down in one of his speedy runs and eluding Parry and also beating Williams, scored easily'. (*The Liverpool Mercury*) The lead lasted seconds as Southworth, signed from Blackburn Rovers in the summer, equalised before putting his side ahead soon afterwards. The striker notched his third before the interval, at which point Everton led 4-1. His fourth was a goal of sheer brilliance as he ran rings round the Wednesday defence before he netted. Everton ran away with the game to win 8-1, condemning Wednesday to a then-record League defeat. Wednesday dropped into the test match zone with a Boxing Day home defeat by Burnley.

Wednesday faced league leaders Aston Villa on 6 January 1894 and they raced into a two-goal lead after Spiksley netted from a return pass from Johnny Webster and scored with a bullet header. These efforts took the outside left's goals for the season to ten, almost 30 per cent of Wednesday's total of thirty-six. Jack Reynolds reduced the arrears before England international Dennis Hodgetts equalised with a close-range finish as the game ended 2-2.

Desperate to avoid finishing in the bottom three, the Wednesday club president John Holmes convened a special meeting to discuss the precarious situation. The outcome was that the players were offered £50 to share if they could win five out of their last six games to ensure they finished outside the test match zone.

The following game was at Clayton against bottom-placed Newton Heath and took place on a very heavy pitch against opponents who weren't afraid to employ some rough house tactics, especially against the Wednesday outside left who, in the circumstances, did well to avoid serious injury. It was Earp, however, who was man of the match for the away side, who won 2-1 with Woolhouse netting twice. Following the heavy rain earlier in the week, the Wednesday players were able to enjoy a bath after the game as Newton Heath's water supply relied on collecting rain water that had ran off the pavilion roof into butts.

Two days later, in a game that had been abandoned at 2-0 on 58 minutes in December, Wednesday beat Darwen 5-0 at Olive Grove. The 1893–94 season witnessed three Wednesday matches abandoned. The two victories meant Wednesday entered the 1893–94 FA Cup in fine heart and for Spiksley, there was the thrill of returning to Royal Arsenal, whose side now contained two great friends: Charlie Booth and Arthur Elliott.

A long, tiring journey to Plumstead was made by the players and 200 Wednesday fans, whose arrival at the Manor Ground was greeted with great cheers by the 12,000 home fans. Early in the game, as Arsenal pressed, Spiksley prevented a goal when he inadvertently fell on the ball just inches from the goal and was kicked black and blue as the home attackers attempted to wrestle the ball into the goal. Amazingly, the ball squirted wide and when the Wednesday winger emerged from the floor he was covered in mud from head to foot. It was almost impossible to recognise him, but soon afterwards he opened the scoring when full back Joe Powell misjudged a cross and he nipped in to net. Sharpshooter Arthur Elliott equalised for the home side but the tie was settled when Spiksley showed pace and poise to put his team into the next round. The Wednesday scorer was again cheered as he left the field at Plumstead.

Before the next cup-tie against Stoke, Wednesday beat fellow strugglers Preston North End 3-0 at Olive Grove, with Spiksley, Earp and Brandon all scoring from free kicks. All of the goals came in the second half, as in the first, a nervous Fred, mocked by Jimmy Ross as he shaped to shoot, had flashed a penalty several feet over the crossbar and was berated by the Preston man afterwards. During the interval Mr Holmes visited the home dressing room and it was agreed that Fred wouldn't take a penalty again for Wednesday. He did in fact, eventually take two, scoring once and also missing a vital last-minute effort against Blackburn in 1899.

Wednesday maintained their good form by beating Stoke 1-0 in the Cup and the draw pitched Wednesday at home to League leaders Aston Villa, who aimed to emulate Preston's feat of 1888–89 by becoming the second club to win League and Cup in the same season. One thousand Villa fans travelled north, buoyed by their team having beaten Sunderland away in the previous round, a result that confirmed Villa's status as England's top club. Villa were favourites to progress, but Wednesday fans were optimistic and there was a tremendous atmosphere among the 22,100 crowd.

Woolhouse opened the scoring and the celebrating home fans sent hats, caps, scarves, and handkerchiefs high into the air. The game then settled down with the Villa half back line of Jack Reynolds, James Cowan (known as the 'Prince of half backs'), and Bill Groves dominating possession. In return, the Wednesday side fed the ball to Spiksley and after two dashing runs and near misses, John Devey, the Villa captain, detailed both John Baird and Reynolds to mark him. With seconds of the first period remaining, Bob Chatt made it 1-1.

Playing with the breeze, Villa were dominant and on 73 minutes Chatt drove his side ahead, after which the Villa faithful sang out, 'We've won to-dye – we've won to-dye'. A Birmingham journalist in the press box predicted 3-1 and it should have been, only for Chatt to miss horribly with only 7 minutes to go, leaving Wednesday still in the game. However, with less than 120 seconds remaining, Spiksley collected the ball. The Wednesday fans stirred, remembering Fred's last minute winner against Derby County in 1893, before crossing their fingers and looking on transfixed.

With most journalists having sent off their telegrams advertising the final score to the 'sports specials', the winger tricked his way round his two markers before leaving Cowan and Groves in his wake. A great roar went up as Villa's players realised they were now under serious threat. As Bill Dunning, Villa's 6 feet 2 inch 'keeper advanced, the Wednesday forward sent the ball with just the right amount of pace around him and into the net. It was 2-2 and absolute pandemonium among the relieved home fans, including those who halted their trek home by rushing back inside the ground to watch the following 30 minutes of extra time.

Amid an intense atmosphere, the game remained at 2-2 on 115 minutes when Spiksley did it again. In an almost exact repeat he beat his markers and defenders before this time pushing the ball into the path of the unmarked Woolhouse who, with every watching Wednesday fan's heart beating strongly, drove home his second goal of the match for the winner. Technically, Villa still had a chance of an equalizer, but Langley was taking no chances and he kicked the ball into the nearby allotments. When another ball was found he belted it on to the railway line. He kicked the next one even further and in an era when referees didn't add on time for interruptions, the away side had no time to force an equaliser.

Fred Spiksley had hauled his side back from the dead. And, unlike in 1893, when his goal against Derby County had afterwards been wiped from the record books, this time there was no preventing Wednesday advancing to the next round. For years afterwards, the Villa game became known as 'Spiksley's match', with his exploits reinforcing his growing reputation as a big match player. An excited crowd hung around for a long time after the final whistle, so unexpected was Wednesday's success.

Before the semi-final, Wednesday boosted their League chances when a Davis goal was sufficient to beat Nottingham Forest 1-0. One victory from the final two League matches would ensure Wednesday's 'great escape'.

On 10 March 1894, thousands of Wednesday fans packed out Midland Line Station (MLS) excursion trains to Fallowfield Station in Manchester. The suburban Fallowfield village was besieged as supporters tramped down the cobbled streets to what was now one of the country's finest football grounds. Eleven months earlier the Manchester Athletic Ground in Fallowfield had staged the 1893 FA Cup final between Wolves and Everton. There were 45,000 spectators in the ground and thankfully thousands were refused entry due to the horrendous crush inside. Indeed, it was a miracle no-one was killed amid the ensuing chaos, especially as there were insufficient policemen and marshals on duty to deal with any disaster. Plenty of people were injured and a considerable amount of fighting broke out, but there were no fatalities. Following the game, J.J. Bentley, the Football League president, personally oversaw much-needed ground improvements.

The Wednesday players and officials arrived at the ground in two horse-drawn decorated wagonettes. On the way, a black cat ran in front of the leading pair of horses. Was this a good luck omen? Blaring trumpets announced the teams' arrival. The Bolton XI were clearly bigger and stronger and, kicking with the sun behind them, employed both full backs, John Somerville and Dai Jones, to hit high balls which their bulky, heavier forwards could chase down.

Wednesday clung on and on 20 minutes, Harry Brandon took possession, advanced, and hit a lovely ball beyond the Bolton backs. As 'keeper Willie Sutcliffe moved to collect, Spiksley beat him to the ball and headed into the empty net. Sutcliffe hated losing and constantly challenged referees' decisions. He rushed over to referee Mr Armitt and vociferously argued that his England colleague was offside.

Fred Spiksley knew there had been five defenders between him and the goal when ball had been released by Brandon. 'It was one of the best goals of my life. The ball travelled diagonally over 20 yards and running at top speed I met the ball perfectly with my forehead and headed it like a bullet into the back of the net.' Throughout his career Fred used his pace and anticipation to judge a cross to score many goals with his head, but this time his effort was disallowed for offside, without the referee even consulting with his linesman. Further salt was rubbed into Fred's wounds when a second effort from him was also disallowed for offside.

Bolton then took the lead after a dubious hand ball decision against Jamieson. When Bob Tannahill knocked the free kick to Handel Bentley, the Bolton player's miskick confused Allan, who was looking into the sun, in the Wednesday goal to put his side ahead. Towards the interval a scything tackle on Spiksley by Alex Paton prevented a possible equaliser.

Bolton's luck appeared to be in after half time when they were gifted a second goal after Allan's attempt to fist away Bentley's shot saw the ball rebound from the crossbar and enter the net off the back of the 'keeper's head.

Bolton, now 2-0 up, were taking no chances as Archie Hughes committed an ugly foul on Spiksley. The worst was to come when Jimmy Cassidy committed a flying rugby tackle on Langley and escaped censure. Spiksley then created a great scoring opportunity, but was wrongly penalised for offside. Jones, Paton and Somerville all hauled him down over the next few minutes before Paton dragged over Woolhouse amid strong penalty claims.

Finally, Wednesday got their reward when Woolhouse brilliantly netted following a speculative long ball from Earp. Brady's ball then sent Spiksley through, but he was felled from behind by a dangerous two-footed Somerville challenge which was so bad that the referee rebuked a Bolton player for the first – and only – time in the game. When the final whistle sounded, Bolton had won 2-1 and advanced to play Second Division Notts County in the final, where they were beaten 4-1.

Wednesday were convinced they had been robbed. Writing years later, Spiksley blamed the referee for Wednesday's misfortune as he had no doubt both of his first-half efforts were goals. He was convinced that Mr Armitt had his back turned when Brandon's ball was hit towards him and the referee was wrongly persuaded by Willie Sutcliffe to disallow his effort, as he was well onside.

Having suffered FA Cup disappointment, Wednesday held their nerve in the following League game when a first-half goal by Spiksley helped overcome Burnley 1-0 at home. When the season ended Wednesday had finished in twelfth place in a League won by Aston Villa. The great escape had been achieved and the Wednesday players were rewarded with a £50 bonus between them.

In the League and FA Cup, Wednesday played thirty-four matches during the 1893–94 season. They netted fifty-six goals, and with thirteen League goals and three in the Cup, Fred Spiksley was the club's top scorer, while Miller second with eight.

Wednesday's most important addition for the 1894–95 season was a local lad. Tom Crawshaw was a player of such great ability that it seemed certain he would play for his country in double quick time, and so it proved. Tom was a Wednesday star from the start and was to perform with distinction for fourteen seasons, during which time he collected two FA Cup and Division One winner's medals as well as captaining his side to the Second Division title. Crawshaw's arrival meant no first-team place for Betts and the centre half retired at the season's end. Crawshaw was rated by Spiksley as the best centre half and finest header of a ball ever. Langley believed that only the Notts County centre back Walter Bull compared to Crawshaw in the air.

Wednesday also signed three Scots in the summer of 1894. Winger Archie Brash was speedy and tricky and played a major role in helping Wednesday win the 1896 FA Cup. Inside forward Bob 'Rabbie' Ferrier arrived from Dumbarton and quickly formed an effective right side attacking partnership with Brash. Ferrier was clever with the ball, could shoot powerfully and worked tirelessly. He later became a fine full back. His son and grandson, both also called Bob, enjoyed successful sports careers with the former making a record 626 Motherwell appearances and the latter being a noted sportswriter.

All four new signings featured in the opening day's 3-1 defeat at Everton. The game's first goal was scored by one of Spiksley's England colleagues from the 1893 Richmond international, Edgar Chadwick, one of the greatest players of his generation and a master strategist and dribbler. Wednesday then beat Preston 3-1 and Blackburn Rovers 4-1 at home. A couple of 2-1 victories, away to Derby County and at home to Bolton Wanderers, when Spiksley opened his season's account, put Wednesday in third place. Three defeats in four, including a 3-2 home loss against Sheffield United, stilled hopes of a title challenge, before five victories and just one defeat in eight established Wednesday in a comfortable League position.

On New Year's Day 1895, Wednesday, with Crawshaw and Spiksley in 'fine form' (*Birmingham Daily Post*) beat Everton 3-0 on a frosty pitch. Four days later, Liverpool were beaten 5-0 at home, with Spiksley scoring two to take his goal tally to a rather meagre five for the season. Wednesday remained fifth, but a single point from three away games saw them drop one place in the run-up to the FA Cup-tie with holders Notts County at Olive Grove. A crowd of 12,000 assembled for the big game.

In 1894, Notts County had become the first side from Division Two to win the FA Cup. The Lacemen, named because of Nottingham's hosiery trade, had in their side Jimmy Logan, whose hat-trick was only the second ever achieved in a final.

The County side were essentially the same from the previous season. They did, however, include debutant Wattie Arnott, the legendary Queen's Park full back who Spiksley had destroyed two years earlier when England beat Scotland 5-2. Facing his nemesis in the 1895 English Cup was going to be another step towards the completion of Arnott's career. Wednesday were five up before County replied with a late penalty, and County's hold on the cup ended after just one game. The *Sheffield Telegraph* reported: 'Watty Arnott is not the man he was' and he only made one more County appearance.

Two days later, Fred Spiksley participated in the Trent River Ice Race in Gainsborough. It was so cold that the Trent had frozen over with ice 11 inches thick. Hundreds of skaters took the chance to demonstrate their skills – or lack of them! Former Trinity captain Billy Brown enlisted the support of local tradesmen to organise a 1-mile ice race, the winner of which would receive a gold medal, the runner-up a silver medal and third a smaller silver medal. Eighteen entrants were cheered all the way by a 2,500 crowd. Fred Spiksley won his heat and was joined in the final by another former Trinity stalwart in Abe Watkin. The race favourite was M.S. Blundell who, by winning comfortably, made it a bad day for bookmaker William Spiksley. In a fierce three-way race for second, his brother, Fred, overtook Mr Robinson but was unable to overcome Watkin and thus finished in third place. After the presentation of the prizes there were great celebrations including one, no doubt, at the Crown and Anchor pub on Bridge Street. The landlord, however, was no longer Fred's father as he had returned to work for Marshall's Yard as a boilermaker.

The reward for Wednesday's success against Notts County was a home tie with Middlesbrough, then an amateur team in the Northern League. With

Sheffield United having drawn a much more attractive home tie with West Bromwich Albion, it was agreed that Wednesday's game would be brought forward an hour to 2.30pm. Unfortunately, Middlesbrough were so outplayed that many in the small crowd of 4,000 left at half-time to rush down to Bramall Lane and watch a more competitive match. In the 1890s, and for many years afterwards, it wasn't unusual for fans in any city or region with two clubs to watch one team one weekend and the other the next.

The Wednesday game ended in a 6-1 success for the League side, with Davis scoring three, but the quarter-final against Everton was certain to be much tougher challenge for Wednesday. In 1895, Everton were reputed to be the world's wealthiest club and were certainly the best-supported, averaging 17,420 at home in the League in 1894–95. Wednesday were the third best supported with 9,625 supporters. Until the 1980s, FA Cup ties tended to attract more spectators than League games and this was certainly the case on 2 March 1895, when 28,000 – nearly three times as many for the League game on New Year's Day – squeezed inside Olive Grove to see Wednesday take a 25th-minute lead through Everton old boy Brady, who slipped home a Spiksley pass. The home side were then reduced to ten men as Davis had to leave the pitch following a rough challenge by Dickie Boyle. Some great defensive work by Earp, Crawshaw, Langley and Brandon kept Everton away from Allan's goal, but the home side then suffered a further blow when Ferrier was lamed with a dead leg, the injured player being moved out to the right wing. Amazingly, with just seconds remaining of the half, the ball somehow made its way to Ferrier at the far post and he tapped it home to double the home side's advantage.

At the start of the second half Wednesday's goal was under siege. Chadwick should have scored before Brady, Brash and Spiksley dropped back to inside the Wednesday half. As the game ticked away from them, Everton pushed the Wednesday defence further and further back, but were unable to fashion a serious scoring opportunity. With minutes remaining, Brash became the third home player to sustain an injury, but Everton still couldn't beat Allan and the game ended 2-0 to Wednesday. After such a magnificent backs-to-the-wall effort, Wednesday fans were certain that this was finally going to be the year when their side won the FA Cup.

Standing in the way of a second final were West Bromwich Albion, the Cup winners of 1888 and 1892, who had defeated Small Heath, Sheffield United and Wolverhampton Wanderers on their way to the 1895 semi-final. Their side contained the irrepressible Billy Bassett and in Joe Reader they possessed one of best 'keepers of his generation and one who, as a player, coach and steward, served the club for a total of sixty-five years, but only played once for England.

The semi-final took place on Derby's Racecourse Ground, where the football field was just a small part of a large plain of grassland between the River Derwent and the town itself. The racecourse and cricket ground were in close proximity and after paying their entry, the 18,000 spectators crossed the circular racecourse and cricket enclosures to reach the heavily-grassed football pitch.

Ferrier's place was taken by Woolhouse. After the referee, Lieutenant Simpson, started the game there was an early attempt by Brady that Reader skilfully saved. However, on 20 sent it to Tom Hutchinson, the West Brom player escaped an ill-prepared Crawshaw to score a magnificent opening goal.

There was a second blow to Wednesday when it became apparent that Davis was suffering from a recurrence of his stomach injury from the Everton tie. To compound Wednesday's problems, an elbow from Billy Richards laid out Crawshaw and play was held up for 5 minutes, after which the Wednesday defender played the rest of the game wearing a great swathe of bandages, with blood continuing to pour from the wound. It was an incident comparable to that many decades later when Terry Butcher sustained a similar injury playing for his country.

Richards added to Crawshaw's problem by laying him out a second time with his elbow, but the Wednesday man was swiftly revived with a sniff of smelling salts and refused to leave the field. Today it would have been Richards who would have been forced to leave the arena, having been sent off. On this occasion, however wasn't even spoken to.

Bassett had been very quiet, but he was a player who was always looking for an opportunity to give him an edge over his opponents. Langley had done well to keep the winger away from the goal and with 35 minutes gone the pair raced for a ball bouncing towards the corner flag and well within the 12-yard penalty area that in 1895 ran right across the pitch. Bassett reached the ball first, trod on it and fell over writhing on the ground as if he had been shot, as Langley flew over the top of him.

The *Sheffield Telegraph* was at odds with many spectators, believing the incident merited a penalty. But that didn't prevent the paper heavily criticising Bassett who, when the referee awarded the penalty, immediately rose from the ground and began dancing a jig. 'From being lame, Bassett recovered instantaneously.'

Billy Williams, a non-stop dynamo at full back, doubled the lead and at the interval the score remained 2-0. The injustice ripped the heart out of the Wednesday side and their 8,000 followers, who had hoped to see a famous victory. There was no chance of that now, but the losing side fought to the end with Crawshaw and Petrie smacking shots against the crossbar.

Albion responded with a horrendous tackle on Spiksley by an unidentified opponent, which meant that the Wednesday player virtually disappeared from the game. With Crawshaw and then Earp suffering injuries, the game was dominated by Albion and when the final whistle sounded it meant Wednesday had lost in consecutive FA Cup semi-finals. Albion went on to face local rivals Aston Villa at the Crystal Palace, the third time the sides had met in the final. Each side had won once before, but this time victory went to Villa, thanks to a goal in the first minute – the quickest ever in a Cup final at the time.

A disappointed Wednesday returned to League football and a week later faced leaders Sunderland, who were sadly too good for them by winning 2-1 and later going on to win Division One for the third time in five seasons.

The Wednesday season came to a much less glorious end as, with only one win and one draw from their last half-dozen games, they finished in eighth place. Since beating Liverpool 5-0 in January, Wednesday had played eleven League matches and won just once: 3-2 at home to West Bromwich Albion. The season ended with a 6-0 hammering against the same team, a result that meant the losing side conceded more League goals than they had scored: fifty-five to fifty. Of the half century scored, Fred Spiksley notched just seven and was outscored by Davis, who got one more. Both men scored three in the Cup.

Chapter 10

No Nets

The home international series, 1894

Wales had beaten Ireland 4-1 in the 1894 Home International Championship opening game. Next up, England began against Ireland in Belfast on Cliftonville's Solitude Ground, named after a former stately home which once stood nearby, on 3 March 1894. An all professional team crossed the Irish Sea which included debutants Josiah Reader, Jimmy Crabtree and Henry Chippendale, while Jimmy Whitehead and John Devey were playing in only their second international. Four of England's finest – Bassett, Goodall, Southworth and Chadwick – were omitted. The impeccable credentials of left half Ernest Needham were also overlooked. Dennis Hodgetts had been selected when his finest days were behind him, and with Spiksley playing at outside left the Villa man was played out of position at centre forward. In response, journalists called the team selection a 'hotchpotch'.

The sea voyage on Thursday, 1 March 1894 was Fred Spiksley's first and he later made a firm resolution that it would be his last. Soon after the players had enjoyed a fine meal, the boat, which had embarked from Fleetwood, began rising and falling so violently that it became impossible to stand up. As passengers headed for their cabins, Spiksley was sent flying down the corridor. Every hatch on the boat was battened down and all of the England players, except Johnny Holt, became seasick.

However, the ship proved her seaworthiness and by dawn the England party had arrived in Belfast. With the ship's stewards sauntering along as though nothing untoward had happened, there was panic when it was discovered that Crabtree was missing. The Burnley man had been given up as lost when a hollow groan was heard coming from under one of the dining room tables and he was found safe, but certainly not well, curled up in a state of semi-consciousness. A cup of coffee and news that the ship had docked soon had the 'dead man' back on his feet.

The England side had just over twenty-four hours to recover from their traumatic experience and the result that followed proved they hadn't done so properly. Afterwards, travel plans to Ireland included the need to use the shortest route, Stranraer to Larne, and allow two additional days to acclimatise for training.

The teams lined up for the match as follows:

England: Josiah Reader (West Bromwich Albion), Bob Howarth (Preston), Bob Holmes (Preston) (capt), John Reynolds (Aston Villa), John Holt (Everton), Jimmy Crabtree (Burnley), Henry Chippendale (Blackburn Rovers), James Whitehead (Blackburn Rovers), Dennis Hodgetts (Aston Villa), John Devey (Aston Villa), Spiksley (Wednesday).

Ireland: Tom Scott, Robert K. Stewart, Sam Torrans (capt), Samuel Johnston II, Robert George Milne, John Burnett, Bill Dalton, George Gaffikin, Olphie Stanfield, James H. Barron, William K. Gibson.

Playing his fourth game for England was Jack Reynolds, who had previously scored against his country while playing for Ireland and is the only man to score both for and against his country. The son of an illiterate mother and a labourer father, Reynolds worked as a weaver before enlisting in the East Lancashire Regiment and being posted to Ireland in 1887, where he played regularly for the regimental football team against local sides, who in turn invited him to guest for them. He did, however, miss some matches as he was in hospital on three occasions for some form of venereal disease.

The Distillery club bought Jack out of the Army on Boxing Day 1889. This was a risky move as professionalism remained illegal in Ireland. In February 1890, Reynolds made his Ireland debut against Wales. He was now known as William and the *Ulster Football and Cycling News* reported that he had been born in Ireland before emigrating to Lancashire.

In Jack's second game he netted Ireland's only goal as they lost 9-1 against England. Reynolds made five appearances for his adopted country, where the fact that football had been introduced by the British Army based in the garrison towns had immediately incurred the hostility of the nationalist community. Reynolds later decided he was really English and signed for West Bromwich, where he collected an FA Cup winner's medal in 1892. Immediately afterwards he joined Aston Villa for £50 and won two more FA Cup winner's medals and three League championships with the club. He later won the Scottish League with Celtic. Highly competitive, Reynolds had remarkable ball skills and his footwork was frequently brilliant.

The Irish crowd were disappointed at the appearance of an under-strength England XI. The selectors were clearly using the game as a trial for the Scotland match. Despite the insult, however, England were given a rousing reception when they entered the arena.

Fred was disappointed when his tenth-minute effort was overruled for offside as he knew that when the ball had been played he had started his run from behind the Irish backs. Soon after Bob Holmes, the England captain, limped out of the game and as the away side reorganized, Reynolds dropped to centre half with Holt going to left full back. This gave James H. Barron and William K. Gibson, of Cliftonville, Ireland's oldest club, who at just aged 17 was making his international debut, some space and time, but it was England who should have scored when Whitehead, who had been quiet throughout, missed horribly after Fred created a simple chance.

On 42 minutes England scored when, following two fine Reader saves, a long punt up field by Crabtree was pounced upon by Devey to put his side ahead at the break. Only just, though, as seconds later Linfield's George Gaffikin smashed the ball home, only for the effort to be disallowed for an earlier harshly awarded foul.

On 55 minutes, England made it 2-0 when Spiksley set off on one of his trademark runs to score a goal that must have borne a striking resemblance to Ryan Giggs's famous 1999 FA Cup semi-final replay goal at Villa Park for Manchester United against Arsenal. This was how the *Athletic News* described it:

'A second goal came through a brilliant individual effort on the part of Spiksley, who, receiving [the ball] from Hodgetts, raced past Cliftonville's Stewart, got almost to the line, and with a slight touch by the side of his foot sent the ball just under the bar.'

The Irish were stunned and should have fallen further behind, but Devey, set up by Spiksley, missed when he was clean through. A grateful Scott cleared long and with Crabtree and Holt up field, Linfield's William Dalton centred and as Howarth and Reader froze, Distillery's Olphie Stanfield, who played thirty times for his country between 1887 and 1897, nipped in to reduce his side's arrears to just a single goal. The great jubilation and excitement that resulted should have been stilled when Spiksley broke clear, only to hit a tame shot.

On 87 minutes the final goal was scored when Cliftonville's Gibson, who made thirteen national appearances and was remembered forty years later by Sir Frederick Wall as one of the three finest Irish players ever, poked a bouncing ball home and caused further excitement among the home fans. The England players argued the shot had gone wide but in the absence of goal nets, the rights and wrongs of what had happened were left to the referee and he decided Gibson's effort had gone between the posts.

A brilliant game thus ended 2-2, following which the 'was it or wasn't it' debate raged and after all the players were consulted and enquiries made of spectators behind the goal, it was admitted that the ball had gone wide. Had

Ireland not lost a goal in 1892 when an effort that flashed through the posts against Scotland wasn't given, thus allowing Scotland to win the game 3-2? For the Irish the 'goal' against England simply levelled things up! It meant that for the first time in thirteen meetings Ireland had scored more than a single goal against England and it was also the first time they had avoided defeat.

The England match against Wales took place in Wrexham on 12 March 1894, with the all-amateur away side winning easily, 5-1. On 24 March, Scotland beat Wales 5-1 in Cardiff and one week later, Scotland overcame a spirited Ireland side to a rather lucky 2-1 win. Football can be a strange sport. Ireland had really lost to England and might have beaten Scotland, but now the Scots needed only a draw against England to become Home International Champions for 1894.

After playing for the Whites in the England trial match against the Stripes at Leyton, Fred Spiksley was selected to face Scotland at Celtic Park on 7 April. The England XI faced a late blow when Jack Southworth was declared unfit. Southworth had been in top form with Everton in 1893–94 and a career-ending injury the following season meant he had played his final international. Gilbert Oswald Smith took his place.

The Celtic executives had gone to great lengths to ensure their ground was perfect for the game. Over £750 was spent, much of it on re-turfing the pitch. A *Glasgow Evening News* column under the pseudonym of 'The Scottish referee' was highly critical of what he considered to be questionable tactics by the SFA for producing a pitch with a rich lush covering of long grass that would slow the pace along the ground and thus neutralise England's speed, especially out on the wings.

On Friday afternoon the England professional players, including debutant Ernest Needham, met up at Preston and took the train to Glasgow where they were booked into the Central Station Hotel. The players were in bed by the time the three amateur players, Gay, Pelly and Smith, checked in.

At 2.30pm on the Saturday afternoon the horse drawn carriages arrived at the hotel and as the England party embarked the crowd outside expressed their condolences and genuine sorrow at their impending defeat!

The teams lined up as follows:

England: Gay (Corinthians FC and Old Brightonians), Tom Clare (Stoke), Fred Pelly (Old Foresters), John Reynolds (Aston Villa), John Holt (Everton), Ernest Needham (Sheffield United), Billy Bassett (West Bromwich Albion), John Goodall (Derby County) (captain), Gilbert Oswald Smith, Edgar Chadwick (Everton), Spiksley (Wednesday)

Scotland: David Haddow, Donald Sillars, Dan Doyle (captain), Isaac Begbie, Andrew McCreadie, David Mitchell, William Gulliland, James Blessington, Alex McMahon, John McPherson, William Lambie

The Scotland side included four debutants in 'keeper David Haddow, Andrew McCreadie, James Blessington and William Lambie. At right back the selectors had chosen Donald Sillars, a soldier, footballer and a gentleman. He was an amateur with Queen's Park and his selection was a surprise. The fastest sprinter in the Scotland team, his job was to stop Fred Spiksley. The *Glasgow Evening News* called him the 'Demon'. It was his fourth cap. Up front for Scotland, Alexander 'Sandy' McMahon had predicted he was going to show Johnny Holt 'the double shuffle' on the new turf.

The English had more international experience, with their players having fifty caps between them against Scotland's twenty-one. Nevertheless, Scotland fans were convinced their side would win and they were intent on employing their greatest weapon – themselves – to ensure that was the case. Overwhelming home support, it was argued, would carry the day and also, wasn't the England side one of the smallest ever with only Goodall of the forwards taller than 5 feet 7 inches, while none of the half backs exceeded that height?

The ground still had electric light posts round the pitch, which had been employed in a failed experiment designed to make night time football possible. The posts became affectionately known as 'Madden's rigging', a reference to Celtic centre forward John Madden who had worked as a riveter in a Glasgow shipyard. A magnificent illustration of one of the Scotland goal's being lustily celebrated clearly shows these electric light posts, which were also mentioned in contemporary match reports of the game.

Huge numbers hoped to see the action and as such despite, careful planning by Celtic and the SFA, the arrangements to house the crowd weren't adequate. It was a sign of the footballing authorities' inability to successfully manage large crowds. This was to have lethal consequences a few years later in this fixture when 25 fans died at Ibrox in 1902. In 1894 there weren't enough police officers on duty outside the ground, not to mention too few gatemen to take the entrance money and no stewards inside the ground to prevent the enclosures from becoming overcrowded.

Once the gates were opened the crowd surged forward and, as people struggled to pay for entry, the pushing intensified. Fearing a catastrophe, the main gate was opened to allow greater access and spectators rushed into already overcrowded enclosures. The palisade fence in front collapsed under the crush and spectators fought for their lives as hundreds spilled on to the cinder track encircling the pitch. Many people were injured before the police and St John's Ambulance arrived to restore order and ensure treatment for those hurt in the melee. With an official attendance of 45,107, a new world record had been achieved, although in truth, over 50,000 had entered the ground. Once again, it was a miracle no one had been killed.

With kick-off delayed due to the crowds the atmosphere was subdued. The mood brightened considerably when Pipe Major Wallace marched his massed band of pipes and drums on to the field, accompanied by referee John Reid and his two linesmen, N.L. Jackson for England and A. Sliman for Scotland.

The sides were met with a great cheer. Scotland, in blue, won the toss and started well as Gulliland, in a sign of things to come, left Pelly for dead before forcing Gay to save. England responded. First Reynolds and then Needham hit the woodwork, but it was soon apparent that the pitch was a problem. Divots could be seen lying on the surface as Scotland went ahead on 7 minutes. Gulliland stormed past Pelly and with Blessington and McMahon acting as decoys, he found an unmarked Lambie who netted.

With the noise in the stadium almost deafening, England responded and Doyle did well to clear after McMahon misdirected a Spiksley corner towards his own net. The England outside left then dashed beyond Sillars. Haddow saved his shot, but before he had time to recover his bearings, John Goodall kicked the ball out of his fingers and coolly netted before turning and walking calmly back to the halfway line.

It was 1-1 after just 12 minutes. The away side, though, were restricted by Southworth's absence as a nervous Smith knew nothing of combination play and was on a different wavelength from his fellow forwards. Smith was a brilliant dribbler and had a great shot on him but passing, link-up play, distribution and finding space were, as an amateur player, alien to him. Apart from the Leyton trial match he had never played alongside professional footballers before.

The other England outfield amateur player Fred Pelly was also out of his depth, having only just undergone a serious eye operation that saw him lose the sight in his left eye, leading to him wearing an eye patch. To make matters worse he was accidentally elbowed in his good eye after 15 minutes and left virtually blinded for the remaining 75 minutes. Pelly became widely known as 'the only blind man to have played football for England'. Pelly's handicap left Clare and Needham sharing the full back duties and they combined successfully to dispossess the Scotland forwards.

With Chadwick out of sorts, Spiksley hardly had the ball and when he did, Sillars, realising that all the pre-match warnings about his speed were true, tugged his opponent's shirt, tapped his ankles and tripped him when he had the chance. With the referee failing to intervene, Sillars floored Spiksley before smiling as he helped the injured man up off the ground.

On 30 minutes, Goodall stepped round the Scottish defence and, with the goal at his mercy, tripped on the turf. He kicked out in disgust. Towards the interval, Gay saved four tremendously powerful shots and was congratulated by his team mates when the half-time whistle sounded.

On the restart, Bassett had his close-range shot saved by Haddow as England piled forward and were only denied by a Doyle goal line clearance from a Spiksley shot. With Holt dominating McMahon, Doyle switched the Scotland centre forward out to the left and put McPherson in the middle. The move paid off on 74 minutes when Davie Mitchell beat Clare and crossed. With Pelly missing, Gay dashed out to intercept but was beaten to the ball by McPherson, who sent it into the net as the stadium erupted in ecstasy. England were stung and were fortunate when almost immediately after his goal, the Scotland scorer missed a good chance.

How would England react? Pelly couldn't see, Smith was out of his depth and Chadwick was clearly out of sorts. The Scottish players and fans were already looking forward to the final whistle. Holt urged his colleagues to double their efforts. Goodall and Spiksley were determined not to be beaten and combined brilliantly only for the former to flash his shot just over the bar. Dan Doyle prodded his team to finish off the game, but in Holt, England had a man mountain and the Scots were reduced to long-range efforts.

With 85 minutes on the clock, England were able to push forward to find Bassett, who had been remarkably quiet until then. The winger jinked past Mitchell before slowing down as Doyle approached and then surprised his opponent by back-heeling the ball to Reynolds, the England pair thus employing a trick they had perfected during their time together at West Brom.

Reynolds advanced from 25 yards, looked up briefly and, using the strong breeze, hit a powerful shot that sped just under the crossbar and into the top corner of the net. It was a sensational goal, one of the best from the 1890s, and left Celtic Park in a silence that was only broken by the cheers of the England players and a small knot of officials.

With neither side able to snatch a late winner (Scotland, in particular, were content since they finished with five points compared with their opponents' four), England were grateful they had emerged with honour after being forced to overcome a number of problems. There was also the case that England would, with goal average not being taken into account at the time, have finished joint top if there had been nets for the Ireland match!

In 1895 the England selectors omitted Spiksley for all of England's Home International matches. In the first, a side consisting of professional players beat Ireland 9-0 with Stoke's Joe Schofield playing his third and last international at outside left. A week later a team of amateur players drew 1-1 with Wales, where Sandilands played at outside left. England then beat Scotland with a team containing two amateur players. Stephen Smith had been in fine form for Aston Villa during the 1894–95 season, notching eighteen goals in all competitions. He marked what proved to be his only game for England by scoring the third from outside left in a 3-0 victory that earned his country top spot in the table.

In 1896, England's first match was away to Ireland on 7 March. The previous season's results had made it clear that England performed better with professional players in their side. Spiksley had been in fine form in January and February 1896 and had played especially well in Wednesday's 2-1 success at Sunderland in the FA Cup. He was picked to play his fifth international for his country and was one of seven professionals selected.

England: George Raikes (captain) (Oxford University), Lewis V. Lodge (Corinthians FC), William Oakley (Oxford University), Jimmy Crabtree (Aston Villa), Tom Crawshaw (Wednesday), George Kinsey (Derby County), Billy Bassett (WBA), Steve Bloomer (Derby County), Gilbert Oswald Smith (Oxford University), Edgar Chadwick (Everton), Spiksley (Wednesday)

Ireland: Tom Scott, John Ponsonby, Samuel Torrans, James Fitzpatrick (capt), Robert Milne, Hugh Gordon, Gideon Baird, Edwin Turner, Olphert Stanfield, Jim Kelly, John Peden.

The England party left Stranraer and embarked on a ferry crossing that left many of them seasick. Billy Bassett was the worst affected and rarely featured in the match that took place at the 15,000-capacity Solitude Ground in Cliftonville, Belfast. Although good weather was forecast, the skies opened half an hour before kick-off and the ground conditions quickly became treacherous. The match referee, Mr James Robertson, was an army man from Dumfries and his Friday night ship from Stranraer had been blown off course and he was in a bad way when it docked, although thankfully he had gathered himself sufficiently to referee the game.

Ireland, wearing their St Patrick's blue-coloured shirts (Ireland wore blue until 1914), started very well and Ollie Stanfield should have put them ahead. In goal for England, George Raikes was extremely nervous and his handling throughout the game was poor.

When England pressed, Spiksley set up Bassett but the Baggie missed an easy chance. However, it was from a Bassett cross that Smith hit a first-time low shot that flashed beyond Scott to give England the lead on 40 minutes and half time arrived with England 1-0 ahead.

With the wind behind them, England had more of the play in the second half and after Spiksley tricked his way round John Ponsonby, he delivered a perfect centre for Bloomer to make it 2-0. The Wednesday man had again delivered on the international stage. A game ruined by the conditions ended in victory for England by two goals to nil before a 12,000-strong crowd.

England's second international match in 1896 took place on Monday, 16 March at Cardiff Arms Park. Sandilands took Spiksley's place at outside left and Goodall replaced Chadwick. England won 9-1 and Bloomer set a record by becoming the first player to score five times for England in an international.

Sandilands failed to score and he was missing for the England trial match at Leyton on Wednesday, 25 March 1896. Four days earlier, Spiksley had rescued Wednesday by crafting an undeserved equaliser against Bolton in the FA Cup semi-final that, after finishing 1-1, would be replayed three days after the England trial game. It was a sign of Fred's patriotism that he was willing to make a 290-mile round trip to play, but knowing his record and ability it was surely unnecessary for the selectors to make him do so.

Representing the Players in the trial match, Fred was in direct competition for a place against Scotland with amateur Cuthbert J. Burnup of Cambridge University, who was at outside left for the Gentlemen. The professional side suffered a blow when Bloomer was forced to withdraw due to an injury. The Rams player had scored six of England's eleven goals in 1896 and it was simply unthinkable that he might not be fit to face Scotland. Manchester City's Pat Finnerham was Bloomer's replacement.

Around 10,000 fans watched the game. The Gentleman, easily recognisable by their greater height, muscular strength and plain rude health, scored early through MH Stanborough. The professionals, much quicker and more skilful than their opponents, then took control of proceedings and Goodall was unlucky to be ruled offside following a superb pass from Spiksley. In the meantime, Raikes was again visibly nervous and appeared unable to catch the ball. On fifty minutes the Players equalised when Lodge and Oakley collided leaving Finnerhan to run clear and score.

On 65 minutes, Raikes spilled a Bassett shot and Goodall put his side ahead. The Gentleman rallied and, using their great strength and physique, they laid siege to their opponents' goal, forcing Sutcliffe to make several impressive saves. However, the Bolton goalkeeper was helpless when on 75 minutes, Cotterill equalised from one of a series of well-placed corners from Arthur Henfrey. The game ended 2-2. Spiksley hadn't played particularly impressively, but neither had his opposite number Burnup, who had never previously played football for his country and was generally regarded as a cricketer.

On Saturday, 28 March 1896, Spiksley was in inspired form and was the man of the match as Wednesday beat Bolton 3-1 in the replayed FA Cup semi-final in which he also scored. Having previously scored seven goals in five England internationals, he was surely a 'cert' to play against Scotland. 'Pa' Jackson, the head of England selectors committee, had other ideas and on Monday, 30 March he used his power over the other selectors to gift Cuthbert 'Pinky' Burnup, a stockbroker, with what proved to be his only cap. In goal, Raikes, a clergyman, was selected and there were also places for amateur players Oakley and Smith, who admittedly deserved his place and Henfrey, who had so little influence on the match that the Scottish papers later suggested he might have been a ghost.

When left half Ernest Needham was forced to withdraw at the last minute with a bacterial infection, the England selectors replaced him with a sixth amateur, Vaughan L. Lodge of Cambridge University and Corinthians FC. This necessitated a switching of positions for a number of players.

Respected journalist J.A.H. Catton claimed he had heard Jackson on one occasion attempt to get someone to play for Corinthians FC by saying, 'Come and play for me and I will get you your international cap.'

Over the previous seven years no England side facing Scotland had contained so many amateur players, as it was generally accepted that when professionals formed the majority of the team then England won. To compound matters, Bassett was picked despite suffering from flu. Scotland had abandoned their previous policy of not selecting English-based Scots and their side included Sunderland's Ted Doig in goal, Tom Brandon from Blackburn Rovers, James Cowan of Aston Villa, John Bell of Everton and Tommy Hyslop of Stoke. Only one amateur player, Lambie of Queen's Park, was selected.

Many of the England side had no idea of what was to face them as they walked out at Celtic Park on Saturday, 4 April 1896. They were without Fred Spiksley, who on that day was playing for Wednesday against Small Heath.

A gate of 51,345 fanatical Scotsmen helped curdle the Sassenach blood and Raikes gifted the home side the opening goal by dropping the ball to allow William Lambie to follow up his original shot to net. Jimmy Cowan then doubled the lead on 40 minutes.

In the second half England provided tougher opposition and Goodall created a chance that saw Bassett reduce the arrears. In the end, though, Scotland had beaten their arch rivals for the first time in seven years and the highest ever attendance at a football match celebrated wildly as a sorry England side left the pitch with their heads bowed. Scotland had won the 1896 Home International Championship. In truth, 'Pa' Jackson had gifted them the top spot. Two weeks later, one of the missing England professionals, Spiksley, scored two of the finest goals ever seen in the FA Cup to give his side a famous victory in the final.

Chapter 11

All The Way to The Palace

Spiksley guides Wednesday to their second FA Cup final

The major development in the summer of 1895 was the signing of Third Lanark's Lawrie Bell, which solved Wednesday's goal-scoring problem and enabled Harry Davis to return to his preferred inside forward position. Bell was an excellent dribbler with a powerful and accurate shot; he linked up well with his wide men and was a clever passer, all enabling him to have an outstanding first season.

In the season's opener, Bell opened the scoring at Everton in a 2-2 draw. Three days later, on Tuesday, 5 September, Fred Spiksley took part in another big match that was attended by just five people when he married Ellen Robinson in Sheffield. The marriage ceremony was conducted by J. Chas Barber, the resident registrar at the Sheffield Register Office, and was witnessed by Mr J. Bennett and Henry Canham, neither of whom appears to have had any previous connection with the bride and groom. It seems that they were approached in the street and requested to witness the ceremony.

On the marriage certificate the groom is listed as 25 years old, living at 19 Talbot Street, Sheffield, and working as a printer with the *Sheffield Telegraph*. Only the age was correct, as Fred Spiksley had quit his newspaper job when he returned to Gainsborough in the summer of 1893. It seems possible that Thomas McCabe, whom Fred had lodged with between 1891 and 1893, had put the couple up for a few days before the wedding.

Ellen had lived with her mother, Jane Robinson, in an extended family that included three brothers and four sisters, all younger than her. Ellen told the registrar she was 21 years of age, but this was a lie as she was only 18. It was said that her father had died two years previously and was therefore unable to give his eldest daughter away.

Why the secret marriage? It was most likely because Ellen was four months pregnant and there was consequently an urgent need to marry without fuss or publicity. Attitudes to sex before marriage were changing – especially among the young – but having a child out of wedlock was still heavily frowned upon in late

Victorian times. If the news had become public then Fred Spiksley would have been in the middle of a scandal. As a result, no one from Gainsborough or Fred's team mates attended the wedding, which went smoothly. Sadly, that wasn't the case with the pregnancy as baby Frederick Walter Spiksley died within a few days of his arrival in January 1896.

Wednesday's opening home League game in 1895–96 was against Sheffield United, and another effort from Bell, following a header from a Spiksley cross, was enough to win the day. It was the only time Wednesday beat United in a competitive fixture in the nineteenth century.

Defeats at Wolves and Derby were a disappointment, but Wednesday played much better at Olive Grove and another double by their outside left saw West Brom beaten 5-3. This was followed by home victories against Wolves and Sunderland. When Wednesday later won at West Brom, they rose to fourth in the table. A 6-1 hammering at Bury, however, showed there was still work to be done.

At home to Burnley, Spiksley provided the talking point when he performed one of the back-heel manoeuvres for which he became famous, putting the ball directly into the path of Brady, who scored the only goal.

Defeats against Stoke and Derby meant Wednesday entered 1896 back in eighth place. If a trophy was to be won it would have to be the FA Cup. Wednesday faced Southampton Saint Mary's away in the first round. Saints were a top Southern League team and although inferior to the Football League, the standard of the Southern League was still good enough to mean the Yorkshire side would need to play well to progress.

The Wednesday party left for the south coast at 11.48am on a Friday and arrived eight hours later, before walking a few yards to the Davis Railway Hotel.

The Cup-tie gave Hampshire football fans a chance to see one of England's top clubs and the game was the talk of the town in the week leading up to it, with some Saints fans being so confused that they turned up on the Wednesday to watch it! The Antelope Ground witnessed a record crowd of 12,000, including some who had climbed on top of the corrugated iron stands to seek a better view. Shortly after the players entered the pitch there was a loud bang as one of the stands collapsed under the weight. Miraculously, no-one was hurt and the game was started when Lieutenant Simpson sounded his whistle.

The away side were swiftly into their stride as the Southampton defence struggled to protect Jack Cox, their young 'keeper. He had leapt from third to first choice due to injuries and military commitment ruling out 'keepers one and two, Tom Cain and Matt Reilly. Unsurprisingly, he looked nervous and was fortunate when Davis failed to net from close in. However, despite enjoying virtually total possession, Wednesday struggled to create scoring opportunities and were grateful when Jimmy Massey, who had kept his place in the side after replacing an injured Bill Allan in goal for the previous League game, made two fine saves. Massey, noted for his bravery, had signed from Doncaster Rovers in 1893 and would remain in goal for the next four and a half seasons. He was to play brilliantly, especially late on, at the 1896 FA Cup final. Without the injured Langley, the Wednesday team selection hadn't been well thought out, with right half back Harry Brandon switched to left back and Bob Petrie, a natural left footer, playing at right half. Earp and Brandon were struggling to work out an understanding when Watty Keay darted between the fullbacks and scored a goal that on another day might have raised the roof. The home crowd were ecstatic, but not for long.

From the restart the ball went out to Fred Spiksley and he curled it inside to Brady, who shot powerfully past Cox to equalise. When the ball was next in Wednesday's possession the young 'keeper made two smart reflex saves, but as the ball ran free, Spiksley controlled it and as he feinted to shoot, the Saints defenders rushed forward only to find the Wednesday winger had rolled the ball into Brady's path, who from almost the same spot as his first goal, knocked it home. Wednesday doubled their lead in the second half through a Davis diving header.

Southampton St Mary's, who dropped the St Mary's from their name in 1897, cut the arrears when Jack Farrell netted following a corner. The game became highly competitive. Massey made a number of good saves and Earp, Crawshaw and Brandon combined to prevent an equalising goal and ensure their side deservedly progressed to the next round.

There is no doubt that Wednesday should have come away from Southampton with a win, but the Hampshire club were a side making considerable progress. The following season they won the Southern League for the first time and would win the title for three consecutive seasons. In 1900 and 1902 Southampton reached the FA Cup final, losing to Bury and then Sheffield United.

Wednesday were handed a second round home tie against the reigning League champions Sunderland, and the match attracted a then-record home crowd of 22,000, who paid £729 to watch the action. Sunderland, three times winners of Division One, had never won the FA Cup. Standing in the Wearsiders path were a side that had turned Olive Grove into a fortress in the FA Cup. Fred Spiksley was nettled when he bumped into Will Chatterton, the Derbyshire and England cricketer, and was asked who he felt would win the 1896 FA Cup. With League leaders Aston Villa out, Chatterton's choices were Derby, Sunderland or Everton. Fred challenged the cricketer, 'Are we out already?' He was told Wednesday certainly would be when Sunderland beat them, and when he argued against this he was asked to place a bet at odds of 10-1. He paid his £1. It was only time Fred Spiksley bet on football.

After losing a gruelling Birmingham Senior Cup match with Aston Villa 4-3, the build-up for Wednesday's players was a recipe of light exercise, fresh air and relaxation.

On match day, the teams ran out to a tremendous roar and the game started frantically before Wednesday began dragging the Sunderland defence out of position and shots rained in on Ned Doig's goal. From a half-cleared corner, the normally reliable Robert McNeil, the Sunderland right back, was too slow in closing down Spiksley and, taking advantage, the Wednesday man chipped the ball to the back post where Bell headed home. With Doig performing heroics, this looked like being the home side's only reward in a first half they had dominated. However, on 44 minutes Bell made another scintillating break. As the Sunderland defenders were sucked towards him he fed the ball beyond them to Spiksley 'who with a really brilliant run and shot put on the second goal for the home side amidst enthusiastic cheering' (*Sheffield Telegraph*).

Sunderland had been outplayed in the first half and understood that they needed to keep much better possession of the ball. The Wednesday players had to work hard to close down the away side. In time, the effects of the hard game against Aston Villa began to take their toll.

Sunderland reduced the arrears when Jimmy Millar's quick throw-in to Johnny Hannah put several Wednesday players out of position. Hannah drew Massey out of goal and squared the ball to Millar who pushed it into the empty net. Their chances grew when a high tackle by Hugh Wilson on Spiksley left the winger incapacitated. It was now the turn of Earp and his lieutenants, Crawshaw and Langley, together with Brandon and Jamieson, to defend for their lives. They did so with great resolution and when the final whistle sounded, the home side were in the final eight of the FA Cup.

The Wednesday players spent the week leading up to the tie in Matlock, staying at the Chesterfield House Hydro, 600 feet above the meandering River Derwent looking north over the ravine to High Tor and Matlock Bath, 2 miles away. Each morning, after a cold shower and breakfast, there was a long walk followed by lunch, massage treatment, an hour of intensive football practice and drills before a sixty-minute game in which no tackling, tripping or charging was allowed in order to avoid injuries. There followed relaxation in the steam baths and a light tea.

The party arrived home on the Friday afternoon. The main concern was injuries to five senior players: Langley, Bell, Brady, Davis and Spiksley, with the latter suffering from a liver infection and the least likely to play.

Inevitably, news leaked out that the Wednesday line-up might be a weak one. In 1896 there was no match-day programme and so, in the days before decent public address systems, never mind giant screens or the Internet, anyone who wanted to know the side prior to kick-off bought a match card, costing a penny, from the legendary cricket and football scoreboard printer, Billy Whitham.

The Wednesday match card was inconclusive. Langley was out and was replaced by Harry Brandon. Bell, Brady and Davis were fit and there was a surprise recall for Brash at outside right. That left the left wing position to be filled and the match card revealed it would be occupied by Anthony Richards, an inexperienced youngster, or Fred Spiksley. Everton were also struggling to field their first team and Tom McInnes, Smart Arridge and the irrepressible Johnny Holt were missing.

Rain had fallen steadily all night and two hours before kick-off the heavens opened. With no paved pathway to Olive Grove, the footpaths were quickly turned into mud, which in turn found itself on to the ground embankments and enclosures, thus adding to the fans' discomfort. Unsurprisingly, the size of the crowd was much reduced to just 12,000. After all, this was an era when catching a cold could be potentially fatal and, with no such thing as sick pay, taking time off from work was a luxury few working class people could afford.

The teams ran on to the pitch to a muted welcome, until the outside left was spotted and a huge cheer went up as though the home side had already won the game. The tie itself proved to be very one-sided: on 15 minutes, a Spiksley header found Brash, who netted, Before Bell doubled the advantage after Jack Hillman spilled the ball.

At the interval, both teams changed into clean shirts. When play resumed a long-range Petrie shot crashed against the cross bar, before a Brash solo run ended with him making it 3-0. The home side then stepped up the pace again and when Spiksley collected the ball 70 yards from the Everton goal, he ran unchallenged before finding Bell who made it 4-0. Wednesday were into the FA Cup last four for the third consecutive season.

Their opponents were their 1894 conquerors, Bolton Wanderers. In the other semi-final the bookies' favourites and Will Chatterton's last surviving tip, Derby County, faced Wolves. Bolton had progressed against Wednesday in 1894 thanks to foul play and poor refereeing, and there was therefore disappointment when it was announced that the referee from that day, Leek's Mr Armitt, would take charge of the 1896 semi-final involving the two sides. Wanderers were going well in the League and were unbeaten in nine competitive matches in 1896.

A tight game was predicted at Goodison Park, the scene of Bolton's defeat by Notts County in the 1894 FA Cup final. Thousands of Wednesday fans journeyed to Liverpool, far outnumbering the Bolton supporters.

Having won the toss the Bolton captain Jimmy 'Surefoot' Somerville chose to defend the Park End goal with the sun behind them, possibly recalling that Wednesday 'keeper Bill Allan had fumbled the ball over his goal-line with the sun in his eyes in 1894. With Langley suffering a twisted knee, Harry Brandon was again asked to play out of position at left back. Bolton also had an experienced full back missing in Dai Jones with E Hamilton replacing the Welsh international.

The game's first goal arrived on 5 minutes when Cassidy hit a shot over the Wednesday full backs and, blinded by the sun, a nervous Massey missed the flight of the ball and parried it to Tannahill, who scored from close range. Somerville's decision had paid immediate dividends. Their confidence high, Wanderers sought to double their advantage and Paton fired home from a free kick. However, the Bolton fans' joy was stilled because no-one had touched the indirect effort and Jack Wright's shot smacked the crossbar.

Having hardly left their own half, Wednesday almost equalised when Brash sent over a cross that Spiksley reached just before Somerville. The Wednesday winger improvised by knocking the ball off the Bolton man's shin pads, which sent it beyond a surprised Sutcliffe. He reacted by diving backwards to push the ball for a corner. It was a magnificent save.

Less pleasant was a deliberate hack on the Wednesday outside left by Jim McGeachan. Wednesday penalty appeals were overlooked as Mr Armitt inexplicably decided to award an indirect free kick on the 12-yard line and failed to speak to the offender. The game was now, however, all Wednesday and Sutcliffe, who had played brilliantly in the 1894 FA Cup final, showing his international class to ensure Bolton stayed ahead. He was eventually beaten twice, Hamilton first clearing a Spiksley shot from the line and then also blocking a Crawshaw header with a remarkable overhead scissors kick.

When the sides returned from their half-time break the sun had dipped and so did the quality of the football. The equaliser all Wednesday fans craved should have been scored by Davis, but he curled wide when clean through. However, with 70 minutes gone the deserved equaliser finally arrived after Spiksley's swerving cross had Bolton 'keeper Sutcliffe coming out to collect before he realised the ball was moving away from him. It was too late and an unmarked Brash rushed in and volleyed home as everything handy – hats, caps, flowers, favours – was flung upwards by delighted Wednesday fans.

With Bolton exhausted and Wednesday down to nine fit men (Petrie was limping and Jamieson was suffering from an injury), the tie failed to sparkle and was set for a replay. Then, in the last minute, Archie Fairbairn beat Brandon and raced in on goal. The Bolton man's nerves failed him at the last minute and his shot hit Massey's shins. When the ball spun free the 'keeper was forced to make a good save from the follow-up shot from Bobby Brown. At full time, the tie ended 1-1 before a thoroughly entertained crowd of 37,000.

The replay was at the Town Ground, Nottingham Forest's home on Arkwright Street. In the 1890s most fans couldn't afford to travel to away games, but an FA Cup semi-final was different and 12,000 Wednesday fans made the short trip – only worrying about how to pay the rent and feed the family on the way home.

Bolton fans were outnumbered 3 to 1 in the 16,000 crowd, which also contained a few locals who were rooting for the Sheffield side. Vail, who had replaced Cassidy, and Langley were to dust each other's jackets pretty well over the following 90 minutes.

Despite a heavy breeze and a difficult pitch, Wednesday took the lead after 2 minutes when Crawshaw hit a 12-yard free kick beyond Sutcliffe. The goal was compensation for another refereeing poor decision as the free kick was awarded for a hand ball so close to the Bolton goal that it should have been a penalty. Bolton equalised on 20 minutes when former Wednesday man Brown headed past Massey, before Vail was booked for a terrible tackle on Langley that left the Wednesday man crippled for the remainder of the game. At the interval the Wednesday fans had the terrible feeling that with the wind behind them, Bolton would again eliminate their side from the FA Cup.

With Petrie performing well to cover for the injured Langley, Wednesday remained in the tie. When Bolton conceded a free kick, Petrie took it splendidly and found Davis, whose diving header restored the Yorkshire side's lead. With Vail performing like a bull in a china shop, Bolton were beaten and in the final minute Wednesday confirmed their 1896 FA Cup final place when, from a Brash cross, Fred Spiksley used his instep to fizz the ball over Sutcliffe and under the bar. 'You would have to attend a great many games of football before you could see a better and more well-fashioned goal', wrote Langley in 1925.

When the referee sounded the final whistle the pain in Langley's massively swollen knee was agonising, and with his mind in torment he was carried from the field by Earp and Petrie in a state of delirium. Thousands of Sheffielders went into Nottingham and celebrated wildly. It had been a famous occasion.

Chapter 12

1896 Hero

Wednesday win the FA Cup for the first time

The Wanderers amateur team first won the FA Cup trophy in 1872. When they also became the first to win the competition three years in succession, from 1876–78, they relinquished their right to keep the trophy on the understanding that any side equalling their feat would also return it to the FA. When Blackburn Rovers were successful three years running from 1884–86 they were awarded a commemorative shield.

After Aston Villa beat West Bromwich Albion 1-0 in the 1895 final they displayed the cup in the window of William Shillcock, a football outfitters. It was stolen on 11 September 1895 and never recovered, despite a £10 reward for its return. Villa were fined, a new trophy was made, and it took 100 years for the truth to become known when evidence surfaced which, according to author Mike Collett, was 'as reliably substantiated as possible'.

Mrs Violet Stait, aged 80 in 1995, had married Jack Stait in 1935, the son of John 'Stosher' Stait. She claimed her husband had told her that his dad 'pinched that cup out of Shillcock's window' and, following further extensive investigation by the Aston Villa club magazine *Claret and Blue*, and later the BBC, it was agreed that Stait had been one of four unemployed men who had broken into the shop through the roof before walking out the front door with the trophy. Little good it did them financially, as the four were double-crossed by their receiver who only gave them 10 shillings (50 pence) to share. Melted down, the original cup disappeared forever.

It had been a surprise when Wolves overcame Derby County 2-1 in their 1896 FA Cup semi-final, with goals from Joe Tonks and Billy Malpass. Tonks had replaced David Wykes in the first team after the latter had died from typhoid fever. It was the third time in eight seasons that the Black Country side had reached the final, losing 3-0 to Preston in 1889 and beating Everton 1-0 in 1893. Unlike Wolves, Wednesday were hoping to capture the FA Cup for the first time.

Sheffield Wednesday played three League games before the Cup final. They won two and lost one, with Fred Spiksley scoring in the 3-0 defeat of Small

Heath, his tenth League goal. At the end of the season, Wednesday had finished seventh. Wolves, meanwhile, needed a 5-0 last-day defeat of Bolton Wanderers to avoid playing in the test match series.

In a surprise move the Wednesday directors departed from tradition by preparing the team for the big FA Cup game at home. Headquarters were established at the Earl of Arundel and Surrey Hotel, and training took place each morning at Olive Grove, with the ground open to anyone interested in seeing their heroes close up.

The Wednesday party departed for London at 2.30pm on Friday, 17 April 1896, with the train stopping momentarily at Nottingham's Midland Station to collect Fred Spiksley and Jack Earp and complete the playing contingent of thirteen. The question remained, however, as to who were going to be the unlucky two not to make the final eleven?

After arriving at St Pancras Station at 6.10pm, the party journeyed across the capital to reach the Queen's Hotel, the name of which had been a close secret with everyone under strict instructions not to divulge it. After the evening meal, Arthur Dickinson reported that the side would be announced in the morning. The papers had been full of reports that if the Crystal Palace pitch was firm and dry then Langley would play at left back. If the pitch conditions were heavy, however, Dr Jim Jamieson would play at half back, with Harry Brandon moving to full back and Langley dropping out of the side.

Fred Spiksley and Ambrose Langley, whom everyone knew better as Mick, shared a twin-bedded room on the night before the big game. Fred had been left bemused by the press reports. Writing for the *Thompson Weekly News* in 1920, he said:

> For a game of this importance and stature, the team chosen should have been announced well in advance to allow the eleven players selected sufficient time to prepare mentally for the game ... I shared with Mick Langley, and neither of us had more than two hours' sleep. I was anxious for him. I kept getting out of bed, going over to the bay window and looking out to see what was happening with the weather ... this state of affairs continued throughout the night. Other players were restless, not least Jim Jamieson, who had played in every Cup-tie that season and yet faced the possibility of missing the final if it didn't rain heavily!

After breakfast on the Saturday morning, the players gathered in the hotel library to discover their fates. Coach Bill Johnson had visited Crystal Palace and had returned with his pitch report.

The team selection up front was a surprise, but the Wednesday selectors knew that Wolves had some big strong players. Brash and Ferrier had performed brilliantly throughout the season, but both were small and so it was thought best to beef up the right flank by using Brady in support of Brash. Davis was switched to inside left to partner Spiksley on the left wing, with Bell at centre forward. In defence, Langley was selected with Jamieson missing out.

Wednesday:

Massey, Earp (captain), Langley, Brandon, Crawshaw, Petrie, Brash, Brady, Bell, Davis, Spiksley

It was six years since Wednesday had last played in the Cup final and no-one from the 1890 match represented the club in 1896. The 1890 side had included nine local lads and it was a sign of how quickly football had changed following the development of professionalism that in 1896, only Crawshaw was from the Sheffield area.

Wednesday were the bookies favourites to win the 1896 FA Cup, but Wolves weren't without their backers. As one of the original twelve members of the Football League, they had appointed tobacconist John Addenbrooke as secretary/manager in August 1885 and he was to continue in the job until June 1922. He was an exceptionally fine administrator and office worker, as well as possessing the ability to spot good footballers and recruit fine scouts. His team for the final lined up as follows:

Billy Tennant, Dickie Baugh, Tommy Dunne, Hillary Griffiths, Billy Malpass, William Owen, Jack Tonks, Charlie Henderson, Billy Beats, Harry Wood (captain), David Black.

The eleven included many local lads: Tennant, the only amateur in the side, Baugh, who had played in Wolves' first League match in 1888, Griffiths, Owen, Tonks, Wood and Malpass. Baugh, Wood and Malpass had played in the 1893 final, while Baugh and Wood had also played in the 1889 final.

The 30-year-old amateur goalkeeper, Tennant, had quickly established himself as a fans' favourite after England international Billy Crispin Rose was injured. Baugh was a Wolves man through and through and played from 1886 to 1896. He was a fine player, with a tremendous appetite for hard work topped off with the ability to head the ball powerfully to safety. His son, Richard junior, played for Wolves after the First World War. Scotsman Tommy Dunne, a no-nonsense defender, strong tackler and a good header of the ball, made 102 Wolves first team appearances. Right half Hillary Griffiths was one of three brothers who played for Wolves and made 201 first team appearances, scoring once. He and Fred Spiksley had frequently tangled in earlier games. Centre half Billy Malpass had played superbly in the 1893 FA Cup final and during his Molineux career from 1891 to 1899 he made 155 League and FA Cup appearances, scoring 9 times including goals against Notts County, Stoke and Derby County in the 1896 FA Cup run. Billy Owen completed the half back line. He was the tallest wolf in the pack at 6ft. In the 1895–96 season he played in every single League and FA Cup match, completing the same feat in 1896–97 and 1897–98.

Jack Tonks was a dashing outside right and fine crosser of the ball. His goals had helped his side overcome Stoke and Derby in the quarter and semi-final stages. Scotsman Charlie Henderson was Tonks's right flank partner in the 1895–96 season, his only one with Wolves, during which he scored eleven goals in thirty-six League and Cup appearances before signing for Sheffield United.

Billy Beats was signed a year after he scored three for Port Vale when they beat Wolves in the 1894 Staffordshire Cup final. He made 218 League and FA Cup appearances for Wolves, his ability to run at defenders being supplemented by fine ball skills, a delicate touch and a powerful shot. He spent seven seasons at Wolves during which he scored seventy-three goals; he represented England twice.

Harry Wood signed for Wolves in 1885 and made 289 Football League and FA Cup appearances, scoring 126 goals. He was the scorer of Wolves' first League hat-trick, against Derby County, in 1888 when, with thirteen goals, he topped the season's scoring charts for his club. He repeated that feat in 1890–91, when he was equal with Sam Thomson, 1892–93, 1894–95, 1895–96 and 1897–98, when he was equal with Beats and Bill Smith. Wood played football with great skill and enthusiasm and won three England caps. He later signed for Southampton where he became a big favourite at the Dell, scoring 65 goals in 180 games. He played in the 1900 and 1902 FA Cup finals where he completed a hat-trick of defeats and also won four Southern League championship medals between 1899 and 1904. Like many footballers, on retirement he took over the running of a pub, the Milton Arms near Fratton Park, Portsmouth.

David Black was a coalminer's son who, after playing internationally for Scotland in 1889, moved south to play professional football at Grimsby and Middlesbrough before signing for Wolves for the start of the 1893–94 season. His tricky skills on the Wolves left helped him score seventeen goals in eighty-four appearances.

In 1896 any visitor to the Crystal Palace would quickly realise it was 'The Home of the English Cup Final' and the 'Finest in the Kingdom'. For starters there was an unequalled opportunity for sightseeing: the Crystal Palace was a gigantic glass building constructed in Hyde Park to house the 1851 Great Exhibition that was a showcase for Britain's industrial and economic might. In the summer of 1851, six million visitors had attended what was the first ever international industrial fair. The building was then dismantled and re-erected in an enlarged form at Sydenham in South London, its location a 200-acre park, being renamed the Crystal Palace. Ornamental gardens, terraces and fountains were added, as were two massive fountains, which were switched on for the first time on 18 June 1856 by Queen Victoria and Prince Albert, the prince having co-organised the Great Exhibition with Henry Cole. Sadly, a massive blaze in 1936 burnt down the palace, but the ruins still remain in the park, along with a couple of statues, some stairs and some dinosaur sculptures, which were finished in time for the Royal Visit.

In 1895 the FA were desperate to return the English Cup final to London after the two previous Lancashire finals. Kennington Oval was clearly too small for the big game and so the FA approached the Crystal Palace company to see if they could assist. J.A.H. Catton, one of the FA council members who was placed on the sub-committee to confer with the Crystal Palace, claimed 'There was nowhere else to go, or so suitable, the arena was neutral as it was not used by any club and was so situated that a massed multitude on the lawn and the rising ground behind could obtain a view of the game'.

It was agreed to create a new football field within the grounds, within which Crystal Palace FC, formed in 1861 and one of the founding members of the FA on 26 October 1863, had drawn 0-0 in the first round of the first FA Cup against Hitchin Town on 11 November 1871. After losing 3-0 away to the Wanderers in round two of the 1875–76 season, the amateur Crystal Palace club, which has no connection to the modern-day club, disappeared from the football scene.

A vast area of the parkland that previously formed the south basin of the water fountain was turned into a massive arena extending to 25 acres of ground. The playing field was laid out in an elipse shape and a cycle track was installed. The goal posts were sited at the north and south ends of the ground and around the playing field was a railed area called simply 'The Ring'. Landscaped banking was introduced to form a natural amphitheatre that could accommodate tens of thousands of football fans in relative comfort, with most having a reasonable view of the pitch. There was an entrance at the north end and a standing area with the banking behind that extending round the goal to the east side. The banking then rose rapidly upwards to the tree line, directly in front of a strong retaining fence. On the other side of this fence was a switchback railway fairground attraction. A magnificent photograph, taken as the game kicked off in 1896, shows the west side, where John Aird and Sons had built a pavilion where 'honoured guests' sat comfortably under cover and were guaranteed a great view when the captain of the winning side received the FA Cup directly in front of them. There were 6,000 additional seats in blocks of 3,000 in two multi-span stands on either side of the pavilion, which contained provision for 100 members of the press.

On 20 April 1895, Aston Villa beat WBA to become the first winners of the FA Cup at the Crystal Palace, when 42,560 fans watched the action. With football becoming more popular a larger crowd of 48,836 witnessed the 1896 final. The occasion was nothing like as big as today's major football matches in terms of its coverage, but there had been plenty in the newspapers in the days leading up to it, including photographs and cartoon drawings of the players. The *Sports* newspaper gave away photographs of both teams, and on the day itself, photographs of action on the pitch were taken and one of which is reproduced in this book.

Excursion trains from Sheffield to Kings Cross and St Pancras railway stations started leaving at 6.00am on 18 April 1896. Thousands of Wednesday fans dressed in blue and white streamed south, where they poured out of the stations and hopped on to open-topped horse-drawn omnibuses travelling into central London. Sheffield blue merged with Wolves black and gold as all along the River Thames the big game was the main topic of conversation. A feature of the journey across London was the music of partisan Wednesday fans, singing songs in honour of their side. At Sydenham Hill and Crystal Palace railway stations, the fans disembarked and after a short walk the multitude of Wednesday fans arrived at the gates.

It was barely noon as they poured into the ground. There were still four hours to kick-off, plenty of time to picnic and sightseeing opportunities to enjoy. Best not miss the kick-off, though, as the previous season had seen the quickest goal ever scored in an FA Cup final. It was timed at thirty seconds and is credited to Aston Villa's Bob Chatt, although many Villa fans, and a certain Steve Bloomer, who was standing behind the goal where it was scored, were adamant that their captain John Devey had got the final touch.

By 2pm many fans were inside the ground and by 3pm the people holding reserved seat tickets were busy taking their places, as the crowd continued to swell right up until kick-off. Wednesday and Wolves players walked out 15 minutes before the whistle and while familiarising themselves with the conditions, the teams also warmed up with exercises and stretches to get themselves loose. The Wednesday XI were all fit, their splendid conditioning undertaken by coach Bill Johnson and his faithful ally John McReynolds. The weather was fine and warm without even the slightest breeze. The referee, Lieutenant Simpson, summoned the two captains to the centre spot. The toss was won by Wolves captain Harry Wood, who elected to defend the southern 'Railway End', although in truth, the conditions meant there was no real advantage in winning the toss.

With the referee allowing the teams time to settle into their formations, Fred Spiksley glanced across at his 'old friend' Hillary Griffiths and saw he was taking up a position a couple of feet across the whitewash. The Wednesday outside left immediately knew his opponent would have a dodge or two up his sleeve and if he was to make an impression then he needed to be at his best from the start. Fred knew what to expect from Griffiths. Little trips and kicks at ankles and knees were routine for Division One and especially at Molineux, which even then had a reputation for being a difficult place to play as the crowd was so partisan. However, Fred was feeling fit and more than ready to perform on what, in 1896, was the biggest stage in football. He also had a point to prove as he had been inexplicably left out of the England side that faced Scotland exactly two weeks before.

At 4pm Lawrie Bell started the game by passing to Brady, who pushed the ball forward to Spiksley out left, with the winger moving the ball back infield to Crawshaw who, under pressure by the advancing Wolverhampton half backs, sent the ball out of play on the Wednesday right around 35 yards out from the Wolves goal. In what proved to be Wolves' only touch of the ball before it entered the net, a hasty throw saw Crawshaw regain possession before sending the ball forward on the Wednesday right to Brash. He beat his marker before reaching the goal line and crossing to Davis, who laid the ball off for Spiksley to beat Tennant from around 25-30 yards out to make it 1-0.

Fred had scored what seems likely to be the quickest goal ever in an FA Cup final, as the newspaper headlines declared 'Sheffield scored in the first few seconds' (*The Times*). Sadly, the exact time of Fred Spiksley's goal cannot be officially confirmed. No-one thought to ask the referee afterwards if he had recorded it in his notebook and there was no reason for him to do so as it wasn't common practice in 1896. According to the former FA historian David Barber, the FA no longer have the referee's notebook and don't even know if it still exists. All this has allowed Louis Saha to become known as the quickest FA Cup final goalscorer, when his effort for Everton against Chelsea in 2009 was recorded at 25 seconds.

However, there is more than ample evidence that the honour of the quickest FA Cup final goal is Fred Spiksley's, with the *Monday Sportsman* reporting how, 'Few will forget the dash with which the Wednesday went off, and the lightning goal credited to Spiksley inside the first minute of the game had a great deal to do with their ultimate victory.'

The same day's *Manchester Guardian* is even more specific: 'Less than 20 seconds had passed, when Wednesday scored the first point of the game. Archie Brash on the outside right passed the ball into the path of Fred Spiksley who scored with a powerful shot that Tennant in the Wolves goal was unable to reach.' Meanwhile, the *Morning Po*st declared: 'In about a quarter of a minute Spiksley registered the first goal'.

The following newspapers reported that the goal had come within 30 seconds: *Sheffield Daily Telegraph, Nottinghamshire Guardian*, with others reporting that the goal was scored in under a minute: *Leicester Chronicle, Pall Mall Gazette, Northern Echo, Derby Telegraph, London Standard, Reynolds' News, Glasgow Herald, Wrexham Advertiser, Liverpool Mercury, Sportsman, Lincolnshire Chronicle, Buckinghamshire Advertiser, Lloyd's Weekly, Dundee Courier.*

As the Wednesday fans celebrated, a shell-shocked Wanderers side restarted the match. However, Harry Davis dispossessed Charlie Henderson and drove forward to hit a shot that was deflected for a corner. It was taken by Fred Spiksley and only just scrambled away by a panic-stricken Wolves defence.

When Wolves made their first advance on 4 minutes, Langley cleared to great South Yorkshire cheers. On 8 minutes the Molineux side had their first real chance from a free kick awarded against Langley. Jack Tonks floated the ball into the Wednesday 6-yard box and when it bounced up kindly, David Black, with his back to the goal, hooked it over his head and towards the Wednesday net. The hush in the crowd was ended when at the very last moment, the ball seemed to dip into the goal: Wolves had equalised thanks to a touch of skill and good fortune. Massey, playing against his hometown club, could only look on in anguish as the black and gold ranks roared their approval at the equaliser.

Four minutes later a determined Petrie hit a fine shot that fizzed just over before Spiksley beat Griffiths and bore down on Tennant's goal; his shot was only just wide. Wednesday, though, were determined to restore their lead, doing so on 18 minutes with what Fred Spiksley believed was the best goal he ever scored.

The initial movements were almost identical to those of the opening goal, with the ball being crossed into the centre from the right wing. Lawrie Bell then helped it into Spiksley's path 35 yards out from Billy Tennant's goal. This was 5 yards further out than from where the Wednesday outside left had shot in the first minute, but those 5 yards were to prove crucial as he drove the ball with great power. This time, he put spin on the ball and the crowd's initial groan meant most believed he had badly miscued his shot. Then, when the spin took hold, the ball swung violently and at just 3 feet off the ground, smacked against the far right-hand goalpost before entering the Wolves' net. So powerful was the strike that when the ball hit the net it rebounded back on to the field. Tennant was so confused that after he kicked it away, he missed Billy Beats restarting the game as the shocked crowd tried to work out exactly what they had just witnessed.

Tennant then kept his side in the match on 25 minutes by denying Brady with a fine stop, but with neither side able to wrestle control, Wolves were happy to concede a number of free kicks in their desire to prevent the quicker Wednesday forwards grabbing a third. The leading side then adopted a neat passing style that forced Wanderers on to the defensive. The interval arrived with Sheffield Wednesday still leading 2-1.

The Black Country side were again pushed back at the start of the second half as Brady and Brash twice combined, with Dunne and Baugh being forced to make last-ditch tackles to prevent a Wednesday third. Spiksley, who had confused his opponents by performing his back heel trick, was then upended from behind by Griffiths.

On 57 minutes there were great cheers among the Wolves fans when Tommy Dunne drove a free kick beyond Massey, but these were soon stilled when it was realised that no one had touched the ball. Griffiths then flattened Spiksley again before Langley denied Tonks a shooting chance.

Pushing forward, Wednesday should have doubled their lead, but Bell failed to direct his header from a Crawshaw free kick beyond Tennant from just yards out. The Wolves 'keeper then performed heroics when Spiksley put Davis through and the Wednesday player was denied by Tennant's outstretched fingers. As the game entered the final quarter, Wolves stepped up their efforts and for the first time became the better side.

Massey needed to rush out to deny a dashing Beats and the Wednesday 'keeper made a fine save from a Black hot shot that brought cheers from the increasingly anxious Wednesday fans. From a corner, Massey punched clear amid half a dozen Wolves players all trying to clatter him. Wednesday were dropping ever deeper and from a second corner there was the remarkable sight of Fred Spiksley making one of the only half a dozen clearances he made during his entire career.

In desperation, Earp, the Wednesday captain, then asked Crawshaw to drop back and, as a foretaste of the general system of defence that was later perfected by Herbert Chapman at Arsenal in the 1920s and 1930s, perform the role of a stopper centre half.

With just 10 minutes remaining, the Wolves' captain Harry Wood knew Wednesday were wilting, urging his defenders to hit the ball high into their opponents' box. The aerial bombardment did create the anticipated panic, but Wolves might have done better to keep playing the way they had been as Wednesday's defenders were exhausted. Hitting in long balls allowed them to stay where they were and when the ball was cleared, the Wednesday forwards could hold it up and run down the clock, which is exactly what Spiksley did when he used all his trickery to prevent Wolves gaining possession.

However, on 89 minutes the goal Wolves craved was only denied by another great Massey save before the Wednesday defenders literally began to throw themselves in front of further attempts on their goal. The game finally ended when the ball was cleared into midfield with the referee's whistle bringing jubilation among the Wednesday players, officials and fans. Wednesday had won the FA Cup.

Bell grabbed the match ball and later declared that it was destined to his home town of Dumbarton, where it would remain for eternity (the current whereabouts of the ball are unknown). While Fred Spiksley was having his hand 'shook-off', as reported in the *Athletic News*, a bizarre story was unfolding in the centre of the Crystal Palace football pitch when one player couldn't understand what all the fuss was about. As the players were walking off the pitch, Billy Tennant innocently enquired of Mick Langley when the date for the replay was.

'Replay, old chap, there won't be any replay, we have won the English Cup by the odd goal in three.'

Tennant was adamant, 'Get away, there were only two goals scored today'.

'Why, man alive, where on earth were you when we scored our second goal?' enquired Langley.

Years later, Fred Spiksley wrote about this in his autobiography stating:

> I was lucky to score the third and winning goal, hitting the ball with such force and spin that when it hit the back of the net the ball catapulted back into the field of play with Billy Tennant still wondering where the ball had vanished. Eventually he turned round to see the ball lying on the ground in front of him. Believing the ball was still in play Tennant leathered it down the ground, blissfully unaware that Lieutenant Simpson had already awarded the goal. In his moments of searching to see where the ball had gone, Billy contrived to turn his back away from the action and in consequence he missed seeing both the ball being returned to the centre spot and Billy Beats taking the kick-off."

At least Tennant was given a medal. Wednesday's unlucky reserve, Bob Ferrier, came running over from the bench, from where he had been watching the game, and congratulated all the players. After shaking their hands he finished up by tearfully saying, 'You know, I should have so liked to have had a medal'. Fred later acknowledged that nobody who played in the final could possibly have understood the true feelings of fellow players such as Ferrier and Jim Jamieson, who had been left out in the cold.

The sheer thrill of winning the FA Cup and collecting a winner's medal in this era is perhaps best illustrated by Roy Massey, grandson of the Wednesday 'keeper. Interviewed for this book, he recalled 'My grandfather always wore his medal on his waistcoat'. Roy played as a forward for Rotherham United, Leyton Orient and Colchester United before undertaking coaching roles at Colchester, Norwich and Arsenal (1998–2014). He was later a scout for Wolverhampton Wanderers. Roy had over fifty years in football and is very proud of his grandfather, who lived to the ripe old age of 91.

> I visited him every Sunday to sit in front of the living room fire listening to his tales. He told me in his first Wednesday game he had gone to catch the ball and was knocked over the line with it in his hands by the centre forward. A goal was awarded, but the next time a similar situation arose he tipped the ball over the bar before crouching down and flipping the forward over him and into the post where he suffered a broken arm.
>
> 'Keepers are a breed apart and to be a good one you have to be mentally tough, but from reading about him he was also very brave, handled the ball well, had good reflexes and was physically strong. In terms of training I understand he did a lot of shot-stopping with the players shooting at him. He was clearly a good player but he made apparent to me that Crawshaw and Spiksley were the best players in the team that won the FA Cup. He really admired both those players.
>
> He told me there was, like in most dressing rooms, great comradeship between the players and of how they were treated by Sheffielders like kings when they returned with the FA Cup in 1896. He said it was a close game and he was proud he had made a couple of good saves late on to keep Wednesday in the lead. At home games he said that Wednesday often attracted big crowds, who were rarely abusive like can be the case today, and who would be very happy if Wednesday won. When he finally finished playing football, he largely worked in the coal mines around Mexborough until he retired."

At the same time that the Wednesday first team had been playing in the Cup final, the second team had been at home against Barnsley St Peter's. Four thousand Wednesday fans shouted with joy when a telegram arrived on 15 minutes with news their side led 1-0 and there was further pleasure when the half-time score arrived. When the game ended spectators assembled in one vast crowd in the main stand and when the tinkle of a telephone bell was heard they could hardly hold their breath. At first there was silent hush, ears straining for news and then there was a cry – 'WE'VE WON THE CUP!'

Two hundred miles south, Lord Kinnaird, the FA president, surrounded by excited spectators, presented the cup to Wednesday's captain Jack Earp, who proudly lifted the trophy high above his head. Tremendous cheers meant few could hear Kinnaird say how delighted he was with the match and spirit in which it was played. Lord Kinnaird then presented the gold medals to all twenty-two players who played in the final. These were memorable moments for the players, before Jack Earp again lifted up the FA Cup, bringing deafening cheers from the Wednesday supporters.

Arriving back at the hotel, the FA Cup was placed proudly in the centre of the tea table. Gleaming in the sunlight it looked magical and quite took the breath away. John Holmes, the Wednesday chairman, stood up to say a few words.

> Gentlemen, I have been hunting this Cup for the past twenty years, and whilst Mr Dickinson has been the huntsman, and his clever hard-working team, the hounds, there has also been a tremendous number of members in the hunt who joined the chase with a will, and yet experienced continual disappointment year after year, but they still kept their courage, and in doing so were in at the kill at the Crystal Palace at Sydenham this afternoon. In closing this part of my notes, I must refer to a great man connected with our great game. I refer, of course, to Mr Arthur Dickinson, our financial club secretary, and I congratulate him upon the success that has at last crowned his work.

Arthur Dickinson rose to his feet and replied, 'Yes, I'm glad we've won it at last, as I can now bow out in a blaze of glory.' This was clearly said tongue in cheek, however, as Dickinson continued serving Wednesday for many years to come.

When the Wednesday players and officials caught the train home from St Pancras on Monday afternoon, they could not have anticipated the massive welcome they would receive in Sheffield when they arrived at Midland station at 5.28pm. Other football fans also wanted to catch a glimpse of the trophy and from Derby onwards the numbers gradually grew, with the Wednesday players holding it up to the carriage windows for people to see.

When the doubled-headed locomotives finally steamed into Sheffield they were met by Fred Spiksley, who had journeyed home independently. Travelling separately to games and living and training in Gainsborough all helped to make Fred a bit of an outsider. The scene was one of absolute chaos as the arrival platform was swamped with thousands of fans all desperate to see the winning players and the FA Cup. Inspector Bestwick's brass band started belting out 'See, the Conquering Hero Comes', but they had hardly got started when the crush of the crowd separated the bandsmen from the conductor. The conquering heroes themselves were forced to retreat to the safety of their saloon carriage and it was a further 20 minutes before the band could form up again and the players were able to board a coach and horses waiting to take them on a parade around Sheffield.

The large crowds had spilled out on to the road as they sought to catch a glimpse of the FA Cup, which for most of the time was held aloft by the player who had scored the Wednesday goals at the Crystal Palace: Fred Spiksley. The sheer numbers of people made it impossible to travel up Commercial Street and, to the disappointment of everyone involved, the coach was forced to go straight to the Royal Hotel, where Councillor George Senior and Mr Arthur Nixon had arranged a dinner for the honoured guests. The band, by this time, had long since disintegrated.

Later that evening the players visited the Empire Theatre where another enthusiastic reception awaited them, especially when the FA Cup was displayed and the reformed band even managed to play a few tunes. Four nights later an official dinner was held at the Masonic Hotel. By this time, the scorer of Wednesday's two goals had received a cheque from Will Chatterton for £11. This concluded Fred's football betting career, but, sadly, not his addiction to gambling.

Fred and the rest of the Wednesday players and directors also received a special jug from Wednesday board member, the Earl of Wharncliffe, who was so delighted at winning the FA Cup that he commissioned a number of jugs from Staffordshire Pottery.

Chapter 13

Number One Footballer in The World

Fred Spiksley's benefit year

At the end of the 1895–96 season, Fred Spiksley was the most talked about footballer in the game. Aged 25, he was the only survivor from Wednesday's non-League days. Since joining the club in 1891 he had scored fifty-two league goals (including those scored in the Football Alliance) and fifteen FA Cup goals. A further thirty-two goals in regional cup competitions and club games meant Spiksley had notched ninety-nine first team goals in just five seasons, and all from playing out on the wing. In the Burnley FA Cup tie, Spiksley had demonstrated how just his presence on the pitch alone was enough to encourage his team mates to play better and believe that no game was lost. The FA Cup ties against Derby and Aston Villa were also legendary games amongst those who witnessed them.

In Spiksley, Wednesday had a player who had performed at the highest level. He had destroyed the Scots in 1893 and had hit two stunning goals at the 1896 FA Cup final. No player in the world was as famous as Fred Spiksley, as proved by an illustration which featured in the national newspaper *Sports*, placing Spiksley's name right next to that of cricketer W.G. Grace.

The 'Olive Grove Flyer' at this time was a feared and respected foe, and many backs could only adopt rough tactics to try to contain him. When he did get away he raced away with the ball seemingly stuck to the outside of his foot. Spiksley was full of tricks that we are familiar with today, dinking his shoulder, feinting one way and then another before invariably putting in defence-splitting passes and crosses.

Wednesday were obviously keen to retain him and Fred happily signed a rolling one-year contract on the same terms as before. Today it's hard to believe that Wednesday offered their star player only a one-year contract, but these were different times and this wasn't unusual. An added sweetener for Spiksley was when the Wednesday committee agreed to a benefit match as thanks for his six years' service. Fred was delighted and his pleasure doubled when the famous amateur club, Corinthians FC, based at the Queens Club in London, agreed to provide the opposition on 30 December 1896.

The only new signing for the 1896–97 season was former reserve Bill Regan, back after a season with non-league Fairfield. The Wednesday committee were content to rely on the thirteen players who had travelled south for the 1896 FA Cup final.

The action began with two 2-1 defeats, at home against promoted Liverpool and away to Everton. Following a 3-1 victory at home to West Bromwich Albion, the Cup holders 'with the exception of Spiksley and Brady' (Charles Francis), fell to pieces in the second half at Blackburn and despite kicking with the wind and rain behind them, in the second half conceded three goals to lose 4-0. There was gloom all round when, next game, Stoke led 3-1 at half-time at Olive Grove, but a brilliant second-half performance saw Wednesday win 4-3. Fred Spiksley scored his first goal of the season and also scored as Wednesday completed the double over West Brom, winning 2-0 away.

Seven days later, a series of remarkable League results began against Sunderland when the home game ended 0-0. In December the same score line was recorded in Sunderland and after that Sunderland won the next five League encounters between the sides without Wednesday scoring. Indeed, this failure to score in seven consecutive League matches against one club is a Wednesday record.

Fred Spiksley scored twice as, backed by hundreds of away supporters, Wednesday drew 2-2 at Nottingham Forest. His first was a real beauty: following a fine passing move involving Brash and Bell, the ball was passed to Brady who let it run into the path of the Wednesday wide man, who showed great coolness and judgement to lift it over the head of 'keeper Dan Allsop and into the net.

A double-header against runaway League leaders Aston Villa saw Wednesday heavily beaten 3-1 at home and 4-0 away. With the home game tied at 1-1 Villa scored twice through Johnny Campbell and Charlie Athersmith. Campbell was a wonderfully gifted and clever inside or centre forward. He was brave, aggressive when required, possessed plenty of tricks and, above all, had an instinctive knack of scoring goals. He had exceptional balance, close control and dribbling skills, and was part of a brilliant Villa forward five in 1896–97 that also consisted of John Devey, Fred Wheldon, Charlie Athersmith and Stephen Smith. Villa ended the League season on forty-eight points, eleven ahead of second-placed Sheffield United.

Three consecutive draws left Wednesday in mid-table prior to the Boxing Day fixture away to Sheffield United, which was lost 2-0. Two days later, Wednesday's best performance of the season saw Blackburn Rovers hammered 6-0, with Ferrier scoring three. Just 5,000 spectators watched the game, although that was at least better than the attendance of just 1,000 against Wolves on 12 December.

Fred's testimonial match against Corinthians FC was on 30 December, fitting in with the amateur club's traditional Christmas tour, and they agreed they would field their strongest possible team including England internationals Gilbert Oswald Smith, Charles Wreford-Brown, John Gettins, Vaughan Lodge and Bill Oakley.

Sorting out the financial arrangements for the match wasn't easy. In truth, the amateur designation was a sham. The expenses demanded by Corinthians FC were always hefty and in this case were double the wages of Wednesday's professionals, who all donated their match fee. These young amateur gentlemen, such as William Moon, who played seven times in goal for England at the end of the 1880s and who left the equivalent of £4.5 million after his death, steeped in wealth and privilege, could tour the country indulging in their favourite pastime, assisted by having their considerable expenses covered by less wealthy opponents.

In the event, a good gate, a cracking game and a well-supported subscription list combined to make Fred Spiksley's benefit an unqualified success. A total of £291 was raised, including £30 from his former club, Gainsborough Trinity, and there were donations from Sheffield United players. It helped that the rain stayed away to allow 8,000 fans to pay a well-deserved compliment to Wednesday's 'Olive Grove Flyer'.

Wednesday: Massey, Earp, Langley, Petrie, Crawshaw, Jamieson, Brash, Ferrier, Davis, Brady, Spiksley.

Corinthians FC: William Campbell, Lewis Vaughan, Bill Oakley, Bernard Middleditch, Charles Wreford-Brown, Arthur George Topham, M.H. Stanborough, Gilbert Oswald Smith, J.H. Gettins, C.L. Alexander, Cuthbert 'Pinky' Burnup.

Fred Spiksley had the honour of leading his team out and he was greeted by a rousing reception that continued when Wreford-Brown led out the visitors.

Facing the wind, Wednesday struggled. Massey dealt with three shots before Burnup missed a glorious chance and then quickly atoned for his error by putting his side ahead. The lead was doubled when the referee, Mr J. Fox, overruled strong offside appeals and John Gettins raced clear from 50 yards out before beating Massey. Wednesday's concerted efforts to get back into the match were thwarted by Campbell in the away goal.

On changing ends Wednesday had the benefit of the breeze behind them, but Gilbert Oswald Smith's low fast shot then made it 3-0. Corinthians FC were determined to show that the amateur game was superior to the professional one. Earlier in the season they had beaten Wednesday 2-0 at the Queen's Club in their annual match with the FA Cup winners. In 1903–04, Corinthians FC hammered the FA Cup holders, Bury, 10-3 and the following season beat Manchester United 11-3, the Manchester club's heaviest ever defeat.

However, fears of a thrashing were quickly ended when Davis headed the ball on to Fred Spiksley, who in turn headed it to his partner Brady, who nodded the ball beyond Campbell. The left wing partnership between the two players was now almost telepathic and according to Fred 'they were my happiest football days in every respect'. Despite the brilliant understanding between the pair, they only once spoke to each other on a football pitch when, following a poor pass, Alec Brady remarked, 'That was a bad 'un, Fred', to which Spiksley replied, 'It wasn't a good 'un, Alec'.

Although it's not clear why the two players didn't speak to each other on the pitch, the reason could lie in Alec Brady's brief association with Gainsborough Trinity in the 1888–89 season. Spiksley had threatened to walk out on the club if Trinity continued to play their 'Scottish Professors' who had starved the local player of the ball. Perhaps when Brady arrived at Olive Grove the pair stayed away from one another? Whatever the reason, this odd stand-off was to continue because Wednesday needed to keep them both on the left wing as together the pair were irresistible and are one of the Yorkshire club's greatest ever partnerships. Spiksley knew that when Brady was on his inside he was much more effective in creating and scoring goals. Ultimately, this must have been much more fun.

Encouraged by reducing the deficit, Wednesday pressed and an under-pressure Oakley, in attempting to clear Petrie's effort, diverted the ball past his own 'keeper. Then on 70 minutes, a well-directed long pass from Brady was thumped past Campbell by Brash to make it 3-3. The atmosphere was now electric as the sides traded blows in their efforts to fashion a winner. When clever play by Davis ended with a powerful shot and the rebound from Campbell was knocked home by Brady, the cheers of the crowd seemed set to herald a famous victory for the FA Cup holders.

The Londoners, though, were not going to go down easily. Massey pulled off a great save from Alexander before Brash failed to wrap up victory when he missed from close in. With the light fading, Gettins sent in a powerful shot that Massey failed to spot until it was too late and moments later a highly competitive game ended 4-4.

Back in the FA Cup, there was major disappointment when any hopes of retaining the trophy were snuffed out when Nottingham Forest won 1-0 with an Arthur Capes goal before a best-of-the-season Olive Grove crowd of 16,639. The trophy would eventually pass to Aston Villa, winning it for the second time in three seasons, beating Everton 3-2 in a thrilling final in which the lead changed hands twice in the first half. By winning the trophy, Aston Villa became only the second side to record the League and FA Cup 'double', a feat first achieved by Preston in 1888–89.

According to Villa historian John Lerwill, the success of the Birmingham side during this period was the result of an earlier revolt within the club when they had lost heavily in the 1892 FA Cup final against local rivals WBA. 'A new committee, which was fairly middle-class and took the Christian view of that time on matters of drinking and gambling, began by looking at the lifestyles of the players…Villa became quite authoritarian and the club demanded the highest standards.' Such an approach would have, of course, ruled out any chance of Spiksley being sought by Villa if they were aware of Fred's gambling habits. At the same time, Villa never had any trouble finding good left-wingers during this period, including Hodgetts and his successor Steve Smith. Core players such as Devey, Crabtree, Cowan, Spencer and Athersmith all played well past the turn of the century for Aston Villa.

After being beaten by Forest, Wednesday had nine League matches to play, winning three and losing two. One of the victories was on the final day of the season, when Bury were beaten 2-0 before another sparse crowd of 1,000.

The game might have marked Fred Spiksley's final football match. During it, one very deliberate attempt to put him out of action almost cost him his life when an unidentified opponent made a back for him, intending to ensure he would come down to earth on his head rather than his feet. As he hurtled towards the turf, the fear that he might come down on his neck had the Wednesday winger frantically trying to break his fall with his flailing arms. The England international failed to prevent the heavy fall, but amid total silence he was able to rise slowly to his feet and stagger through the remainder of the game. A doctor later told him that if the fall had happened to a heavier man then a broken spine was the most likely outcome. The injured player later said: 'Only two things saved me from paralysis: a miracle and my light weight.'

Wednesday finished in a respectable sixth place, the club's highest ever. In previous seasons, Wednesday had never conceded fewer than fifty-three goals, but in 1896–97 the goals against column was just thirty-seven, the second best in the table, with Sheffield United conceding only one fewer. At the same time, Wednesday's goals total of forty-two was their lowest ever with only one player – Fred Spiksley on ten – reaching double figures. After the previous season's excitement, the Wednesday fans had been left disappointed.

A few weeks after the season ended, Sheffield Town Hall was officially opened on 21 May 1897, having taken seven years to build. On the roof of the building was a Vulcan with its hand in the air. Wednesday fans quickly began referring to it as 'Fred' as it appeared to show him appealing for a foul.

During the 1897 close season, which saw existing regulations on the dimensions of the field of play adopted, Wednesday signed right-winger William Dryburgh from Cowdenbeath and his good form during the 1897–98 season allowed Brash to depart. Albert Kaye had been spotted playing for non-League Eckington and the new Wednesday centre forward was to play impressively, finishing with ten goals in twenty-seven League and Cup matches. Wednesday finished in their highest ever League position, fifth, but this feat was overshadowed by Sheffield United, who roared to the League title.

Wednesday began badly and lost four of their first five matches, with the only success coming at home to Liverpool. In the sixth match, Wednesday beat champions Aston Villa 3-0 with Spiksley scoring twice. In a 3-1 defeat of Notts County, he again scored twice and was also on the score sheet as Bolton were beaten 3-0 at Burnden Park, after which the victors lay in fourth place in the table on eight points, five fewer than top-placed Sheffield United.

The two great rivals faced each other in the ninth League game. It took place at Olive Grove and having lost just once in the eight previous meetings, Sheffield United were confident. The away followers in the 24,000-plus crowd breathed a sigh of relief when Billy Foulke, who joined United at the start of the 1894–95 season, made a great early save from Fred Spiksley. Foulke was 12st 5lb when he signed for United from Blackwell and steadily grew to over 25st by the time his career ended at Bradford City in 1907. Fred and Bill were to become close friends as both shared a great love of horse racing. Fred, like many others, appreciated Bill's wry sense of humour.

The United followers were elated when their side took a fourth-minute lead. The goal came when John Cunningham cut into the centre before laying the ball off to Walter Bennett, a fine marksman whose confidence and incisive play earned him the nickname 'Cocky', who fired his shot beyond Massey. Bennett, twice capped for England, was later killed in a colliery accident in 1908.

With right half Rab Howell again sticking close to Fred Spiksley, the Wednesday wide man was left with little room to manoeuvre and the away side might have doubled their lead before half-time, but Bennett's shot clipped the top of the bar before going over. An injury to Almond meant the United centre forward had missed much of the first-half action and although he returned for the second, he was unable to make any serious contribution to the game. There was a further blow to the visitors when Bennett was injured on the restart and struggled thereafter.

Wednesday now dominated and would have equalised except for a poor miss by Fred Spiksley. United were then stunned when Fred Priest was injured and, not surprisingly, the home side controlled possession. Such was Wednesday's

Willoughby Street, Gainsborough, the birthplace of Fred Spiksley.

Fred Spiksley's first medal as a professional footballer, the Gainsborough News Charity Cup winner's medal from his first season with Trinity. These competitions were bigger events for clubs and supporters in the early years of football than they are today.

Gainsborough Trinity 1887. (Players only) Back Row: G. Vamplew, R. Sharman, C. Howlett, C. Jubb, Curtiss. Front Row: R. Fergus, S. Smith, H. Chambers, J. Madden, W. Brown, F. Spiksley, H. Robinson.

Baines card featuring Teddy Brayshaw, who accidentally broke Fred Spiksley's leg on Spiksley's nineteenth birthday.

Gainsborough Trinity 1889-90. Fred Spiksley stands in full length knickerbockers (shorts) on the far right of the team.

The Wednesday 1891-92. (Players only) Back Row: T. Brandon, Smith, Darroch. Middle Row: H. Brandon, Mumford, Thompson, Cawley, Spiksley. Front Row: Gemmell, Betts, Richardson.

A newspaper illustration describing the Olive Grove ground, looking towards the city centre with a passing train.

SPORTS, MONDAY, DECEMBER 2, 1895.

CRAWSHAW BEATS ALSOPP WITH A BEAUTY.

MR. WEST SENDS F. J. FORMAN BACK FOR THE BALL.

Fred Spiksley c.1893.

The Graphic newspaper illustrates one of Spiksley's three goals against Scotland in 1893.

The England team that faced Scotland at Celtic Park in 1894. (Players only) Standing: Ernest Needham, Fred Spiksley, Gilbert Smith. Seated: Thomas Clare, John Reynolds, William Bassett, John Goodall (Captain), Fred Pelly, Edgar Chadwick, Leslie Gay. Cross-legged: John Holt.

Illustration of the crowd celebrating a Scottish goal during the 1894 international. The drawing captures Celtic Park's failed floodlighting system, nicknamed 'Madden's Rigging'.

Fred Spiksley c.1894.

Front cover of the *Daily Graphic* showing The Wednesday's 1896 FA Cup final triumph.

Fred Spiksley pictured 'mid-air' as he athletically challenges for the ball during the 1896 FA Cup final.

Illustration of Spiksley's second goal in the 1896 FA Cup final that gave Wednesday their first FA Cup success.

The Wednesday team pictured with the FA Cup in 1896. Back Row. H. Brandon, Langley, Johnson (trainer), Brash, Holmes (President) Jamieson, Dickinson (Hon. Secretary), Nixon (Director). Middle Row: Bell, Brady, Earp, Davis, Spiksley. Front Row: Crawshaw, Petrie.

The second FA Cup trophy, first awarded in 1896 after the original was stolen in 1895 and never recovered.

The Wednesday play Everton at Olive Grove in March 1899.

The incorrect spelling of Spiksley's name was commonplace as shown on these collectable cards.

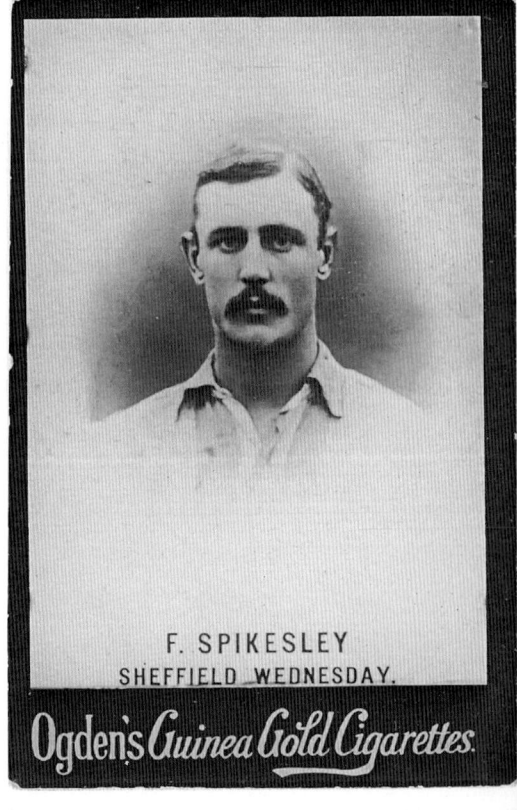

F. SPIKESLEY
SHEFFIELD WEDNESDAY.

Ogden's Guinea Gold Cigarettes.

ENGLAND.

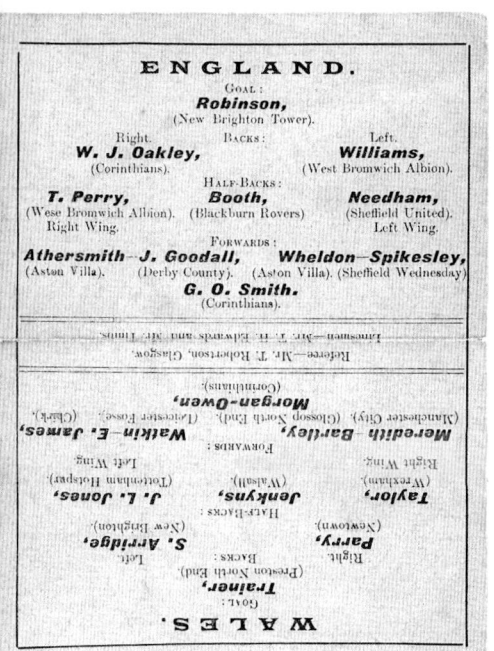

GOAL:
Robinson,
(New Brighton Tower).

Right. BACKS: Left.
W. J. Oakley, **Williams,**
(Corinthians). (West Bromwich Albion).

HALF-BACKS:
T. Perry, **Booth,** **Needham,**
(West Bromwich Albion). (Blackburn Rovers). (Sheffield United).
Right Wing. Left Wing.

FORWARDS:
Athersmith—J. Goodall, **Wheldon—Spiksley,**
(Aston Villa). (Derby County). (Aston Villa). (Sheffield Wednesday).
G. O. Smith.
(Corinthians).

Linesmen—Mr. T. B. Edwards and Mr. Tims.
Referee—Mr. T. Robertson, Glasgow.

WALES.

GOAL:
Trainer,
(Preston North End).

Right. BACKS: Left.
Parry, **S. Arridge,**
(Newtown). (New Brighton).

HALF-BACKS:
Taylor, **Jenkyns,** **J. L. Jones,**
(Wrexham). (Walsall). (Tottenham Hotspur).

FORWARDS:
Right Wing. Left Wing.
Meredith—Bardley, **Watkin—E. James,**
(Manchester City). (Glossop North End). (Leicester Fosse). (Cliftonville).
Morgan-Owen,
(Corinthians).

Spiksley returned to the England team in 1898 to face a Wales team that now contained Billy Meredith, one of the greatest players of all time.

An illustration of England's third goal against Scotland in 1898, scored by Steve Bloomer from a Spiksley cross.

The England team that faced Scotland at Celtic Park in 1898, featuring possibly the greatest forward line fielded by England during the pre-war era. (Players only) Back Row: Athersmith, Forman, Oakley, Robinson. Front Row: Bloomer, Williams, Smith, Brown, Needham, Wheldon, Spiksley.

Fred Spiksley (far right) is pictured in front of a packed Olive Grove main stand in 1898 during the last ever Steel City Derby to be played on the ground before Wednesday's move to Owlerton (Hillsborough).

The Wednesday team pose for a photograph in front of a packed Olive Grove main stand during their disastrous final season at the ground in 1898-99. Spiksley is the second player from the right.

The Wednesday team are photographed here in September 1899 prior to the first match at the Owlerton ground that subsequently become known as Hillsborough. From left: Ferrier, Earp, Pryce, Brash, Massey, Crawshaw, Spiksley, Wright, Millar, Langley, Ruddlesdin.

Fred Spiksley photographed wearing his knee support prior to the start of the 1902-03 season that was to end with The Wednesday winning the league title for the first time.

Fred Spiksley aged 33.

Football League Champions 1902-03. (Players only) Back Row: Ferrier, Hemmingfield, Thackeray. Middle Row: Layton, Langley, Lyall, Crawshaw, Ruddlesdin. Front Row: V.S. Simpson, Davis, Wilson, Malloch, Spiksley, G. Simpson.

BLACKBURN.

PALACE.   "Football Match."

Harry Weldon, Will Poluski, jun., Chas. Chaplin, Bob Lewis, Jimmy Fletch, James Monrow, R. J. Hamer, Bert Royston, Frank Hayter, jun., Fred Newham, Fred Onzella, C. Turner, J. Thuro, Harry Fergusson, Harry Douglas, Jock Roberts, J. Jackson, L. Calvert, Jack Melville, H. Reeves, Clifford Walton, Fred Spiksley, F. Gamble, J. Fitchett, W. Wragg, F. Arkesden, Elsa Beresford, Irene Wood, Lucy Waldon.

Manager, FRANK CALLAGHER.
Stage-Manager, T. ELLIS BUXTON.

Fred Karno's popular Football Match theatre production featured Fred Spiksley performing on stage with Charlie (Chas) Chaplin.

IT'S A FACT

THE HIGH QUALITY OF MODERN SWEDISH FOOTBALL CAN BE TRACED BACK HALF A CENTURY TO THE FORMER SHEFFIELD WEDNESDAY OUTSIDE LEFT **FRED SPIKSLEY**, WHO WAS ONE OF THE EARLIEST BRITISH COACHES IN SCANDINAVIA.

FRED LEFT ENGLAND WITH THIS IMPOSING RECORD:—
BOTH GOALS FOR SHEFFIELD WEDNESDAY WHEN THEY FIRST WON THE F.A. CUP IN 1896.
THREE GOALS IN TEN MINUTES FOR ENGLAND v. SCOTLAND IN 1893.
FIRST AND SECOND DIVISION CHAMPIONSHIP MEDALS AND A GRAND TOTAL OF 350 GOALS.

This newspaper clipping, believed to have come from *The Daily Mirror* in the 1950s, illustrates Spiksley's reputation as an international coach and acknowledges his hat-trick in the game against Scotland in April 1893.

Coach Fred Spiksley (far left) stands alongside his 1FC Nuremberg side shortly before the outbreak of the First World War in 1914.

Spiksley was a well-known coach across the London area and was captured here in one of Jimmy Seed's many cartoons.

An autographed impression of Fred Spiksley.—By Jimmy Seed.

Spiksley (in a hat) stood next to a trophy with an unidentified Mexican side. Spiksley won twenty-two trophies in two seasons with Real Club Espana.

Fred Spiksley in 1925 when he was employed as a special skills coach for Fulham.

Spiksley in a 1929 photoshoot for the *London Evening News*. He demonstrated skills that featured in a series of coaching articles aimed at helping young boys develop their football skills.

A still from Spiksley's 1929 *British Pathé* film. He looks on as one of his 'Scheme of Sticks' training drills is demonstrated by England international footballers Len Oliver and Bert Barrett at Craven Cottage.

The players of the Spanish side Badalona are put through their paces by Fred Spiksley and his unique training methods.

EN BADALONA

F. C. Badalona, 1 - F. C. Barcelona, 0

En una espléndida manifestación de entusiasmo el Badalona dió la gran sorpresa batiendo a los campeones

Badalona was the only side to keep a clean sheet against Barcelona during the 1930 Catalan League Championship. The translation in this local newspaper reads: 'In a splendid display of enthusiasm, Badalona created a great surprise by beating the champions.'

The plaque erected by The Delvers in 2018 at Gainsborough Trinity's Northolme ground.

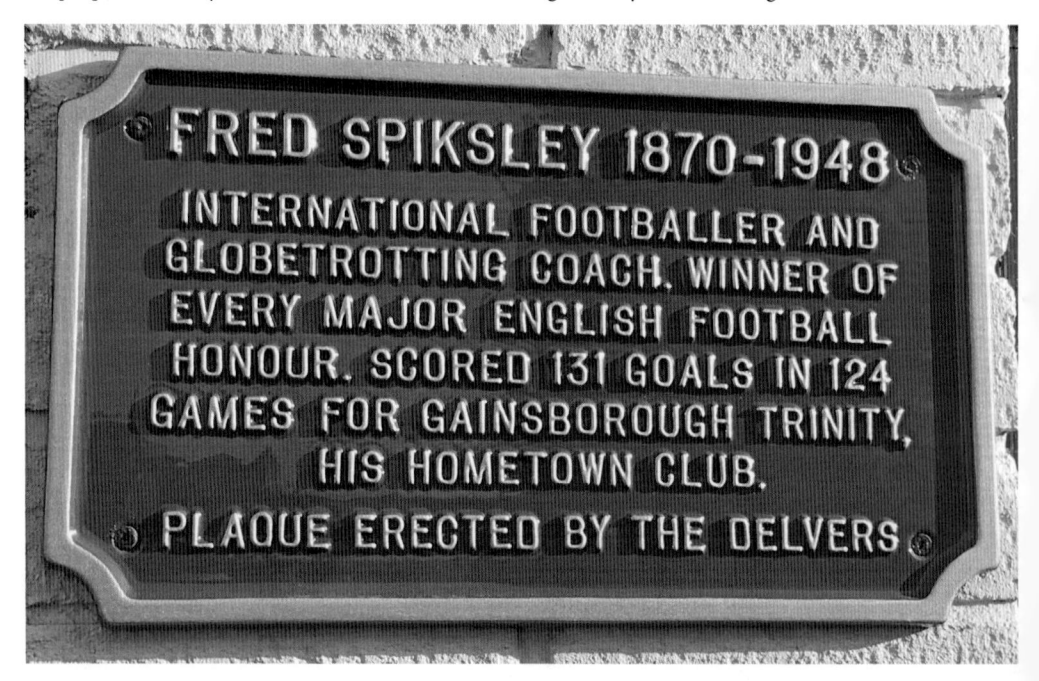

FRED SPIKSLEY 1870-1948
INTERNATIONAL FOOTBALLER AND GLOBETROTTING COACH. WINNER OF EVERY MAJOR ENGLISH FOOTBALL HONOUR. SCORED 131 GOALS IN 124 GAMES FOR GAINSBOROUGH TRINITY, HIS HOMETOWN CLUB.
PLAQUE ERECTED BY THE DELVERS

determination to equalise that Foulke was even bundled over the line only for the 'goal' to be disallowed. It took two Wednesday forwards to achieve the feat. United followers, who worshipped their giant 'keeper Bennett, regularly sang 'Who ate all the pies?' in his honour. United in general were a weighty side, during what was the most successful period in their history. Between 1897 and 1902 they captured the League title and twice won the FA Cup, while also finishing runners-up twice in the League and once in the FA Cup.

Plenty of chances were made but all were missed and, remarkably, it was United who went closest when a shot hit the bar and dropped to the injured Priest, who fired an easy chance wide. The winners retained top spot in a game that had been a typical no-holds-barred local derby in which quality had been lacking.

Off the pitch, the conduct of the fans was starting to become a problem. What had been friendly rivalry between supporters was making way for unruly behaviour. The reporter "Looker On" in the *Sheffield Telegraph* wrote that 'scores of really good sportsmen are heartily glad' when the derby matches are over due to the 'bad blood too often engendered and the unhealthy, almost ferocious, excitement manifested by the crowd'. There was press criticism of the verbal abuse directed by fans of both clubs towards the match referee, Mr Brodie.

By the time of the return match at Bramall Lane on 27 December, both Sheffield teams were in the top three, with Wednesday having taken twelve points from eight games. Fred Spiksley had scored seven goals in these games including netting on Christmas Day when Stoke lost 4-0 at Olive Grove. However, the outside left failed to complete the game as he was sent off. The referee was Lincoln's Mr West, well known to Fred from his Gainsborough days as being so biased that when he acted as the Lincoln City linesman he was reported by teams in the Midland Counties League for intimidation. Fred was unhappy to discover that Mr West had been elevated to referee status and feared he might use his new powers to get his own back on those who had objected to him acting as Lincoln City's 'twelfth man'.

The ground at Olive Grove was rock hard from the frost, which made the ball unusually bouncy and difficult to control. Stoke right back John Robertson, who later captained Liverpool to the League title, was a dashing, daring and slightly reckless opponent who seemed to make no allowance for the treacherous underfoot conditions when he tackled for the ball. From a high kick the ball bounced to a tremendous height and when Fred used his shoulder and ball skills to manoeuvre away from his marker, it was a masterful move that went unappreciated by Mr West, who blew for a free kick. When Fred politely enquired why he had been penalized, he was ignored.

When the Wednesday winger proceed to complain, Mr West shoved him over on to the icy ground, causing him to fall on his bottom, much to the amusement of the crowd. West then told the player to retreat down the pitch, but when he positioned himself back the 6 yards required under the then rules, this failed to satisfy the referee who told him to retreat further. When Fred stood his ground and informed the referee that he was abiding by the rules, he was informed by Mr West that for deliberately ignoring his instructions he was dismissing the player. Fred initially refused to leave the field, but eventually gave way for what was the first and only sending-off in his football career.

As a result of his actions, Fred appeared before the FA's disciplinary committee on 5 January 1897. He was exonerated of any blame and was neither fined nor suspended and his unblemished record and good name in football remained intact. That record wasn't to be sustained over the following two seasons, as in 1898–99 he was involved in a heated argument with the referee at the end of the home game with Everton on 4 March 1899. Afterwards he was forced by the FA to apologise and Wednesday were warned about the conduct of their players.

Fred was fortunate as earlier in the same season he had been involved in another confrontation with the referee at the end of the FA Cup-tie at home to Stoke on 28 January 1899. The match ended 2-2 and although an injured Fred hadn't played in the game, he'd been left angry at what he felt were two unfair challenges on Massey in goal, both of which resulted in Stoke goals. The second in particular was disputed by the home players. Fred limped into the dressing room after the final whistle and berated the referee, even telling him to make a detailed study of the laws of the game. Luckily for Fred, the referee took no notice and Fred later reflected, 'He did not even report the matter to the FA as I had expected him to do. Had he done so, I have no doubt that I should have been suspended for a lengthy period.'

With both teams entertaining title aspirations, there was massive interest throughout Sheffield in the lead-up to the return game with United on Boxing Day. The Bramall Lane gates were opened at 12.45pm and the then largest ever attendance of 37,389 – paying £916 at the turnstiles – packed the ground for a game where both sides were at full strength. Pre-match entertainment saw the band play 'Auld Lang Syne' and 'Lead Kindly Light', the entire crowd singing along to create a great atmosphere.

The rain had left the pitch greasy, and with the wind behind them, the away side almost scored in the first minute as Alec Brady fizzed a shot across the face of Foulke's goal. A long shot from Harry Thickett was only just scrambled away by Massey, but it was Wednesday who created most of the scoring opportunities.

The away side had strong penalty appeals when Spiksley was upended from behind by Thickett and although it seemed a bad foul, referee Aaron Scragg waved play on.

It was a Wednesday player who opened the scoring when, after Massey was forced to save from Bennett, the unfortunate Earp sliced the ball into his own net on 25 minutes. The Wednesday captain later blamed the band for playing 'Lead Kindly Light' on a gloomy day!

With the away side continuing to push forward, the game was finely balanced at the interval and in the second half it continued to be an exciting affair. On the Wednesday left, Brady and Spiksley continued to probe and when the latter curled over a cross to Brash, the right winger was clean through with only Foulke to beat. The United 'keeper's presence put off Brash, who fired wide to the groans of the Wednesday supporters.

The home side were determined to keep Spiksley quiet and Rab Howell was detailed to help Thickett, but the England international managed to escape both before finding Kaye, whose shot was blocked by Bob Cain. Unfortunately for the home side, the ball rebounded into the path of the Wednesday outside left who smashed it beyond Foulke to level the scores.

The game was all-action from then on, with half chances for both teams before Brash yet again created a one-on-one situation with Foulke, but, as previously, the 'keeper won the contest. Consequently the game ended 1-1. It was generally agreed that the game had been the best so far between the two top Sheffield sides and the *Sheffield Independent* paid tribute the following day:

> Yesterday there was little scrambling and less roughness. Both sides played out their hardest and their best. Lovers of good football, who attend such matches, will have thoroughly enjoyed themselves. Wednesday showed that they understood the kind of football that was required for the occasion by passing and crossing the ball into the danger area in front of the goal, whilst United combined beautifully whilst being dogged and steady in defence, proving that they were back to their top form.

Despite their performances, both teams lost their following matches with Sheffield United going down 2-1 at home to Liverpool and Wednesday beaten 6-3 at home by Nottingham Forest on New Year's Day. However, whereas United went on to win their next seven, Wednesday then lost away to Everton and their poor form soon had them dropping out of the title race. This meant that the match at Sunderland in the FA Cup first round had assumed even greater importance. Wednesday needed a good Cup run to boost their finances, and with John Holmes determined to give his team the best chance of winning, they were taken to Saltburn by the Sea to concentrate on the task in hand.

With miles of beautiful golden sand and a shelved beach stretching for miles up the North Yorkshire coast, Saltburn was literally a breath of fresh air. A cold breeze brought colour to the footballers' cheeks in a week when the aim was to build up a great team spirit with an emphasis on hard physical training.

After winning the League title three times in four seasons, Sunderland had struggled in the previous two seasons. Manager Tom Watson had departed for Liverpool and prolific striker Johnny Campbell to Newcastle United. Sunderland had played well over Christmas and January and had won all six of their League games to rise to second place in the table, the position in which they would finish the season. They were also playing in their final season at Newcastle Road. Work was under way at nearby Roker Park, which would become their home for the next 99 years. Having beaten Wednesday twice earlier in the season, the home fans were in a confident mood and a 17,893 crowd turned out for the big occasion.

Sunderland had undergone their own special training at Gosforth for a match that was keenly anticipated. They also demonstrated why the decision to move to Roker Park was the correct one as by 1.45pm, one hour before kick-off, Newcastle Road was full to capacity with the gates locked. Hundreds of spectators that had been turned away were determined to see the game. At each end of the ground people climbed onto each other's shoulders and scrambled up 20ft high walls before reaching down and assisting their helpers to gain entry and then leaping into the packed crowd. It was a miracle nobody was killed.

With Earp having joined up with the Wednesday party, the players were lined up ready to run out when Bill Johnson roared, 'Go on my little beauties – you can win'. The away side was given a rousing reception by their supporters, many wearing blue and white favours. The home fans were in great voice and after cheering for their own favourites, a number began to abuse Langley, who had previously played extremely vigorously when the sides had met.

Sunderland attacked with the wind at their backs and from the off the away side were pegged back. Massey rushed out to prevent Hugh Wilson scoring and then made two brilliant diving saves. Meanwhile, Langley had managed to further anger the Sunderland crowd with some robust tackling. One supporter threw his breakfast can at the Wednesday full back which instead hit a policeman who, displaying not the slightest degree of surprise, simply pocketed it. No doubt it would come in handy for his lunch.

High balls into the Wednesday goalmouth was Sunderland's preferred option, but all they did was prove that Crawshaw was the greatest header of a football in the English game, with Langley not far behind. Corner after corner was headed clear and when Sunderland did get the ball and Wilson ran clear, Crawshaw timed his tackle perfectly to come away with the ball.

When Wednesday got forward, an overhead bicycle kick by Davis was brilliantly saved by Doig amid huge cheers. Dryburgh was then denied by a last-ditch Peter Boyle tackle as Wednesday began to dominate possession, and Doig did well to save a Kaye effort. With the interval only minutes away, Langley prevented Hugh Morgan getting his shot away and this prompted another bout of jeering, booing, hissing and missile-throwing at the Wednesday man. Langley ignored the abuse as he left the pitch at half-time.

With the wind in their favour, the visitors were confident they could now go on to success, although in the first 10 minutes of the second half it was Sunderland who threatened. When Spiksley did get away he was hauled over. Minutes later a terrible Philip Bach challenge on the Wednesday player left him writhing in agony, convinced the kick he had received to his arm had left it broken. There was a two-minute delay while the doctor examined the severely bruised arm, after which the England international continued despite his obvious discomfort. Minutes later, he hit a great shot that Doig tipped over.

When Sunderland pushed forward, Massey saved at the expense of a kick to his head, but after he recovered the play was from then on virtually all at the other end of the ground. Spiksley had a shot cleared off the line and Kaye rifled a shot over the crossbar. Doig fisted away a shot from Dryburgh as the game entered the final 10 minutes, at which point, true to tradition, the Sunderland flag on the flagpole was lowered as a signal to players and fans that time was running out. On 82 minutes the goal that the away side deserved arrived when Brady and Spiksley combined to send Kaye clear. The Sunderland defenders chased him down but the Wednesday centre forward held them off before dinking the ball over Doig. As the ball nestled in the net the Wednesday fans let out an explosion of noise while, in stark comparison, the Sunderland fans and players stood disbelieving in stunned silence. Sunderland were beaten and the better team had won.

Many in the crowd were unhappy with the result and were looking for someone to blame. Their target was Langley and when the game ended, a number of home fans were threatening to spill on to the pitch and get their hands on the Wednesday man. Fortunately, there were sufficient policemen on hand to protect the Wednesday players by escorting them to the safety of the dressing room.

In view of the hostility towards Langley, the Sunderland executive thought it wise if the crowd didn't see him again. Unruly elements had gathered around the main entrance shouting 'Where is he – the bastard'. Langley left by the back door with a police escort. Sunderland hired a hansom cab to take him to the hotel where they had hired a private room and laid on food, drink and refreshments for the Wednesday party. The rest of the Wednesday players left Newcastle Road an hour late, and after running the gauntlet of the Sunderland mob were taken by a circuitous route through Sunderland as they shook off any remaining pursuers. On arrival at the private dining room they found Langley sitting quietly in front of a roaring log fire, sipping tea and consuming buttered toasted muffins.

Fred Spiksley was keen to get moving south as he wanted to catch the train at Retford that would get him back to Gainsborough around 10pm. Nellie was on her own with a new young baby, Frederick Hayward Spiksley, otherwise known as Fred Junior. When the train did leave Sunderland, it was too slow to allow Fred to catch the London Express from Newcastle and when he finally reached Retford, it was after midnight and too late to find overnight accommodation. It was 12 miles by road to home and with no fire in the station waiting room, Fred decided to walk, calculating he could shave a mile and a half off the journey by walking along the railway track. Having played in a hard physical game the Wednesday player wasn't in great shape, but set off at his best pace and, in dense fog, he whistled to keep up his spirits.

At Clarborough Bridge, where the railway line crossed the turnpike, he hesitated before deciding it was unwise to leave the railway track for the road in such foggy conditions. Sticking to his guns, he pressed on, but when he reached Clarborough Tunnel, he quickly realised that his plan to climb Clarborough Hill and then rejoin the track on the far side of the tunnel was impossible. The hill was simply too steep to clamber up.

The Wednesday man didn't want to walk through a tunnel that hardly seemed wide enough for two trains to pass, but on the other hand he didn't want to retrace his steps. Plucking up the courage, he plunged into the pitch dark tunnel and by keeping his left hand on the tunnel wall, he made slow progress, discovering recesses were built at intervals into the tunnel walls – knowledge that ultimately saved his life.

Suddenly he heard a great roar as a train entered the tunnel. He had only seconds to decide what to do when another roar indicated a second train had entered the tunnel on the opposite track. Fred froze like a rabbit caught in the headlights. In a flash of inspiration, he remembered the recesses and threw himself blindly to the far side of the track. Miraculously, he managed to land in one of them and proceeded to press his backside as close as he could against the wall. Seconds later, the first train, the Lincoln Express, whistled by and the frightened man's ears were blasted by the fierce noise. The second train was a mineral one bound for Grimsby, with two double-headed engines pulling it at around 8 miles an hour. Fred saw one of the stokers shovelling coal into the fire box. Evidently, one of the train drivers had spotted him and yelled out, but Fred could neither hear nor understand. Once both trains had passed, Fred threw caution to the wind and raced as fast as he could through the rest of the tunnel. He was delayed when he ran into a spoil heap at the side of the track and fell head over heels. However, after removing the grit from his teeth, he scrambled to safety as quickly as possible.

Fred's tribulations were not over yet. Before the railway track reached Gainsborough, it crossed the River Trent on a wooden trestle 150 yards in length and high above the river. The trestle bridge beams were 3 feet apart and if Fred missed one of them then it was a sheer drop into the fast swirling river below. Doing his best to steady his nerves and keeping his eyes wide open, Fred negotiated the bridge safely, after which shock quickly set in and he began shaking uncontrollably as sweat poured down his face and neck.

After managing the final half mile walk home, the Wednesday player stumbled through the front door before lighting the gas and looking at his grimy face. He only had cold water to wash with and it took five bowls before he could recognise himself in the mirror. When he finally stumbled into bed, he had nightmares about his experience.

Wednesday's defeat of Sunderland raised hopes of another FA Cup run, but these were ended in the following round when West Bromwich Albion beat Wednesday 1-0 thanks to a neat piece of gamesmanship by Bassett in which he tricked the referee John Lewis into awarding his side a free kick from which the Baggies scored the winner. Defeat in the FA Cup left Wednesday just seven League games to play. Away to Derby County, Fred Spiksley scored his fifteenth league goal of the season as Wednesday won 2-1. He scored his sixteenth at Stoke, although this time Wednesday lost 2-1.

On 9 April, a day after Sheffield United had beaten Bolton Wanderers to clinch the League title, Fred Spiksley scored his seventeenth League goal of the season in a 3-0 defeat of WBA at home. It meant he finished in second place behind Villa's Fred Wheldon at the top of the Division One scoring charts. This was a remarkable feat for an outside left in an era where the focal point of a side's attack was always the centre forward. It was to be another seventy years before any winger finished in the top two of the scorer's chart in Division One, George Best notching twenty-eight to finish equal top with Ron Davies in 1967–68 (Best played many games that season at inside forward after Denis Law was injured).

The victory put Wednesday third in the table but heavy away defeats at Liverpool (4-0) and Wolves (5-0) saw them drop down to fifth. It was still Wednesday's highest ever League placing, however, and raised the prospect of a stronger challenge in the following campaign.

United's success meant it was the first time the Football League championship had come to Sheffield. Under captain Ernest Needham's direction, the champions had introduced a new style of football with long swinging passes from the centre forward out to the wings, wide passing between the half backs, all backed up by tremendous dash and strength. Fred Spiksley was a great admirer of Needham as a player, captain and tactician. 'I give him the honour of being the greatest player association football has ever seen,' said Fred in 1907. Needham had played particularly brilliantly on the day that his side had clinched the title. Switched to play further forward, he scored a sensational goal to win the game at Bolton.

Chapter 14

Best of The Best

Spiksley gives a man-of-the-match performance in England's greatest pre-1900 forward line

Fred Spiksley's absence when England played in Scotland in April 1896 had contributed to his country being easily defeated. The Wednesday man also never played in the 1897 international games in which England first beat Ireland 6-0, with the Liverpool outside left Tom Bradshaw failing to net in his only international appearance. Wales were beaten 4-0 at Bramall Lane, where Foulke played his only international match and Everton outside left Alf Milward, playing internationally for the first time in six seasons, scored twice. Milward also played against Scotland, who triumphed 2-1 with goals from Tom Hyslop and James Millar against an early Bloomer opener. Milward missed three good chances in a match played at the Crystal Palace where a year previously Fred Spiksley had scored twice for his club in the FA Cup final.

By 1898 professionalism had prevailed to the extent that professionals could be selected for both the Wales and Ireland matches, meaning players like Fred Spiksley could now earn a maximum of three England caps a year. The FA realised that England were definitely a more competitive outfit when the side contained a majority of professionals.

Fred Spiksley's form in the early part of the 1897–98 season had seen him score fourteen goals in twenty-three League and Cup matches, placing the Wednesday winger in second place in the scoring charts. Nevertheless, he was omitted in favour of West Brom's Ben Garfield for the England side selected to face Ireland. England struggled in Belfast and only a fine display by 'keeper Jack Robinson enabled them to squeeze home 3-2. Against Wales in Wrexham, Fred Spiksley was restored to the England team at outside left. The game was played six days before the Scotland game and the selectors chose a strong team.

England: John Robinson, William Oakley, Billy Williams, Ernest Needham, Tom Perry, Tom Booth, Charlie Athersmith, John Goodall, Gilbert Oswald Smith, Fred Wheldon, Fred Spiksley

Wales: James Trainer, Charles Parry, Smart Arridge, John Taylor, Caesar Jenkyns (captain), John Leonard Jones, Billy Meredith, Thomas Bartley, Maddox Morgan-Owen, Alfred E. Watkins, Edwin James

Directly inside Fred was the man he was competing with to finish as top scorer in Division One: Fred Wheldon. Nicknamed 'Diamond', Wheldon ended the League campaign with twenty-three goals, six more than his England colleague. Wheldon had scored three times against Ireland in 1897.

With the selectors telling the England side that they should treat the match as a final trial for the Scotland game, the away side started quickly on a sodden pitch. After some early misses England struck on 9 minutes when, from a Spiksley free kick, Wheldon hooked the ball towards goal where Trainer made a valiant effort to keep it out, only for it to creep over the line and send visitors from the neighbouring English counties jumping for joy. The game afterwards became a tight struggle, but came to life when Robinson was penalised for running with the ball. The 'keeper was beaten from the resulting free kick, but the home fans' celebrations were swiftly stilled when the referee overruled the effort as it had been taken from an indirect free kick and at half time, England held a narrow lead.

Although the away side were forced to defend deeply in order to neutralise the danger of Billy Meredith, then of Manchester City, they played much better in the second half and really should have extended their lead before the Welsh winger drilled a shot beyond Robinson. Welsh celebrations were once again cut short when the referee ruled that Maddox Morgan-Owen, the Corinthians FC centre forward, had held down Robinson. The Welsh players and spectators believed there had been an injustice.

There was further Welsh disappointment when a Spiksley cross was superbly hit home by Wheldon to make it Wales 0 England 2. The England left wing partnership had won the game and the away side completed the scoring when Charlie Athersmith, who had previously hardly made a run down the right wing, crossed for Smith to score with a header.

The performance and result were deemed so satisfactory that by the time the England party had reached Chester, the selectors had chosen the team to play Scotland. Steve Bloomer came back in for Goodall, Frank Forman of Nottingham Forest was selected to replace Tommy Booth and, to the surprise of many, the amateur Charles Wreford-Brown replaced Tom Perry at centre half and was also made captain.

With Sheffield United locked in a battle with Sunderland for the League title, Ernest Needham had written to the England selectors asking to be excused from playing against Scotland. When this request was refused, Fred went over to Bramall Lane to discuss travelling with him to Scotland. He met Bill Foulke and, before he could ask him where Needham was, they were interrupted by a keen, enthusiastic footballer from Sheffield United's reserve side.

'Please, Mr Foulke, I wonder if I might ask you a question?' enquired the nervous youngster.

'Fire away, lad.'

'Well, sir, I was wondering why I am always played in United's second team.'

'Are yer sure yer want t' kna th' answer lad?'

"Yes, sir, I'm sure.'

'Well, if tha really wants t' kna it's because we 'aven't got a third team t' play you in.'

England arrived in Glasgow for a game that all of Scotland was talking about. The England team and Goodall, the travelling reserve, trained on Celtic Park on the Friday lunchtime before taking a guided tour around Glasgow and returning for high tea at the Central Station Hotel.

Charles Wreford-Brown had previously played in just three internationals and had been selected out of the blue to captain England in his fourth. Unlike many other amateur players who played for England, he had few airs and graces and his energy and enthusiasm knew no bounds. He was a born optimist and after tea he delivered a great speech in which he admitted he would be the proudest man alive if England gave the Scots a good hiding the following afternoon. Every player left the room determined not to let the England captain down.

England: John Robinson, Billy Williams, William Oakley, Charles Wreford-Brown (captain), Ernest Needham, Frank Forman, Charlie Athersmith, Steve Bloomer, Gilbert Oswald Smith, Fred Wheldon, Fred Spiksley

Scotland: Ken Anderson, John Drummond, Dan Doyle, Neil Gibson, James Cowan (captain), John T. Robinson, John Bell, John Campbell, William S. Maxwell, James Millar, Alex Smith

The Scottish fans, though, were convinced that England had no chance. Yet the home side had been weakened by the withdrawals of Sunderland's Ned Doig and Hughie Wilson. The Wearsiders were going head to head with Sheffield United for the title and the sides clashed on Thursday, 2 April at Bramall Lane, where a Sunderland side containing the two Scots had lost to a home side missing Needham. Needham was to be back to play for his club side in the next game when he scored the only goal as Bolton were beaten and Sheffield United became Division One champions for the first and only time.

Celtic Park had been upgraded since the last time Spiksley had played there for England in 1894. It now had thirty-five turnstiles and they were certainly worked overtime as the action was watched by 62,000 fans, who paid £3,229 in total. However, many young boys were excluded from attending after the SFA decided not to offer reduced prices for youngsters. The size of the crowd, slightly more than what the Emirates Stadium in North London holds today, was the biggest Fred played in front of during his long career. It was a sign of how football had grown in importance as when Fred had signed his first professional contract with Gainsborough in 1887, the crowd for the England–Scotland game at Leamington Street, Blackburn, that year was 12,000. The first time Fred had played at Celtic Park against Scotland it was a miracle that no one had been killed as the facilities couldn't cope with a large crowd. Not so in 1898, and the scene was a remarkable one as the match passed off without the least disturbance.

Before kick-off, Scottish pipers and half a dozen men with kettledrums entertained the packed crowd. The noise was almost deafening when the heavens opened and umbrellas went up. They had been taken down by the time a brass band began a selection of Scottish tunes that are always guaranteed to set the blood racing. The swirl of the Argyll and Sutherland Highlanders' pipes ended the pre-match entertainment as England strode out on to the pitch. Fred Spiksley was certain his side would win as he felt it was the greatest England team he had ever had the privilege to play in. The huge roar that followed when the Scots then came out meant not everyone agreed with him!

Despite the earlier rain, the pitch was in good condition, although there was also a strong breeze blowing down the ground. England lost the toss but from the kick-off they made great headway into the Scottish defence. It was a sign of things to come over the following 90 minutes.

The Scots were chasing shadows and on 3 minutes, Wheldon and Spiksley ripped apart the home defence with a series of passes and moves that left the latter in front of the goal with only John Drummond and Kenny Anderson to beat. As he was about to shoot his teammate shouted 'Mine!' Taken unawares, Fred had the ball whipped from under his feet as Wheldon put England ahead.

How could he complain? But what was this the England captain was handing to the goalscorer? It turned out to be a gold sovereign and the Wednesday man couldn't help thinking that Wheldon had known before the game of Wreford-Brown's intention to reward any scorer with that valuable item. Wheldon asked the referee to look after the sovereign until the end of the game, but the incident still rankled enough with Fred that he wrote about it in his autobiography more than twenty years later.

Try as they might, Scotland saw their attempts to make space for a shot confounded by an England half back line in fine form. Ernest Needham was constantly collecting the ball and finding Wheldon and Spiksley out wide, and Drummond simply couldn't cope with the Football League's most prolific goalscorers playing together. Their understanding was almost telepathic. It soon nearly became 2-0 when Smith shot narrowly wide after ghosting away from Cowan, the hero of Scotland's victories in the previous two matches against England.

A second England goal wasn't long in coming, however. Smith slipped through a pass for Bloomer to put his side 2-0 ahead. The Scots appealed energetically for offside, but Mr Thomas Robertson, the Stirling-born referee, was certain the goal was a good one.

At half-time the Scottish forward line was rearranged with Campbell moving to centre, Maxwell to inside left and Millar to inside right. When Millar netted on 50 minutes it seemed that the switches had worked but, in truth, the goal owed more to England's over-confidence and Wreford-Brown swiftly let his colleagues know how disgusted he was with their attitude. Despite this, the goal remains historic as a photograph taken at the time means it is the oldest ever to show a goal being scored in an international match. Featured in this book, it shows Robinson clearly beaten as the shot from Millar speeds past him with the Scottish forwards celebrating.

A third England goal wasn't far off, though, as Fred Spiksley left the Scots' dependable right-half Neil Gibson in his wake, hurtled past Drummond and then delivered a great pass into Bloomer's path. Derby's finest man hit a shot that rocketed home off the underside of the crossbar. Bloomer was rewarded with a second gold sovereign.

The game was already over with 35 minutes to go. Scotland never threatened the away goal and left the field well beaten. Fred moaned about the loss of 'his' sovereign, taken from him just as he was about to shoot for the first goal. When, many years later, he finally wrote about the 1898 game at Celtic Park he said:

> To put it kindly, the Scots were completely and utterly outplayed from start to finish that day. England won by 3 goals to 1, humbling the Scots in front of their own fanatical supporters. In my opinion the amount of possession we had, the territorial supremacy that we maintained throughout the game, the number of shots at goal and on target, and the meagre scraps of possession that Scotland had to feed off; England were a good five goals better than our opponent on the day. It was a comprehensive dismantling of the Scottish team, the England fans were on top of the world, and I was a proud man that evening.

According to Needham, this match 'produced the finest football I ever saw an English eleven play during my career ... and, if I am permitted to say so, I played one of my best games that day. I attribute this to the fact that I was so used to Fred Spiksley's methods, having combined with him in many internationals and inter-association matches.' Needham was also full of praise for the Scotland 'keeper Kenny Anderson for keeping the score line respectable.

The newspapers were fulsome in their praise of the England side, with many complimenting the England left partnership. At the same time there was little doubt that a special role had been played by Wreford-Brown, who was everywhere and never failed to encourage and support those under his direction. For many years the 1898 England forward line was considered the finest of all time and it was generally agreed across the press that the man-of-the-match was the little Lincolnshire fellow on the left flank.

Fred Spiksley was a proud man. He had returned to the England side after a two-year gap and they had won both matches. Success in Glasgow meant England recaptured top spot in the Home International Championship. The Wednesday winger had played seven times for England, winning five and drawing two. He had scored seven times, including becoming the first player to score hat tricks in his first two internationals, and had also set up a number of goals for his England colleagues. His partnership with Wheldon against Scotland in 1898 had been brilliant.

Despite this, Fred had played his final international. The following season he and Wednesday both struggled. In 1900 Needham wrote, 'Spiksley had been a certainty for selection in all the 1899 Home Internationals, but was unlucky to miss out through injury'. This was the first of a series of persistent injuries that would dog Spiksley's career until he bowed out of top flight football in 1904. However, Spiksley was never forgotten by those who regularly watched England over many years. In 1926 a book of his personal reminiscences by J.A.H. Catton was published and in it he named his all-time best England XI:

E. Taylor, R. Crompton, H. Burgess, J. Crabtree, W. Wedlock, E. Needham, W. Bassett, S. Bloomer, T. Lindley, J. Goodall, F. Spiksley

Catton claimed:

> Spiksley was a natural footballer who had the advantage of playing at Gainsborough and Sheffield with some Scotsmen who had the characteristic quality of their race – ball control. Thus a youngster who could use either foot with equal facility had the advantage of developing his gift to the top of his bent. Whenever I saw him he played well, but never better than at Richmond, for he scored the last three goals in about ten minutes.

He was also adamant that the disputed goal Fred Spiksley scored against Scotland at Richmond was onside:

> The moment the ball left Bassett's boot Spiksley was off in a flash. He would trap the ball with his right and crash it into the net with his left. This seemed like one movement because he was so rapid ... Spiksley had sleight of foot. He did most of his dribbling with the outside of his right foot ... I do not like making sweeping statements, but I have never seen so thoroughly competent an outside left as Spiksley, who relied not on weight, or even on speed alone, but upon his craft and power over the ball.

Chapter 15

End of an Era

The sad end to Wednesday's years at Olive Grove

Following their league entry, Wednesday struggled in their first two seasons before finishing in eighth, seventh, sixth and fifth place respectively. Winning the title seemed unlikely in 1898–99, but there was surely no fear of relegation, which following the abandonment of the test match series, was the fate of the bottom two clubs in a division now containing eighteen sides.

The new season brought bad news. The Olive Grove lease had expired. Renewal was expected to be a formality, but out of the blue, however, the new landlords gave notice to quit at the end of the season. Wednesday were unaware the land had been sold by the Duke of Norfolk to the MLS Railway Company, who were planning to expand. Wednesday faced an uncertain future and the committee would need to devote a lot of time to finding a new ground.

Spirits were further dampened after an opening day 4-0 thrashing by Liverpool. Nevertheless, there was a healthy crowd of 11,000 inside Olive Grove for the first home game. Goals from Dryburgh and debutant Bill Hemmingfield meant Nottingham Forest were beaten 2-1. Then, after drawing 0-0 at Bolton Wanderers, the same two players scored in another 2-1 home victory, this time over Preston. Hemmingfield had arrived from Mexborough and had a decent first season, finishing top scorer with eight goals.

Wednesday rose to second when goals from Spiksley, Brady and Hemmingfield saw Derby beaten 3-1 at Olive Grove, which turned out to be the season's highlight. After defeat at West Bromwich, Wednesday drew 1-1 at home to Sheffield United. Action photographs were taken during the game by Jasper Redfern and include one in which Fred can be seen in front of the packed main stand at Olive Grove as the ball is cleared by a United defender.

Jasper Redfern was a Sheffield optician who, by 1898, was also taking photographs. He specialised in local films of interest, including football and cricket. He appears to have toured Africa in 1900 before moving into the moving picture business. He later engaged in research into X-rays and the treatment of cancer, from which he eventually died, through exposure to ionising radiation. Redfern loved taking photographs of Spiksley and Foulke.

Harry Ruddlesdin played his sixth Wednesday game in the derby. Barnsley-born 'Ruddy' arrived from village side Birdwell in the summer. Over the next five seasons, Ruddlesdin was to be the man behind Fred Spiksley and he formed a brilliant defensive trio with Ferrier and Crawshaw.

With Brady injured, the Wednesday committee experimented against Blackburn Rovers at home by selecting club captain Jack Earp up front. The gamble looked like it might pay off when, from a Spiksley cross, Dryburgh headed home. Thereafter it was the away side that dominated. It was no surprise when Ben Hulse scored an equalising goal before the interval. With Earp struggling he reverted to right half with Ferrier pushed up to support Dryburgh. On 60 minutes, John Moreland gave the away side the lead with a fine finish.

The home side were then denied a clear penalty when referee John Adams was so far behind play that he missed that the foul by Booth on Spiksley when he was inside the area. The resulting free kick came to nothing, before Carter made another fine save from a Spiksley shot. Wednesday finally gained their reward when, in the last minute, former Wednesday man Tom Brandon came from behind and chopped over Spiksley for a penalty. The Wednesday outside left dusted himself down, but as the crowd held their breath he flashed the penalty a yard wide of the goal, following which the final whistle sounded. A disappointed Fred Spiksley was adamant that the spot kick was his last ever one.

The following home games saw Wednesday beat Bury 3-2 and then Wolves 3-0, with the latter proving a personal triumph for Albert Kaye as he scored all three goals; his last for Wednesday. After not scoring in his next eleven games, Kaye departed for Kent non-league side Chatham.

At Stoke, Brady played his final Wednesday game as an injury kept him out for the remainder of the season, following which he returned home to play for Clydebank. John 'Jocky' Wright was signed for £200 from Bolton Wanderers to play inside Fred Spiksley. Wright was a skilful player but nowhere near as good as Brady and the Wednesday left was the poorer for the enforced change.

Wright debuted in what proved to be the longest League match ever. Aston Villa were again fighting for top spot when they arrived at Olive Grove on 26 November 1898. The game had been earmarked by the Wednesday committee as decision day on the new ground's location. One suggestion had been to play at Bramall Lane with the Sheaf House Ground employed for both Sheffield clubs' reserve team matches. However, when negotiations over Sheaf House stalled, the project was abandoned.

A huge effort had gone into finding suitable locations. Four were selected with the merits of each extensively discussed in the local press. Two were in Carbrook and two in Owlerton. Fans were asked to vote at the Aston Villa game for their preferred choice.

Around 10,000 voted and after a number of spoilt votes were deducted the results were:

Carbrook: 4,767
Owlerton: 4,115
Neutral: 124
Sheaf House: 16

However, when negotiations began with Carbrook Cricket Club, who owned the land on which Wednesday hoped to make their new home, the discussions foundered and it wasn't until early April 1899 that John Holmes could report that a plot of land at Owlerton could be purchased by the club.

In the meantime, however, there was the matter of playing Villa. With Wednesday's office personnel occupied with the ballot, everyone missed a telegram sent to the Earl of Arundel and Surrey Hotel from match referee Aaron Scragg saying he had missed his connecting train to Sheffield. A new referee was going to be required. With panic setting in, the advertised 2.30pm kick-off time passed before it was discovered that Fred Bye, an experienced local referee, was present and would take charge.

The match started in gloomy conditions at 2.45pm. Heavy ground made passing difficult and Crawshaw's opening goal was quickly cancelled out by Frank Bedingfield. Dryburgh restored the lead before the interval, at which point Scragg arrived to take charge. A Hemmingfield diving header made it 3-1 but with the light deteriorating, the players, already caked in mud, could hardly recognise one another. On 79 minutes and 30 seconds, Scragg, under pressure from Villa captain John Devey over the conditions, abandoned the match at 3-1.

An almighty row now ensued with Wednesday arguing that Villa should concede the points. Villa contended that the home side should have arranged an earlier kick-off time as it was known that November days were short. Scragg notified the Football League that he had abandoned the game because of bad light and following an inquest, the Football League management committee decided that Aston Villa must return north and play the remaining 10 and a half minutes. To Wednesday's annoyance, they were instructed to pay the away side's travel expenses. Stuck in a battle with Liverpool for the title, Villa argued that the whole game should be replayed.

The 'loss' of two points meant that when Wednesday were thrashed 5-0 at Burnley they fell to fifteenth place. This was the seventh away game and Wednesday had yet to score in any of them. There was thus real relief when goals from Wright and Spiksley ensured a 2-2 draw at Newcastle. However, a 2-1 Boxing Day defeat at Bramall Lane saw Wednesday drop into bottom place, staying there when Liverpool won 3-0 at Olive Grove on New Year's Eve. A 0-0 draw at Bury, a 1-1 draw at Nottingham Forest and then a 1-0 home win over relegation rivals Bolton Wanderers did, however, lift Wednesday out of the relegation zone.

On 21 January, Wednesday made the short trip to Derby with an unbeaten record in 1899, but it wasn't to last as they suffered a 9-0 hammering. The result was, at the time, Wednesday's heaviest defeat in the club's professional era and much of the blame for the shambles was due to the sprint training the players were forced to endure in the days before the game.

With the FA Cup only weeks away and Wednesday struggling in the League, the club had organised a special training week in Matlock Bath. Strict instructions were given to the coaches who accompanied the team to improve the players' fitness and skill levels, while also building team confidence. Wednesday enthusiast Mr Ernest Bowling was placed in charge.

Alas, continual rain made it a depressing week. After three days of indoor work the players, ordered to bed early, were restless, but training outside was impossible as the ground was waterlogged. With the week proving disastrous, Bowling fastened on to using an old 'clinker path' for sprint training. The surface hadn't been rolled for many years and when Fred saw it he used his status as a senior player and selector to assert his contractual rights to train on his own. He feared ending up with a sprained ankle or even ligament damage. However, he could do nothing to prevent Bowling insisting the other players use the treacherous surface. After a lengthy walk, Fred returned to Matlock Bath and was instructed to join the other players. Rather than standing his ground, he relented, and over the next couple of days the Wednesday squad did their best to avoid getting injured.

Fred knew the England selectors would be at the Baseball Ground and would be watching his performance with interest. He was therefore left heartbroken when, after 6 minutes, he was carried off on a stretcher with a snapped right hamstring. He was out of match and was to miss the next four games.

Wednesday's ranks fell further when Ferrier pulled up lame. Later, the Wednesday side became just eight fit men when Earp began limping and, although he remained on the pitch, he could hardly move. Taking full advantage, Steve Bloomer was simply irrepressible and he used the space left by his injury-ravaged opponents to drill home three goals in the first 20 minutes and six goals in all.

Bloomer's best was his fifth when he combined with Billy MacDonald before blasting home, not to mention forcing Massey into making a series of fine saves. Bloomer was certain to play for England after this performance. Yet, earlier in the season, he had been suspended for insubordination and dropped to the reserves in a dispute over wages. Derby's greatest footballer was never truly appreciated by the East Midlands club and it was surprising he remained loyal. Especially as more successful clubs such as Aston Villa and Sheffield United sought to sign him. Bloomer scored thirty League and FA Cup goals in 1898–99, with Derby again earning a place in the FA Cup final where they lost 4-1 to Sheffield United.

Speaking after the Wednesday game, Bloomer said: 'It was one of those days when I could do nothing wrong, if I had shot with my eyes closed I would still have scored.' According to Fred it was 'the most miserable day in my footballing life ... but as I sat on the sidelines I was amazed to see such brilliant shooting ... had it not been for good goalkeeping I hate to think what the final score might have been.' Bloomer and Spiksley never played together for England again and Fred was certain it was because of the clinker path.

Wednesday's dismal form continued when they were beaten 1-0 by Sunderland. A return attempt by Fred Spiksley failed when he played on the right wing and hardly featured. He missed the 0-0 draw at Wolves, where Langley became separated from his teammates after the game and was kicked and punched by home fans angered by his severe treatment of some of their players. There then followed a third consecutive home defeat for Wednesday as Everton won 2-1. The game marked the debut of forward Jack Pryce, who had been signed from Glossop North End, and although it was hoped he would do better than Kaye, he failed to net in eight games.

The realities of being trapped in a relegation fight were starting to envelop the Wednesday players, and at the end of the match there was a heated confrontation featuring Earp and Spiksley and the match referee, Mr Price. An emergency League disciplinary meeting followed; Earp was cleared, but Spiksley was found guilty and made to apologise to the referee.

Then came a 1-0 defeat at Notts County, where Crawshaw missed a penalty after Ernie Watts had scooped away Fred Spiksley's shot that appeared to have crossed the goal-line. To add to the misery the Notts County goal by Fletcher seemed well offside. Following this defeat, Villa returned on 13 March 1899 to play the final few minutes of the original November game.

Around 3,000 Sheffield fans turned out to watch the completion of the longest Football League game. Villa's slim chances evaporated when Spiksley dashed clear before squaring the ball for Richards, who hadn't played in the original fixture. He netted to make it 4-1 at the final whistle. It meant two valuable home points had been earned from a fixture in which everyone who played some part in either game is counted in the record books as making one appearance.

When the sides met again in the League twelve days later, Villa won 3-1. With four games remaining, Wednesday lay in seventeenth place. One angry Wednesday fan decided to take his revenge on the players. A letter containing a team photograph arrived at Olive Grove addressed to 'The Blind Eleven'. The sender had carefully drawn a pair of spectacles around the eyes of each player and then pricked out their eyes. Underneath he had written in bold black capitals 'THE BLIND XI!' Generally, the Wednesday players accepted the supporters' attempts at black humour, but this time it left them very upset and offended. The letter did little for team morale.

Wednesday were beaten 3-1 at home by Stoke and looked doomed, but a 1-0 victory over Burnley at home raised hopes of avoiding the drop. However, these were dashed thanks to a defeat against Preston, which meant that Wednesday were as good as relegated when they faced Newcastle United on 15 April in the final game at Olive Grove. For the many who had enjoyed watching Wednesday play there it was a very sad occasion, and not made any easier by fears that the new ground would require loyal supporters to make quite a trek out into the countryside. Home fans' spirits were dealt an additional blow when Newcastle won 3-1. Wednesday ended in bottom place with twenty-four points from thirty-four games. Only thirty-two goals had been scored – just seven more than Brady and Spiksley on the Wednesday left had scored between them the previous season. Brady's loss was crucial in Wednesday's unsuccessful relegation battle.

The 1898–99 season ended with Villa as champions, while Sheffield United won the FA Cup. Bramall Lane was easier to get to and Wednesday fans feared that the more successful United side might now become much more popular than their own with the Sheffield public.

Chapter 16

The Owlerton Gamble

Wednesday bounce back after a risky move away from their heartland

F red had no wish to play Second Division football, but the Wednesday directors persuaded him to back the club in their time of trouble and focus on winning promotion. Rejoining Fred at the club was Archie Brash, his confidence restored after a successful season at Crewe Alexandra. Dryburgh left for Millwall Athletic, while centre forward Harry Millar from Bury cost £100. Of the forwards who had started in the Wednesday first team on the previous season's opening day, only Fred Spiksley remained. Dryburgh, Davis, Kaye and Brady had been replaced by Brash, Pryce, Millar and Wright.

Changes off the pitch mirrored those on it. Paul Firth became trainer, replacing Johnson, who joined Tottenham to help train them to FA Cup glory. Pre-season training was conducted at the Sheaf House Ground, and the Niagara Grounds at Wadsley Bridge hosted three public practice matches as Wednesday's new ground in Owlerton was still unfinished. The fact that it was to be ready for the opening League fixture against neighbours Chesterfield on 2 September 1899 was largely due to Arthur Dickinson's efforts.

With finance needed to buy land and construct a stadium, and with only £250 capital, the Wednesday committee was dissolved and 'The Wednesday Football Club Limited' was formed in June 1899. The share prospectus stated it had:

> Been formed for the purpose of providing another suitable ground whereon to continue the old Club. After considerable difficulty, the Company have fortunately been able to acquire a most suitable piece of land on the Penistone Road, near the High Bridge, Owlerton, containing 10 acres, for £5,000. There will be good approaches to the ground from the Penistone Road, and also from Leppings Lane. The Corporation Tramcars will run within 1 minute's walk from the ground, and the present Railway Station at Wadsley Bridge is about 5 minutes' walk from the ground.

The share issue raised £7,000, with George Senior, Charles and William Clegg, Alfred and John Holmes, Colonel Robert Hughes and Dickinson all subscribing. Senior, a self-made man who owned Ponds Forge, became chairman. A £500 deposit was paid to wealthy local silversmith Wilf Dixon, the owner of the land, which was on the north bank of the River Don at High Bridge, Owlerton.

Uncovered terracing was constructed at each end of the ground using deposited rubbish, the brick stand from Olive Grove with a capacity of 2,000 was transported to the new venue and another new stand, with a capacity of 3,000, was erected in record time. The dressing rooms were good and included full bathing facilities, not to mention a pleasant refreshment room, a separate ladies' tea room and a bicycle room. A small fence ran round the pitch perimeter.

J.A. Brierley of the *Lancashire Evening Post* visited the new arena and felt that,

> Owlerton will in future challenge Bramall Lane very strongly for such welcome plums as cup semi-finals, internationals and inter-league matches, while in due course it will be almost equal to accommodating such great gates as the Association have been getting at the final in recent years. Having such an excellent pitch, the Wednesday authorities are determined to make the appointments and accommodation thoroughly worthy of the club and city. They have succeeded admirably.

Season tickets costing 10 shillings and sixpence (52.5p) were available with match day prices of 1 shilling (5p) for seating and sixpence for standing; boy's tickets were half price. Would the Wednesday fans turn up, though? First, unlike at Sheffield United, the fare on offer was Second Division football. Secondly, Owlerton was several miles beyond the city boundary and was poorly served by public transport. Would fans consider a long walk to the ground, especially in winter? Despite the uncertainty, Sir William Clegg delivered a rousing speech to the players and promised each of them a 10 shilling (50p) bonus for every point won at home and a pound for each one won away, the bonus being paid at the season's end.

The Wednesday team for the club's first ever Division Two match against Chesterfield, was: Massey, Earp, Langley, Ferrier, Crawshaw, Ruddlesdin, Brash, Pryce, Millar, Wright, Spiksley.

Before the game, both sides had their photograph taken by Jasper Redfern in the goalmouth at the Leppings Lane end of the ground. The famous Sheffield optician also used this game as an experiment in recording moving image by using his stereoscopic camera, which took a series of photographs that then could be used to create short animations of the action. It was a technique Redfern had been experimenting with from around 1898, and his first trials at recording a football match took place when he took his camera to the 1899 FA Cup final to record Sheffield United defeating Derby County 4-1.

More than 12,000 people were in the ground for the opening match, a testament to the loyalty of the Wednesday fans. The Lord Mayor of Sheffield, Alderman William Clegg, a Wednesday director, started the match at 3pm. The first goal at the new stadium came from the Chesterfield captain Herbert Munday, when the experienced Fred Geary, a title winner with Everton in 1890–91, saw his shot rebound off the post for Munday to score, all to the utter joy of hundreds of away fans.

The home fans were less pleased and some even began questioning the Wednesday players' desire. This scepticism, however, was unfounded as Fred Spiksley became the first Wednesday player to score at the new home when he ran past the Chesterfield defence and levelled. Ferrier put the home side ahead and in the second half, two Spiksley crosses were knocked home by debutant Millar before Brash made it 5-1.

The following weekend had the potential to be a special occasion for Gainsborough-born Fred Spiksley when he returned to play on the Northolme Sports Field, where he had first established his reputation as a player. Gainsborough Trinity had finished as Midland League runners-up in 1895–96. Their subsequent Football League entry application saw them finish above existing League sides Port Vale and Crewe Alexandra in a ballot, and thus break into Division Two in 1896–97. Following a highly creditable seventh place finish, Trinity had finished in the bottom half of the table in the following two seasons.

Four thousand spectators packed out the small ground, generating almost £100 receipts. Scott, the Trinity captain, lost the toss and found his side had to attack with both the sun and breeze in their faces. With Earp having badly injured himself against Chesterfield, there was an opportunity for Bill (Willie) Layton to establish himself as the regular Wednesday right back, while Arthur Dickinson selected Langley as captain. Earp was to play just four more games and left to become Stockport County coach at the season's end. Not long afterwards, Earp joined Lord Baden Powell's First Battalion and served in the Boer War.

Wednesday won 2-1 with goals from Millar and Wright. Fred Spiksley, however, didn't enjoy the match as he had a goal wrongly disallowed for offside and was the victim of some very heavy challenges from Pycock and Hall that were greeted with delight by some onlookers. He was also upset at being booed. The hostility was picked up on by the *Gainsborough News* journalist, who hoped that the fans who had acted so ungraciously to a former Trinity favourite might feel ashamed of themselves. As an experienced professional, though, Spiksley shouldn't have allowed the abuse to get under his skin.

Wednesday won their third game of the new season the following weekend when, before another 12,000 crowd, they beat Bolton Wanderers 2-1 with goals from Spiksley and Millar. The latter was a real comic off the field and his tricks included turning up at the Empire Theatre in Sheffield and conducting the orchestra until being chased out by the theatre manager. Langley believed Millar might have done better as a footballer by taking the game more seriously.

The Bolton game had its own comic moment when a local dog turned up to assist his fellow townsmen. He joined the attackers and when the second goal was forced home he seemed delighted, although he didn't join in the handshaking afterwards. After youngsters attempted to secure him, the dog was finally removed from the pitch when Massey caught him before pitching him into the crowd.

Wednesday played impressively at Lincoln City, where a 2-1 victory was secured by goals from Wright and Spiksley. The latter's success was in contrast to when he had played as a young man against Lincoln City. At that time the home captain Joe Duckworth had regularly dished out good hidings to the frail winger on the sloping pitch on the John O'Gaunt's Ground. However, Duckworth was long since gone and City now played on the level playing field at Sincil Bank. In 1899 the Lincoln City side included Scotsman John Walker, signed from Leith Athletic during the summer. Walker was Lincoln's first black player, and also the first black player to appear in both the Scottish and English Leagues.

On 2 December 1899, Fred Spiksley became the first player to score a hat trick at Owlerton when, along with two from Pryce and one from Wright, Wednesday beat Luton Town 6-0. Edwin Daw in the away goal prevented a massacre and had no chance as Fred netted the Wednesday second, hit home the third from a free kick and finished off the scoring with a glorious shot.

Only two days before the start of a new century, Wednesday lost a Second Division game for the first time. Despite enjoying the backing of a good number of the 4,000 Saltergate crowd, Wednesday were beaten by Chesterfield 1-0. On New Year's Day, there was a return to winning ways when Grimsby Town lost 2-1 at Owlerton with Wright notching his eleventh goal of the season, taking him one in front of Spiksley and four ahead of Millar. However, Millar drew level with Wright five days later when he netted four times as Gainsborough Trinity were beaten 5-1.

The following game pitched first against second when Wednesday travelled to Bolton Wanderers. Following their defeat at Owlerton, Wanderers had embarked on a sixteen-match unbeaten run and were in the middle of a run of six straight victories which included 5-1, 5-0, 6-1 and 7-1 successes. The biggest home gate of Wanderers' season, 12,235, witnessed a fine game in which Bob Jack's goal gave the home side both points. The losing side were forced to play 80 minutes with just ten players when Spiksley sustained an injury that virtually ended his season. He made a few failed comebacks but would be sidelined for a year.

The moment that ruined Fred's season came after the referee had whistled for offside. As he was the nearest to the ball, the Wednesday winger went to retrieve it. He had just put his foot behind the ball when the Bolton right half Jack Fitchett gave it an almighty kick. Fitchett later claimed he hadn't heard the whistle and was going for the ball, but the impact of his kick against his opponent's foot sent a shock wave up the leg to his knee and hamstring, forcing Fred to be carried from the pitch. He was unavailable for the 5-0 home defeat of Loughborough Town, but did return for the FA Cup first round home tie against Bolton Wanderers, which was won by Wednesday courtesy of a Jack Wright goal.

The following weekend, Wednesday included in their forward line a £200 signing from Barnsley, Harry 'Joe Pluck' Davis, who went on to become an automatic first team choice at Owlerton for many years. His nickname came from his courageous, never-say die attitude and he was to become a full England international in 1903 when he was capped three times. He formed an effective partnership with Harry Chapman and became assistant trainer at Wednesday in 1907. Missing Spiksley, Wednesday lost 1-0 in a very rough game at Newton Heath. A clearly rankled home side sought to take revenge on Mick Langley for his challenge during the fixture at Owlerton earlier in the season, which had left his opponent with a fractured wrist. The game was stopped on more than fifty occasions for foul play and there was a near riot when Langley sought revenge for the punishment he endured by dumping one of the home forwards into the crowd.

Thankfully, there was the FA Cup to look forward to. It couldn't have generated greater excitement in Sheffield as United, the cup holders and Division One leaders, had drawn Wednesday at home. It was the first time the sides had met in the competition and a crowd of 32,381 packed out Bramall Lane.

Fred Spiksley was persuaded by the Wednesday directors to play, even though he wasn't fully fit. The Bramall Lane pitch also wasn't fit for such a big match as it was frozen. As the game got underway snow continued to fall and when it turned into a blizzard, the referee Mr Lewis took the players off and then waited unsuccessfully for 15 minutes to see if there was a change in conditions before abandoning the game after 53 minutes. The decision was certainly less favourable to the away side, who had proven the superior outfit and should have led at half-time, only for their unfit outside left to miss two great chances. On 52 minutes, Fred had found Brash with a great ball and his shot was cleared off the line. Wednesday fans complained bitterly that the referee had robbed their side of success.

The rearranged match before a 23,000 crowd at Bramall Lane took place on Saturday, 17 February 1900. It had been planned to hold the game on the fifteenth and the groundsmen had worked hard to make the pitch playable, only for another blizzard to force another postponement. Two days later, a thaw had reduced the ground to a muddy one. Nevertheless, referee John Lewis pronounced it as being 'fit for play'. The home side were boosted by the return from injury of Fred Priest, scorer of United's winning goal in the semi-final against Liverpool the previous season, and who also netted one of the United goals in the 4-1 defeat of Derby County in the final.

Despite being the top flight side, United were largely outplayed by their Second Division opponents in the first 20 minutes. The Cup holders responded by trying to kick Wednesday off the park, but United were fortunate when a Spiksley 'goal' was harshly overruled for offside. In the twentieth minute, Wednesday finally retaliated when Langley and Ruddlesdin sandwiched Cocky Bennett, who had been putting himself about quite a bit. The result was a warning to the two offenders. Whenever the Wednesday and United sides contained Langley and Bennett, the crowd witnessed a rough duel between two men who off the field were close friends. Despite this, Bennett's mother promised to fell Langley if she saw him in her home town of Mexborough. Like all the Wednesday players, Langley rated the United players and was adamant that Foulke was the greatest 'keeper ever, while Needham was 'head and shoulders above any other half back in the country'.

The opening goal arrived in the twenty-fifth minute when Spiksley and Wright combined before the former produced a weighted cross beyond Foulke and into the path of Brash, who sent the Wednesday players and fans jumping for joy by netting. Thereafter, the game continued at a fast pace but it was the Division Two side that led at half time.

On the restart, United resorted to some very rough challenges, as Harry Thickett hacked Fred Spiksley down from behind. It was an offence that would be a straight red today, but carried no punishment in 1900. The injured player had his knee strapped up and carried on. Massey was then badly hurt in a crude challenge and the serious injuries to two of the Wednesday players were compounded by knocks to Millar, Brash and Crawshaw. Still suffering from what happened to him in the first half, Bennett had to go off during the middle period of the second half, but his absence was temporary. On Bennett's return,

Jack Almond pounced to make it 1-1 and afterwards it was something of a miracle that the away side held on to obtain a creditable draw.

The replay two days later attracted a record attendance for the new ground of 23,000. Massey, Millar and Spiksley were all ruled out of the match. Bill Mallinson came in for his third game in goal, youngster George Lee was selected at centre forward for the last of six first-team appearances and Jack Topham, a prolific scorer in the reserves, replaced Fred Spiksley.

Meanwhile, United named a full strength side. Their tactics had paid off but only because of weak refereeing. Mr Lewis must have realised that he had performed badly at Bramall Lane and prior to kick-off, he entered the dressing rooms and told the players he would be severe on dangerous play.

The opening period of the game was poor, and Jasper Redfern was again present with his stereoscopic camera to film it. While, sadly, no footage has survived, there is a stereoscopic image still in existence which belongs to the Sheffield City Library collection.

Several free kicks were awarded. Brash then caught a stray Jack Russell dog and brought the largest cheer so far. On 38 minutes, Lee sustained a serious fracture to his right leg after a careless Thickett challenge that despite the tricky conditions, should have led to the United man's dismissal. The incident virtually ended Lee's professional football career. He was released in the close season and thereafter struggled financially and died five years later aged just 29.

At half-time, ten-man Wednesday reshuffled, putting Layton at centre forward and leaving just the one full back, Langley. The intent was to use the three-man offside rule of the time to catch the away forwards offside, but within 2 minutes, Almond beat the trap and when he was brought down from behind by Langley, Needham scored from the spot. Eight minutes later, Langley brought down Bennett with a rough challenge before a great Foulke save kept his side a goal ahead.

Immediately afterwards, John Lewis dismissed Pryce for what he deemed was an over-the-ball challenge on George Hedley, after the United player had gone down heavily for what was little more than two players running into each other. Eleven-man United sought to finish off their nine-man opponents. With only minutes remaining, Bennett and Langley collided and although the Wednesday captain made only glancing contact, he was dismissed, the referee ignoring Needham's plea that the collision had been an accidental one. The Wednesday fans were outraged at the referee's performance and told him so in direct language. Down to eight men, the home side finally yielded when Beers scored a fine goal as United progressed to face Bury. The Shakers were to beat them and later win the FA Cup by beating Southampton 4-0 in the final.

Langley was forced to appear before the FA disciplinary committee. Despite J.J. Bentley, a prominent Football League official, travelling to support him and telling everyone Langley hadn't made one bad foul in all three matches, he received a one-month suspension when the linesman insisted the player's challenge on Bennett demanded a sending-off.

With Fred still injured, Topham retained his place in the starting line-up for the following four matches, which saw Wednesday win three, lose just once and go top of the table. Fred returned to the side as Wednesday beat Woolwich Arsenal 3-1 at home, thus earning a further £1 bonus. He wasn't fully fit, though, and his final appearance of the season was at Grimsby Town. A then record Blundell Park attendance of 8,000 was delighted when, with 7 minutes remaining, the home side led 1-0. Throwing caution to the wind, Langley went up front and it was later reported by Grimsby fans that he had run amok. Certainly, John McAvoy was badly injured following one of his challenges and soon afterwards, Crawshaw equalised. Then, with just 2 minutes left, the Wednesday captain scored the winning goal.

When the final whistle sounded, William Bellamy, a Grimsby Town director who was also a Football League management committee member, stormed on to the pitch and demanded that Langley be dismissed for persistent foul play. When the player told Bellamy to mind his own business, the latter didn't speak to him for many years.

The victory put Wednesday within touching distance of an immediate return to Division One. This was confirmed the following day when Burslem Port Vale were beaten 4-0 at Owlerton before a crowd of 5,000 on Easter Saturday. Three points were then gained from a 1-0 victory at home to Lincoln City and a 1-1 draw at Walsall. Middlesbrough were beaten 3-0 in the final game and the victory established a club record as it meant that Wednesday had won every home League match during the season. The club had returned to the top flight by finishing in top spot to capture the Division Two Victory Shield, with Bolton in second place.

Fred thus added another medal to his collection. Now all he needed was a Division One winner's medal. However, he was in no rush to celebrate even though there was also the additional financial reward of £26 earned from the nine home victories, seven away victories and three draws in the 21 League games he had played. Thickett's challenge had put his recovery back substantially. Having twice attempted a comeback, he was now ordered by Dr Lockwood to take a complete rest to allow for the natural healing of the ligaments. He could do daily leg exercises for an hour and go for some light walks, but it was going to be a while before he could play football again. At aged 30, Fred must have feared for his future as a professional footballer, especially as many playing careers were cut short in the Victorian era.

When it became clear that Fred Spiksley was going to be incapacitated for many months, the Wednesday committee agreed to renew his contract for the 1900–01 season, but only on the condition that it would be immediately terminated if he broke down again and was unable to play. Four years after winning Wednesday the FA Cup and the club were not even guaranteeing him a full season's contract!

Fred's absence left Wednesday seeking a replacement for him in the summer of 1900. John 'Jock' Napier Malloch cost £50 from Dundee, and the Scot would use his superb ball control over the following seven seasons at Owlerton.

Another Scot, Andrew 'Andra' Wilson, was also signed from relegated Clyde at £200 record fee, plus a £10 signing-on fee. Those who questioned the wisdom of spending so heavily would prove to be mistaken as Wilson went on to become Wednesday's all-time top scorer and appearance maker. It took the Ayrshire teenager some time to get going, however, Wilson stating later that after his first game he thought 'it was no game for me as the speed simply staggered me. English football is played at breakneck speed … making it less clever than in Scotland where the crowds do not tell a player to get rid of the ball quickly.' However, he soon blossomed into one of the greatest players of his generation, with his professional attitude, allied to a thunderous shot, making him a dangerous opponent.

Wilson, who preferred playing at left back, went straight into the first team with Millar. Trouble lay ahead for the latter, however, and he was later suspended without pay in October 1900 for missing training, relegated to making just four appearances during the season, following which he moved to QPR.

The campaign got under way with Wright notching Wednesday's goals in a 2-2 draw with Manchester City at the antiquated Hyde Road and a 1-0 home victory over Bolton. In the third game, FA Cup holders Bury enjoyed a 2-0 success at Gigg Lane with goals from Jasper McLuckie and Jack Plant, both of whom scored against Southampton in the 1900 FA Cup final.

Andrew Wilson scored his first two goals as Wednesday beat Notts County 4-1, before the promoted side collected just a point from the following four games. Relegation fears were calmed with successive 3-2 home victories against Aston Villa and Liverpool and over Christmas and the New Year there were victories at home against Derby County, Wolves and Manchester City. On 1 January 1901, Wednesday lay tenth out of eighteen teams.

On 27 October 1900, Fred Spiksley had played well in a 3-0 success for the Wednesday reserves at home to Montrose Works in a Sheffield Association

League match. It was reported in the *Sheffield Independent* that 'his appearance in the first team may be expected shortly'. He was selected at outside right for the following fixture at home to Aston Villa with Malloch retaining his place at outside left. Wednesday managed to win the game and match reports praised Fred for his efforts but, despite Dr Wharton Hood declaring that Spiksley was as 'sound as ever', he clearly wasn't ready for regular action and he wouldn't return to the side until 19 January 1901 against Notts County. Back at outside left, he was impressive, but County 'keeper Harry Pennington played better than anyone else to ensure his side won 2-0.

At Owlerton, four weeks later, Fred continued his rehabilitation as Wednesday drew 1-1 with Blackburn Rovers with the home goal being scored by debutant inside left Harry Chapman. He was to make another 298 first team appearances and became a big favourite with Wednesday fans for his tireless enthusiasm, solid tackling, acute tactical brain and his great versatility. Chapman netted again in his second match as Wednesday beat Stoke 4-0 at home, the season's biggest victory.

The following weekend saw Fred Spiksley score his first goal of the new century, a header, but his side, weakened by Crawshaw's absence on England duty, lost 2-1 at Aston Villa. Two weekends later, the scorer nipped in front of Bill Perkins to head home at Anfield in a game that ended 1-1.

Playing against Everton at Owlerton, Fred scored with his head in a game that was played in gale and, at times, hurricane-force winds. Crawshaw was again absent on international duty, but with Chapman netting twice the home side won 3-1.

Wednesday thus rose to eighth place, but the following match they conceded three goals for the first time in the season, losing 3-2 at relegation-bound Preston. Fred Spiksley had driven his side ahead late in the game before the home side netted twice in the final few minutes. It was a futile gesture of defiance by North End, as they later lost their last game at home to WBA, who accompanied them into the Second Division.

The Preston game almost had dramatic repercussions for Langley, who was angered by constant abuse from a passionate farmer standing behind the goal. Finally, when taking a goal kick, Langley thrust his left arm back into the farmer's face. A broken nose and two black eyes resulted in the Wednesday man being summonsed to appear at Preston Police Court, but Langley and his solicitor Mr Dronfield were able to persuade the injured party to meet them along with his solicitor Bob Holmes, the former Preston and England full back. The matter was settled out of court for the sum of £9, after which Langley advised the younger players to keep a cool head. Years later, the Preston chairman, Tom Houghton, told Langley that he had, in fact, done the club a good turn as the farmer, previously notorious for his abuse of Preston's opponents, never offended again.

On 13 April 1901, Wednesday hosted title challengers Sunderland in their penultimate home game of the season. The Sunderland side's success was based on a solid defence, who conceded just twenty-six goals in thirty-four League games. Up against right back Andrew McCombie, Fred Spiksley had the better of his opponent and from his cross, Chapman set up Wilson for what proved to be the only goal of a wind-affected match. Sunderland's defeat allowed Liverpool to win their first Division One title.

Meanwhile, Wednesday ended the season by winning 1-0 against a Sheffield United side that two days earlier had lost 3-1 against Southern League side Tottenham Hotspur in the replay of the FA Cup final.

Wednesday thus finished in eighth place with new man Wilson scoring thirteen times, three more than Wright. Fred Spiksley's shortened season saw him score four times in thirteen League matches. Although the Wednesday winger had turned 31 in January 1901, having played well on his return he was rewarded with a new contract for the following season. This allowed him to pluck up the courage and successfully ask for a 10 shilling (50p) a week increase to cover his travelling expenses from Gainsborough, taking his wages up to £3 10s (£3.50). Unlike in 1899–1900, however, there was no end-of-season bonus.

This new deal was a great relief to Fred Spiksley as he had come through what was probably his most frustrating time as a professional footballer. By 1901 football had already become a sport where there was little room for sentiment and with hundreds of young men aspiring to become footballers, there were plenty willing to fill the boots of a player who was seen to be past his prime. Malloch had proven a more than capable deputy for Spiksley and Fred must have been worried that Wednesday might stick by their recent signing and look to a future without him.

Unfortunately, Spiksley's difficulties didn't end there, as off the field his gambling addiction was catching up with him. Around the start of the 1901–02 season, he became embroiled in a regrettable episode that resulted in him being publicly cross-examined in court. Fred's usual support when he was in financial difficulties was his brother William. However, William was going through a difficult time of his own and his marriage had broken down. After being found guilty of assaulting his wife, William was imprisoned for a month.

Instead, Fred turned to Gainsborough money lender Mrs Bell. She was well known and Spiksley was aware that banking a cheque from her would draw suspicions from his bank. Trying to be discrete, Spiksley gained help from a friend called Joseph Nash, who later said that Spiksley was 'in such desperate measures that he was prepared to help him all he could'. A cheque was made out to Nash for £10 and Mrs Bell was handed security from Spiksley in the form of pawnbroker tickets for his English Cup winner's medal and other medals. Nash was right: Spiksley must have been at rock bottom at this point to consider using his Cup winner's medal as surety.

Mrs Bell was happy for the transaction to proceed, as she considered Nash to be someone who would 'joggle' Spiksley along into paying off his debts. However, it appears that at some point Nash double-crossed Fred by pocketing some of the repayments for himself. It turned out that Nash had a string of debts and was more financially stricken than Spiksley. The result was that Spiksley took Nash to Sheffield County Court to try to recoup his losses. The court found in his favour, but it wasn't long before Nash was in front of the bankruptcy court and Spiksley had lost a friend and his money. In addition, Fred, who was still a famous top-flight footballer, had had to endure the embarrassment of his financial difficulties being widely reported locally. Despite what had happened, Spiksley continued to search out other gambling opportunities.

The 1901–02 season began with a 3-1 home victory against promoted Grimsby Town, who were backed by a following of several hundred spectators in a crowd of 17,500. With Massey injured, Frank Stubbs retained his place in goal. The giant 'keeper had been signed in the summer of 1900 from Loughborough Athletic, where he played one Second Division game: a 12-0 hammering by Woolwich Arsenal. Stubbs's first season with Wednesday was a success after he replaced Massey and played the final fourteen games, conceding just fifteen goals.

When Wednesday played their second game of the season, at Notts County, they led 1-0 at the interval. Towards the end of the first period, Stubbs had gone down bravely to grab the ball at the feet of on-rushing forwards, but had taken a kick to the head. Wilson said later that Stubbs had asked what the score was as he left the field at half-time, but as he was a great practical joker everyone thought he was just being funny. However, the 'keeper was clearly concussed and conceded six goals in the second half and Wilson said: 'Most of the goals were given to them by Stubbs, who saved the shots, and then turned the ball behind him.' County won 6-1. Stubbs only played once more for Wednesday and he rejoined Loughborough in the summer of 1903, later becoming Mayor of Loughborough.

In February 1901, Wednesday sign Scottish-born 'keeper Jack Lyall from Jarrow. Replacing Stubbs, Lyall was beaten just once on his debut as Bolton Wanderers were crushed 5-1 at Owlerton. Lyall quickly established himself as the club's undoubted number one.

When on 12 October 1901, Wednesday beat champions Liverpool 2-1 at Anfield, it was their first away win in Division One since they had beaten West Bromwich Albion at Stoney Lane on 12 March 1898, thirty-nine games previously. A goal down, the away side equalised with a Chapman header before Wilson followed up a Spiksley shot that was saved by Bill Perkins to net the winner. Any hopes of a title challenge were soon dispelled as Wednesday's form was indifferent, although there was the pleasure of beating Sheffield United 1-0, with Foulke beaten when Wilson's shot glanced off Peter McIntyre and deceived the 'keeper. Fred Spiksley wasn't playing as he was out injured.

The following home game brought a 4-1 victory over Bury. The Lancashire side were late in arriving and were soon on the back foot following a thrilling Spiksley dribble that was rounded off with a goal. Then two fine crosses by the winger were netted by Dryburgh and Malloch respectively. The Wednesday winger also scored at home to Stoke, who were beaten 3-1. Earlier, he was twice denied by eccentric amateur goalkeeper Leigh Roose. It was Roose who took great advantage of the law that allowed 'keepers to handle – but not carry – the ball anywhere in their own half. It eventually prompted a change in 1912, forbidding the handling of the ball outside the penalty area. Roose, like Billy Foulke, was notorious for being able to withstand some heavy barging by opponents, as he bounced the ball towards the halfway line before launching it into the opposition danger area using either his hands or feet. Roose, who also played for Aston Villa, Arsenal and Sunderland, was killed at the Battle of the Somme in 1916. His body was never recovered.

Fred's third goal of the season also came at home when Manchester City were beaten 2-1 on Boxing Day, his effort coming after he ran on to beat Francis Barrett amid great cheering. On 11 January he then netted in a 4-0 thrashing of Notts County that put Wednesday in sixth place. Three consecutive away defeats in the League and a 1-0 defeat before a 30,096 crowd at Sunderland in the FA Cup meant that any Wednesday fans who hoped to see their side win silverware in 1902 would be disappointed.

In early April, Wednesday faced the two sides that were competing for the League title and gained a creditable 1-1 draw at home to Everton before beating Sunderland 2-1 at Roker Park, with goals from Chapman and amateur Vivian Simpson, a solicitor who played football purely for pleasure. Simpson ended up back in Sunderland in 1917 when he was invalided home from France during World War I and trained junior officers there. He later returned to the Front and was killed by a sniper in the Belgium village of Outtersteene, where he is buried.

The performance against the Wearsiders demonstrated that on their day Wednesday could compete with the best, but the season then ended in disappointment as, despite a Fred Spiksley goal, relegation-threatened Small Heath won 2-1 at Owlerton. This was especially disappointing as before the game an unknown team member had told Fred he had in his possession £55 to be divided between the Wednesday players if they won the match. It was believed that the money had come from someone connected to relegation strugglers Notts County. It later transpired that a further £55 had been on offer from a gentleman in Grimsby, where the local club were also threatened with relegation

Wednesday completed the 1901–02 season in ninth place, ten points behind champions Sunderland and four above relegated Small Heath. The final match was at home to FA Cup winners Sheffield United. It was played before a 4,747 crowd whose entrance fees went to the Ibrox Disaster Fund that was set up after twenty-five supporters had been killed when a new stand at Ibrox Park collapsed during the Scotland–England game on 5 April 1902.

Fred had ended the season with a run of seven games without an injury. As he had shown some signs that he could still be of use, Wednesday were content to award the player a 10s (50p) a week wage rise to £4 a week for the 1902–03 season.

There was no doubt that this was a worrying time for Fred. His recent years at Owlerton had been frustrating and he had clearly not enjoyed playing in front of a home crowd that became increasingly impatient for the old hero to reproduce the form that made him a household name in the footballing world. Some of the crowd at Owlerton may never have seen him play at Olive Grove and may have been excused for asking what all the fuss was about. However, there were surely plenty of people inside the ground who would have put them right.

Fred was keen to recover his international form and status and shortly after the annual team photograph was taken before the 1902–03 season started, he gambled by deciding to throw away the bandages he had been using for knee supports over the previous two seasons.

Chapter 17

Champions of England

Spiksley defies injury to win elusive medal

Throughout the summer of 1902 Fred maintained an intensive training regime aimed at strengthening his leg and thigh muscles in order to protect his right knee. The programme of swimming, running, sprinting and special weight-lift training was a lonely one, but Fred understood Wednesday would end his contract if he failed to perform on the pitch.

At the start of the 1902–03 season he was as fit as he had ever been. That particular season saw the introduction of a radical change in pitch markings, with a new rectangular 6-yard box to replace the previous 6-yard semi circles – within which goal kicks were taken – and a new penalty area, 44 yards wide and 18 yards deep, with a penalty spot exactly 12 yards from the centre of the goal. Two years later, 'keepers, who could previously advance up to 6 yards, were restricted to staying on their line until a penalty kick was taken. Later, 'keepers became required to wear a different-coloured jersey from those worn by their teammates.

Despite his efforts to return to full fitness, Fred received abuse during the opening League match at Sheffield United. A friend told him afterwards that when the ball was passed out to him, a spectator had shouted out 'What's the point of passing to him? He's an old man.' Fred proceeded to show why he should have the ball as he delivered a wicked curling cross that left Foulke stranded, allowing Wilson to head his side into the lead. Fred had earlier equalised with a low close-range shot that confirmed he was coming back to his best and further impressive runs increased his confidence enormously. Davis proceeded to make it 3-1, and although Lipsham reduced the arrears, the final result of United 2 Wednesday 3 was a fair reflection on a day when Harry Chapman faced his brother Herbert, a debutant for the home side. Herbert would go on to become a highly successful manager with spells at Northampton Town, and later Huddersfield Town and Arsenal, transforming both the Terriers and Gunners into the best sides of their eras. Universally acknowledged as the finest football manager of his generation, Herbert Chapman was also instrumental in introducing new tactics and formations to the game. When asked in later life to name his finest football XI from the past, Chapman picked at outside left one of the opponents on his debut – Fred Spiksley.

Wednesday maintained their highly impressive away form of four wins and a draw in five matches when they played at Bolton, where the highlight of a poor first half was the ball bursting. Davis's blistering shot put his side ahead and then he headed back a Spiksley cross for Wilson to hit a rasping volley that ended the scoring. Davis and Wilson also scored in the first home fixture of the season, as promoted Middlesbrough were beaten 2-0 in a Yorkshire derby which, by attracting a 20,000 crowd, showed that Wednesday had now established themselves in their new home.

A 3-0 defeat at Newcastle United ended Wednesday's unbeaten run, but after drawing 1-1 at home to Wolves, Wednesday advanced to top spot by beating Notts County at Trent Bridge 3-0, a Friday match played on the day of the annual Nottingham Goose Fair. All three goals were scored by Fred Spiksley. The first came on 28 minutes when he sped past Tom Prescott and hit a powerful shot beyond Harry Pennington. On the interval, Spiksley scored from close in and then in the 77th minute he and Malloch combined superbly before Spiksley, despite a tight angle, left Pennington with no chance as the ball flew into the net. Spiksley thus became the first player to score a hat trick in a Sheffield Wednesday away league match.

Following this success, Fred also netted the first goal 'with a brilliant shot' the following day, but Wednesday lost 4-2 at Liverpool, who having last played the previous Saturday were much fresher. Two of the Liverpool goals came from Sam Raybould, the First Division's top scorer that season with thirty-two goals.

Sheffield United then took revenge for their earlier defeat when Fred Priest scored the only goal of the game at Owlerton after his penalty had been saved in the 50th minute. Each side played without a key player as Crawshaw and Lipsham had been selected to represent the English League against the Irish League in Belfast.

The derby was, as usual, played at a frantic pace. In the first half, Wednesday were the superior side but were handicapped after a late foul on Spiksley left him injured for the remainder of the game. Davis also missed the first part of the second half while his fractured thumb was bandaged up. Towards the end of the game, tremendous Wednesday efforts to equalise produced some great saves by Foulke.

Harry Chapman helped Wednesday return to form by scoring the only goal at Grimsby and Wednesday then won their fifth away game of the season when they returned to Nottingham and beat Forest 4-1. However, after returning from a 2-1 defeat by Blackburn at Ewood Park on 15 November 1902, the Wednesday scorer, Mick Langley, said to Fred 'There's no championship for us this year'. Sunderland were favourites to retain their title, but started the campaign disastrously, and when Wednesday beat them 1-0 in late November it seemed their chance had gone. However, a strong run over Christmas and into January was to put the Roker Park club back into contention. Fred Spiksley played well in the victory against Sunderland, with J.H. Catton, writing in *Athletic News:* 'Spiksley was brisk, speedy and clever, and many years as he has played can yet hold his own with the best.'

Wednesday enjoyed a good spell over the festive period. They played superbly on 6 December 1902 to beat Everton 4-1 on a hard Owlerton pitch, when Wilson cracked an early shot off the underside of the bar and into the net before Jimmy Settle equalised. Wilson then drove a fast low shot beyond 'keeper George Kitchen. After Spiksley made it 3-1, Wilson prodded home his third goal after a dropping Spiksley corner led to a goalmouth scrimmage.

Promoted WBA had surprised everyone by challenging for top spot and it was a delighted Wednesday side who returned from Stoney Lane with both points in a thrilling 3-2 victory on 20 December 1902. With Lyall laid up with flu, Stubbs was back in goal and he saw his half backs force the home side back before Chapman opened the scoring on 10 minutes. In response, Albion worked energetically and with the wind at their backs, they pushed forward. Stubbs was forced to save smartly and the interval arrived with Wednesday still leading. However, the lead lasted only another 10 minutes but was restored following some brilliant wing play, when Spiksley flashed past Daniel Nurse and Jackie Kifford, before squaring the ball to Davis who beat Ike Webb. West Brom made sure there was to be no repeat performance as the Wednesday winger was hacked down and thereafter was unable to contribute anything worthwhile to events. However, Davis sealed the victory by netting from a superb Ferrier pass.

Back in the West Midlands, Wednesday lost at Aston Villa on Boxing Day but this was then followed by victories against Notts County, Aston Villa and Bolton Wanderers, in which nine goals were scored without conceding. The return match against Aston Villa on New Year's Day attracted a large crowd, as 28,000 spectators witnessed a brilliant performance from Wednesday, who won 4-0.

Against Bolton two days later, Davis scored all the goals in a 3-0 home win to become the third Wednesday player to score a hat-trick that season. Wednesday rose to second place and although Davis had clearly been the man-of-the-match, there was praise for Fred Spiksley by J.H. Catton in the *Athletic News*: 'Spiksley, the evergreen, showed the pace of youth and the art of experience.'

Davis also scored in Wednesday's following two away matches, but the team's inconsistency continued as Middlesbrough and Wolves both won 2-1. In between those two defeats, Wednesday, maintained their challenge with a 3-0 home win over Newcastle, as Chapman netted twice before Spiksley rounded off the scoring.

Wednesday stayed in second place and their ability to field almost an unchanged side throughout the season undoubtedly helped their championship bid. A strong team spirit and work ethic was naturally encouraged as a result, with the two full backs combining well together, the half back line playing superbly, supplemented up front by some great wing play by Davis and Spiksley, plus the steadily improving form of Wilson. Three players – Langley, Ruddlesdin and Wilson – played in all thirty-four League games in 1902–03, and four – Crawshaw, Ferrier, Malloch and Lyall – missed just one match each. Chapman missed just two games, as did Spiksley, who survived the season injury free. The other two mainstays, Layton and Davis, missed five and eight games respectively. The highest number of appearances by any other player who featured in 1902–03 season was five by right back Fred Thackeray, while eight players made one appearance each.

At home to Liverpool, Wednesday won a hard-fought battle 3-1, with Chapman scoring twice and Davis once. Wednesday, though, were to struggle in front of the goal over the following weeks. The side were therefore grateful to Langley when he netted twice from the spot at Owlerton to earn a 1-1 draw against Grimsby and a 1-0 victory against Nottingham Forest.

The following match saw Fred Spiksley missing only his second League game of the season: he was at Celtic Park for the Football League XI against the Scottish League XI. It was the second time he had played in the game, his first being a 1-1 draw at Goodison Park in 1894. Fred, who was joined by his teammate Harry Davis, hoped to repeat his 1898 performance on the same ground when England had crushed Scotland in a full international. Coming a decade after he had made his international debut, Fred's appearance for the Football League was, in this particular era of football, a truly remarkable achievement.

Before a crowd of 40,000, the Football League were grateful to the impressive Wolves 'keeper Tom Baddeley for keeping them level at the interval before the away side moved up a gear. When Davis sent the ball across to his Wednesday colleague, he left Drummond helpless to open the scoring. Raybould was set up by Spiksley for the second. Davis made it 3-0.

The reporter in the *Dundee Evening Post* was impressed, stating 'Spiksley is still a great player, fit for a place in any team'. Consequently, the Wednesday man harboured hopes of again representing his country when the full international with Scotland was held at Bramall Lane in April 1903.

The selectors called up seven of the successful Football League side to face Scotland. Davis was among them, but not Fred. Instead, the left wing place went to Liverpool's Jack Cox, a reliable winger who had previously played twice for England. England had left out a local hero who was in fine form and loved playing in a big game. Evidence of this can be seen in the fact that in nine matches for England and the Football League, Spiksley never finished on the losing side. Yet in this match, without Spiksley, England were beaten 2-1.

Fred returned to the Wednesday side at Sunderland, who had won nine and drawn two of their previous eleven League games. A crowd of 22,000 were inside Roker Park for a thriller which was decided when Wilson beat his Scottish compatriot Doig in the Sunderland goal with a magnificent 20-yard shot early in the second half. The first had seen neither side able to exert any authority, with few chances created in a fierce affair largely conducted in the middle of the pitch.

One behind, the home side pressed strongly, but Crawshaw, Ruddlesdin and Ferrier at half back played excellently, while in goal, the ever-reliable Lyall was alert as always. The crowd were angered by referee Mr Armitt, from Leek, when he disallowed a goal for a challenge on Lyall that saw the 'keeper bundled into the net. The referee was booed, heckled, jeered and sworn at and even pelted with oranges, the game only continuing after consultation between the referee and his linesmen. Wednesday moved to the top of the table. Not that the players had cause for wild celebrations, however, when some home fans later gathered outside the main stand on a road that was being repaired. Picking up stones, Sunderland supporters pelted the Wednesday team's wagonette as it departed Roker Park on its way to the railway station. It was a miracle that no-one was seriously injured as the players threw themselves on to the floor of the conveyance as rocks hammered off it. Those that missed smashed nearby house windows. The police, who also came under attack, smuggled the referee out of the exit on the opposite side of the ground. While the glaziers worked overtime, the fans' actions meant the FA ordered Sunderland's next home match, against near neighbours Middlesbrough, to take place away from Roker Park. It was, in fact, played at St James' Park, but it didn't affect handicap the Wearsiders, who won 2-1 to maintain their title challenge.

In the following game, Wednesday defeated Stoke 1-0 at home with debutant Tom Marrison scoring in a game conducted mainly in the middle of the park. The win meant Wednesday recorded a clean sheet for the fourth consecutive game. The following Saturday, with England facing Scotland, Wednesday travelled to Everton and were a goal down at the interval after Jimmy Settle netted. Langley again proved his worth with a precious equaliser from the spot, before the away side got lucky when a Bruce Rankin shot was fisted away on the line by a Wednesday defender without the referee noticing. The hard-earned point meant Fred could dream of adding to his medal collection.

Everton would end the 1902–03 season under investigation when the Blackburn Rovers secretary, Mr J. Walmsley, was suspended from football management after he was found to have unsuccessfully attempted to arrange for his club to beat the Toffees in their penultimate fixture. Rovers did win the fixture 3-0, but no action was taken against either side after it was decided Walmsley had acted on his own initiative. The early twentieth century saw a number of similar incidents, such as Billy Meredith unsuccessfully attempting to bribe Aston Villa captain Alex Leake in a title-deciding fixture in 1905.

Easter setbacks followed for Wednesday as they lost 4-0 and 1-0 respectively away to FA Cup finalists Bury and Derby County. Bury later crushed the Rams 6-0 in the final. An early injury to Davis at Derby, where the Wednesday side were missing flu victim Spiksley, proved to be too great a handicap. Lyall made some fine saves, but when he parried Yorke's shot on 40 minutes he was left helpless as Billy Richards followed up.

The chances of winning a first title appeared to have disappeared, but on the same day as the Derby defeat, Sunderland lost 2-0 away to already-relegated Bolton Wanderers. The Wearsiders then lost 5-2 at Nottingham Forest before defeating Middlesbrough in their penultimate match, played on the same day that Wednesday won their final League game by beating WBA 3-1 at Owlerton. Wilson made it 1-0 with a lovely rising shot on 8 minutes, only for Ted Smith to draw his side level before the home side were awarded a penalty. When Langley netted a huge roar rang out from the crowd who were delighted to see the home side go into the interval ahead.

The second half was a thriller and Wilson was denied by Joe Lowe in the Albion goal. A Spiksley corner then hit the bar. Albion weren't finished and when they broke quickly it was only through a superb Lyall save from Jim Stevenson in the final minutes that blocked an equaliser. It was described in the *Sheffield Telegraph* as 'one of the grandest things of its kind on this ground'. A flowing forward move ended with Spiksley scoring his side's third goal with a well-judged shot. Rapturously received by the crowd, it was the scorer's eighth goal of the season and just reward for a fine performance. Wilson's goal was his twelfth, but the top Wednesday scorer in the season was Davis with thirteen. Fred didn't know it, but he had scored his final competitive League goal for Wednesday in that match and, like many times before, it was a crucial effort. Years later Ambrose Langley said,

> Our last match was against WBA at and we won 3-1. All through the game the result was in doubt and it was one of our hardest games of the season. But you could always count on Fred Spiksley in the top

matches when the circumstances dictated that Wednesday had to win with so much at stake. Fred Spiksley played brilliantly that day and I can still see his performance that remains vividly in my mind.

Wednesday's victory meant Aston Villa's charge up the table, which had seen them collect twenty-four points from a possible thirty, had been in vain. Wednesday had finished a point ahead of Villa, but for them to collect the championship trophy they needed Newcastle to avoid defeat against Sunderland when the local rivals played each other the following Saturday at St James' Park. The Wearsiders needed to win if they were to finish top due to Wednesday's superior goal average.

Sunderland had drawn 0-0 against Newcastle earlier in the season at Roker Park, but had won on all three previous occasions when they had played at Newcastle. It was generally assumed in the press that Wednesday would miss out on the title because Newcastle would prefer their local rivals to win it. In 1925, Langley wrote: 'Throughout the country there was talk of a "squared" match in that Newcastle was going to let Sunderland win.'

The Wednesday board had arranged a West Country and South Wales tour at the completion of the League season and the team were playing Notts County in an exhibition match at the home of newcomers Plymouth Argyle when Newcastle met Sunderland. A special Plymouth Bowl was the beautiful trophy awarded to Wednesday after goals from Malloch and Ruddlesdin saw them win 2-0 before an appreciative crowd of 16,000.

Almost 400 miles north, the Tyne–Wear derby was tied 0-0 at half-time before a 26,500 crowd. Victory for Sunderland would give them their fifth title in twelve seasons but on 49 minutes, Robert McColl scored the home side's winner. McColl, who captained Scotland on the day of the Ibrox Disaster, scored thirteen goals in thirteen international appearances and later founded the R.S. McColl newsagents' chain. Defeat ended the most successful period in Sunderland's history.

When news of the result reached Owlerton during a Midland League match between Wednesday reserves and Worksop Town, the crowd's enthusiasm held up the game for several minutes. However, the news took longer to arrive in Devon. According to Andy Wilson, the party were 'having tea when someone dashed in saying that Newcastle had beaten Sunderland. We thought that it was a joke at first, but soon telegrams of congratulations started coming in, and we found that we were League champions.' In return, Wednesday quickly sent a telegram to Newcastle United thanking them for their 'true sportsmanship' in defeating their local rivals.

Wednesday's hosts were equally delighted. In the evening, Football League president J.J. Bentley presented the Plymouth Bowl to captain Mick Langley at a local theatre, and the Wednesday captain made a speech before the players returned to their hotel for a party.

Two days later, the League champions drew 2-2 at Bristol City before crossing the border to play Aberaman Athletic, the Welsh Cup finalists. The English side were too good for their hosts and, despite playing within themselves, won 6-0, with Fred scoring two, possibly three. Either way, they were to be the last Wednesday goals he scored.

The touring party arrived back in Sheffield on 29 April 1903 at 4.30pm. Many people began gathering around the Midland Station hours before their arrival and Police Commander Scott was forced to guarantee a strong police presence in order to ensure the crowd's enthusiasm didn't lead to any problems. Emerging from the station, the Wednesday contingent scrambled on to an Old Times coach and with the police band blasting out 'See, the Conquering Hero Comes', they headed up Commercial Street and High Street before alighting at the Carlton Restaurant for a slap-up meal. Enthusiastic crowds of workers lined the streets, having been given special dispensation to leave work for a few minutes.

The restaurant gathering was presided over by Wednesday board member Mr Whitley Fearnehough, who praised the title-winning team for their 'fair play and thrilling brand of football'. Mr A.J. Dickinson praised the players as being 'a credit to the club' and added: 'I am proud to take them anywhere.' Fearnehough reported that although the Football League didn't award medals to players of the title-winning team, the Wednesday players would be getting commemorative medals presented to them by the club, and everyone was looking forward to flying the League champions flag at Owlerton. Afterwards, the players adjourned to the Empire Theatre to see the Fred Karno company perform 'The Dandy Thieves' starring Fred Kitchen. The players were cheered to the rafters when they were taken on to the stage. A more formal celebration banquet was organized for 24 August 1903 and with skipper Langley absent, Fred Spiksley made a short well-received speech on behalf of the players.

Chapter 18

The Bell Starts to Toll

Injury ends Spiksley's illustrious first class career

Whatever else happened in his playing career, by capturing the League Championship Fred had achieved every honour available at the time, including Division One and Division Two titles, FA Cup success, and playing and scoring for England. He scored exactly 100 League goals for Wednesday and another 15 in the FA Cup. Add in his Football Alliance goals for Wednesday and his total reaches a staggering 170, making him the club's third highest scorer across all first team fixtures, behind Andrew Wilson (233) and John Fantham (193).

At the start of the twentieth century, few footballers – especially those at the height of the game – played on or past the mid-point of their fourth decade. One player who did was Billy Meredith who, as a winger like Fred, was never expected to chase back and whose responsibility was to concentrate on breaking down opposition defences. Fred had suffered a number of injuries in his career but there seemed every chance that in 1903, aged 33, he could go on playing for many seasons to come. He continued to enjoy training and stayed away from heavy drinking, which until relatively recently was a major curse for working-class footballers such as Paul Gascoigne, whose ability with the ball can be compared to Fred Spiksley's.

Both Wednesday and Fred would have been encouraged enough to believe that he would have a few more seasons in him, especially after coming so close to another England cap just earlier. Wednesday therefore awarded their star outside left a new contract for the 1903–04 season. In early August he reported for fitness training and ball practice and played for the first team against the reserves. The opposing right back, marking Fred, was a 22-year-old local lad, Joe Ryalls, who had made the first of what proved to be two Wednesday appearances the previous season.

Receiving the ball, the Wednesday winger set off along the touchline when Ryalls attempted a tackle and somehow the players' legs became entangled. Fred's legs were crossed placing great strain on his knee joint and ligaments and so great was the downward pressure on his knee that it caused a complete dislocation and severe ligament damage. When club physician Doctor Lockwood examined the injury the prognosis wasn't good: if Fred was to have any chance of ever playing again he would need prolonged rest and recuperation. His place at outside left instead went to Georgie Simpson, from Jarrow. He played well and Wednesday started the season in fine form.

Patience was never one of Fred's virtues and his early attempt at a comeback in the Wednesday reserves ended almost before it had started. The doctors vetoed any further attempts for the foreseeable future. The Wednesday directors, though, were keen to know when he would be returning as the club were paying him the maximum weekly wage of £4.

Meanwhile, Fred was selected to play against Corinthians FC in a benefit game for Bill Layton on 29 December 1903, but lasted just 5 minutes; his knee was unequal to the strain. Layton, who is the great-grandfather of Michael Knighton, the former Carlisle United owner and Manchester United director, made over 300 appearances for Wednesday and twice won the League title and the FA Cup once in 1907. He was unlucky to be in competition for the right back spot in the England side with Blackburn Rovers' Bob Crompton, a brilliant player, whose 41 caps was a record until it was beaten by Billy Wright in 1952.

Over the next few months the pain in Fred's knee eased and with inflammation and swelling reduced, he could walk unaided. His right knee joint, though, was still unstable and playing football remained unlikely for the foreseeable future. His last competitive match for Sheffield Wednesday was for the reserve team against Gainsborough Trinity reserves on 26 September 1903, scoring after 4 minutes in a 7-1 success. However, after playing impressively, he was forced to leave the field early in the second half 'owing to the failure of his knee, which had given way on several occasions'. (*Sheffield Telegraph*) It was also reported that as Spiksley left the field 'he could not hide his frustration'.

On 1 May 1904 he received a letter from Arthur J. Dickinson informing him that the club he had represented since 1891 were terminating his contract. It was a bitter blow, but there is rarely room for sentiment in football and it cannot have come as too great a surprise that the club had decided to let him go, especially as without him, Wednesday had retained the Division One title, finishing three points clear of Manchester City with Simpson scoring six times in twenty-five League appearances. The title had been won because of the magnificent Wednesday defence, who in thirty-four matches conceded just twenty-eight League goals.

Fred left convinced that if it hadn't been for his unfortunate accident, he would've continued playing for Wednesday well into his forties. His departure saddened his colleague Mick Langley who, commenting in 1925, said:

> For what he did for Wednesday, the club ought to erect a monument in his honour. Fred could start at the halfway line, stop dead twice,

and go on before he centred. Opponents were out manoeuvred. They would run full tilt, Fred would stop, and before they had pulled up and recovered he would be off again. Spiksley used to play the ball with the outside of his foot, pushing it along, and when he centred he crossed the ball so it swerved, not inwards towards the goal, but outwards towards the advancing inside forward. He never placed corner kicks too near the goal. Defences had to come out. Fred Spiksley made Wednesday.

Fred now needed alternative employment and income. Sporting papers were advertising for professional footballers and when he wrote to several clubs he was buoyed to receive a number of replies indicating they'd be happy to employ him on the maximum wage. He was then left stunned when he discovered that Wednesday expected any new club to pay a transfer fee of £250 for him. It was common knowledge that his knee was injured and so no club were ever going to take such a gamble if they were also expected to pay a fee. Wednesday had not only dismissed him, but also stopped him from earning a living as a footballer. Such was the ruthlessness of football in Edwardian times.

Archie Goodall was player/manager at Glossop North End and he told Fred that Wednesday would have to drop their £250 transfer fee. Wednesday refused to budge and so Fred decided to attend the Football League's AGM and put his case directly to the management committee. In the meantime, his brother William, who had several different enterprises (including an under-the-counter betting operation through one of his shops in Trinity Street in Gainsborough), gave him a chance to earn some. Fred was in his element and he received a weekly wage for running the illegal trade.

Fred attended the Football League AGM at Manchester's Midland Hotel in June 1904 to put his case for a free transfer, which was granted. Having overcome one obstacle, another was quickly placed in his way when Goodall informed him that he must undergo a rigorous examination. If this proved successful, the former Derby County player, brother of John Goodall, would approach Glossop's wealthy owner, Samuel Hill-Wood, about financing his contract.

Glossop had been elected to the Football League in 1898 and had immediately won promotion. This proved to be the height of their journey and immediate relegation was followed by a series of disappointing seasons culminating in seventeenth place (second from bottom), in Division Two in 1903–04. The club survived re-election and Hill-Wood gave Goodall the job of rebuilding the side, starting with sorting-out a leaky defence, followed by the recruiting of an experienced player with a cool head to galvanise a misfiring forward line. This was going to be difficult as in addition to not having a good side, Glossop's location in the High Peak area of the Peak District means it wasn't exactly the most hospitable place in the winter. Attracting good players was a problem. Praying for Fred Spiksley's knee to recover and then getting him fully fit was perhaps Goodall's best chance of reviving his new club.

There was consequently dismay all round when Fred failed his fitness test; his knee still required rest. Goodall was reluctant to throw in the towel just yet and successfully persuaded his chairman to give Fred a contract on the basis that he would soon be fit and would move permanently to Glossop. Fred thus became a Glossop player on Thursday, 1 September 1904, and made his debut in the first game of the season for his new club on 3 September 1904 at Anfield, where Liverpool, First Division champions in 1902, were back in Division Two after being relegated two seasons later. The game saw Fred up against Ted Doig, whom Liverpool signed from Sunderland in the summer of 1904. The 'keeper was beaten twice as Glossop grabbed a point in a 2-2 draw. At right back in the Liverpool side was David Murray, who later enlisted at the start of the First World War for the Argyll and Sutherland Highlanders, and was killed, aged just 32, in Loos, France, on 10 December 1915.

Glossop lined up as follows:

Frank Davies, William Synott, Willie Orr, H. Maginnis, John Boden, J. Brown, Leon Gall, T. Cairns, Archie Goodall, Eddie Murphy, Fred Spiksley.

Two-one up, Glossop missed out on a point when Joe Hewitt scored in the final minute of the match. In the combined Everton/Liverpool programme for the weekend of 10 September 1904, it was reported 'Fred Spiksley is light of other days, and his usefulness is much diminished'.

Fred was missing when Glossop drew 0-0 at home to Burslem Port Vale before a 4,000 crowd, and was also absent in the following three games that were all lost as Glossop dropped to the foot of the table. Fred returned for the sixth game of the season on Saturday 8 October 1904 at Chesterfield.

This time the Glossop lineup included: Davies, Orr, Synott, Phillips, Boden, Maginnis, Gall, Cairns, Brown, Murphy and Spiksley.

The away side were one ahead when Spiksley scored an easy tap-in to double the score in a match that ended 2-1. Victory came at a cost, though, as the outside left, having enjoyed no protection from the referee, had been badly kicked throughout the match and was forced to sit out the next game that Glossop won 3-1 against Bradford City. The winger returned at Lincoln City where Goodall also played. Glossop were beaten 3-0, but there was enough in their display and Fred's performance to suggest they could comfortably survive come the end of the season. A week later, Glossop beat non-league Nantwich away in the FA Cup third qualifying round 2-1, with both goals made by the outside left.

Four games, two wins, one goal scored and two goals made. It was an impressive start, but Fred wasn't happy as it was clear his pace had gone and he was going to have to rely on a more measured, relaxed approach. So when he received a letter from Samuel Hill-Wood stating he was suspended because he had failed to relocate permanently to Glossop, Fred was quite philosophical, believing Glossop wanted rid of him because of his performances. He wrote back to the club requesting they forward him his final week's wages. Instead, he was informed he was getting nothing as he was in breach of his contract and in consequence, his registration documents were being retained. This effectively meant he was unable to play for another club.

Apart from his two years working in Sheffield, Fred had lived in Gainsborough his whole life. His family were still there and it would be possible for him to work for his brother's turf accountancy business during the week and then play football at the weekend. There were also opportunities to attend the Doncaster and Lincoln racecourses. In truth, Fred was never going to move permanently to Glossop, but had hoped to do enough on the field to demonstrate that his services were worth retaining even without keeping his earlier commitment. The *Glossop Chronicle* reported that he had been sacked, which led Fred to conclude it was his performances rather than his failure to move from Lincolnshire that had seen his contract terminated.

Nevertheless, it would now be difficult for him to keep playing football as Glossop had retained his registration papers. Fred thought again of applying to the Football League for a free transfer, but soon put that to the back of his mind while he continued to work for his brother William. Fortuitously, early in 1905, Fred bumped into the respected Blackburn referee John Lewis, who was also an influential member of the Football League management committee. When the conversation turned to the documents being retained by Glossop, Lewis promised to raise the matter at the next League meeting.

A few weeks later, Fred received confirmation that he had been granted a second free transfer. Despite this, he played one more League game for Glossop, featuring at inside right when North End played at Grimsby, just forty miles from Gainsborough, on 25 March 1905. The home side won 3–0 and according to the Glossop club historian Tom Sutcliffe, it's possible that Fred's appearance at Cleethorpes was made 'as an amateur'. In return for their expenses, owner Samuel Hill-Wood was known for shipping players in to 'do him a favour'. Glossop didn't do too badly in the 1904–05 season and went on to finish in twelfth place in Division Two and thus avoided the need to apply for re-election.

Chapter 19

Lobbying at Elland Road

Spiksley's role in the development of first class football in Leeds

Following the end of his Glossop contract, Fred Spiksley needed to continue playing, having no wish to return to the newspaper trade and not having sufficient to retire on.

In August 1904 a new club had been formed: Leeds City. The West Yorkshire public had demonstrated little interest in football as they much preferred rugby league, with 30,000 spectators watching Batley play Warrington in the 1903 Northern League Challenge Cup final. Rugby league's domination extended to the local playing fields, forcing football clubs into ground-sharing arrangements with rugby league clubs who dictated terms and fixture lists. Where disputes occurred, football usually lost out. The round ball, however, remained popular among young people, especially as playing in the street was easier.

Hunslet Athletic had been Leeds's premier football club but, after the West Yorkshire League (WYL) was disbanded in 1897, they had joined the Sheffield and Hallamshire (S&H) League. They did well and also made good headway in the FA Amateur Cup. But when their ground lease was lost and they were unable find a suitable alternative venue to satisfy the S&H, Hunslet disbanded. Club officials were later present at the Griffin Hotel at which everyone voted to set up a new football club in the largest English city without one.

Leeds City joined the FA and negotiated with Bentley's Brewery to lease Elland Road football ground. A new group of players were enlisted to play in the WYL and on 1 September 1904, a 2-2 draw was recorded in the first ever game, away to Morley. Two days later, the first home match was played at Hunslet Rugby Club's Wellington Road ground with visitors Altofts winning 2-1. On 15 October, Leeds City played their first game at Elland Road against Hull City. In early November, club representatives signed a one-year lease at an annual rent of £75 with an option to buy the land for £4,500 in spring 1905.

However, Leeds City failed to set the world alight and league fixtures were treated with scant respect. Games were cancelled at the last minute and they were eliminated from the local Hospitals Cup. Yet none of this mattered to the club's executive, who were firmly set on joining the Football League. This appeared to be a pipe dream, except for the fact the Football League hierarchy were desperate to extend their influence into the West Riding following newly-formed Bradford City's successful election into the League for the 1903–04 season. Burnley director Charles Sutcliffe, a Rawtenstall lawyer, was the most powerful man on the Football League management committee and in 1903, his proposal to extend the League to twenty clubs in each division was agreed upon and was set to start two years later.

Leeds City now needed to demonstrate to other Football League members that their application was good enough to justify election. With its new 'Scratching Shed' stand and accommodation for 5,000 spectators under a 30-foot high wooden barrel roof, Elland Road was clearly good enough to stage Football League matches, especially as the new club had the valuable option to buy the freehold. Additionally, wealthy wholesale clothier Mr Norris Hepworth had agreed to become the club's first chairman and principal benefactor.

However, the indifferent quality of the playing staff meant gates were poor, which fed doubts about whether professional football could compete against rugby league. Determined to demonstrate that there was an appetite for football, the Leeds City executive began organising a series of high-profile exhibition games against seven top sides that were generously paid to play at Elland Road. The games needed to be on a Saturday, which created problems as most League clubs were already fully booked up. In response, Leeds City invited clubs who had been eliminated from the FA Cup and were without a League fixture.

West Bromwich Albion were the first side paid for their services in a game arranged for 4 February 1905. Further games against Sheffield United, Derby County, Preston, Leicester Fosse, Lincoln City and non-league Hull City were arranged. What was now needed were good quality professional footballers, who were almost impossible to obtain in January and February as there few available and there was no possibility of senior clubs releasing players during the season. With no scouting network, Leeds City also had no hope of identifying young amateur footballing talent in time for the big games.

Two professional players were available who might help: Fred Spiksley and Tommy Morren, formerly of Sheffield United and England, who was just 5ft 5in tall and under 10 stones. Fred agreed to a 'pay as you play deal' of £3 a game and it's likely that Morren signed a similar agreement. Fred's excitement was boosted by the warm greeting he had received in the local press and his knee had healed beyond expectations. His confidence fell when he realised that Leeds

City had just two professionals. It was going to be tough to compete against some of England's best sides.

The Leeds City committee were delighted that Fred had accepted their offer and were keen to cash in on his popularity with players, coaches, committeemen, directors, referees, League and FA officials. Hepworth asked him to greet visiting officials and dignitaries, introduce them to the Leeds City committee and generally highlight Elland Road's impressive facilities. Fred happily accepted the new role for which, presumably, he was paid, particularly as it gave him the opportunity to meet and chat about old times with such notables as Billy Bassett and Steve Bloomer.

West Bromwich Albion were in Division Two when they faced Leeds City before an excited crowd of 3,000 people, who paid gate receipts of over £50, which easily covered the visitors' match fee.

Leeds City side: Chaffer, Bintcliffe, Burton, Storey, Hunt, Dixon, Morren, G. Howard, F. Howard, Nelson, Spiksley

On a sticky pitch, the away side paid Leeds the compliment of fielding their first team. With the wind behind them, the home side's enthusiasm initially helped them push back the League side. But after that Albion dominated. The game was goalless at the break, but in the second half Leeds City collapsed and were heavily beaten 5-0. Afterwards, Morren left his new club by mutual consent.

Fred Spiksley was very disappointed when he met up with Billy Bassett, now an Albion director, and Harry Keys, the Baggies chairman. The West Midlands club had also been through some difficult financial times and had recently survived a banker's writ for moneys that were owed. The pair had set up a fundraising committee and done everything they could to put the club back on an even keel. Fred and Billy chatted about their England experiences before the former broached the question of Leeds City's application to join the Football League. Winks from Billy and Harry had Fred convinced there was at least one tick in the box.

On 18 February, Leeds City welcomed an under-strength Sheffield United side to Elland Road. The party did include two great personalities from the reserves in Bill "Fatty" Foulke and William "Cocky" Bennett as well as first team captain Ernest Needham, trainer George Waller, director Joseph Tomlinson and club secretary John Nicholson. All were strong characters whose views were respected by the Cutlers' board of directors, who would decide whether to back Leeds City's application to join the Football League.

Another 3,000 crowd witnessed a match that was played in atrocious conditions and in which Hunt scored a last-minute equaliser for the home side in a 2-2 draw, with G. Howard scoring the other Leeds goal.

Hunt also scored against Leicester Fosse, but the home side lost 5-1 before a crowd of around 1,000. Leeds City then lost their remaining four fixtures against Hull City (5-2), Lincoln City (3-1), Derby County (2-0) and Preston (4-1). Fred Spiksley didn't score in any of the matches, but was one of only four players to play in all seven games, the others being Bintcliffe and the Howard brothers. The former Wednesday winger may have been disappointed at the standard of the side he had played in, but he was pleased that his knee hadn't given way.

The exhibition games, attended by an average of 1,850 spectators each, meant Leeds City had a backlog of West Yorkshire League (WYL) fixtures to complete and when the season ended, the new club still had five outstanding fixtures – it was a small wonder they weren't kicked out of the WYL, in which they finished in eleventh place. It appears that Fred actually played twice in the WYL, scoring a penalty when Beeston Hill Parish Church were beaten 5-1, and also scoring in a 2-2 draw against Upper Armley Christ Church.

Despite their lack of success, the Leeds City committee remained enthusiastic. On 5 June 1905, Leeds City AFC became a limited company, with £10,000 capital put forward by the club's benefactors. In the meantime, Fred Spiksley departed after it was reported he had 'helped convince club officials that entry into the Football League was not just a dream'.

This proved to be true, as with twenty-five votes from the current clubs, Leeds City were elected to the extended Second Division. Chesterfield manager, Gilbert Gillies, came to Leeds as boss and put together a team in which only one local player, Charles Morgan, was among the fourteen professionals recruited.

In their first ever Football League game in September 1905, against Bradford City at Valley Parade, a crowd of 15,000-plus witnessed a 1-0 success for the home XI. In Leeds's first home League match, a 6,800 crowd saw WBA collect both points in a 2-0 victory. On 23 September, Leeds beat Hull City 3-1 before an Elland Road crowd of 13,654 and 22,000 watched the home derby with Bradford City in December 1905.

Leeds City averaged 9,000 spectators at home in the 1905–06 season. Meanwhile, the average gate for the Leeds rugby league club fell from 9,000 to 5,600. Football had replaced rugby league as the number one spectator sport in Leeds. Fred Spiksley had played a small part in making that happen and although Leeds City went out of business in October 1919, the subsequent rise of Leeds United has meant rugby league rarely matches football in terms of attendances.

Chapter 20

London Calling

Chelsea, Southern United and saving Johnny Allgood's skin

In early April 1905, Fred Spiksley successfully responded to an *Athletic News* advert for the post of secretary-manager with Southern United Athletic Company Limited. Established the previous summer by eight shareholder directors with modest incomes, the club believed that with half a million local residents in South East London there would be enough football fans to justify their endeavours as they set out to build for long-term success. A successful application to the South Eastern Football League (SL) saw the new club placed in Division Two, where at the end of the season Southern finished in bottom place.

The search for a suitable playing home had led to 'Brown's Field', which is still used today. King Edward VII had regularly gone shooting at the ground when he was Prince of Wales and it was reputed that W.G. Grace had frequently played cricket there in the 1890s. Most people reached the ground by walking up the hill from Nunhead Railway Station, before turning into an alleyway that led to the backs of terraced housing in Ivydale Road and the ground entrance. Brown's Field was well drained and the football pitch was one of the largest in the country at 117 yards long and 75 yards wide. It was well served by buses and was only a short walk from New Cross Gate station, which today is one of the stations that bring football fans to Millwall's ground. In 1904, however, Millwall (Athletic) played their football north of the river, on the Isle of Dogs.

Despite a poor first season, the club's general secretary William Moody achieved some success over the summer of 1905 in recruiting new shareholders and it was reported that there were now 911 issued shares and £236 had been raised towards the 1905–06 season's running costs. The hope now was that Southern United would be able to recruit a professional playing staff and move up the table. Southern United had actually performed reasonably well in 1904–05, particularly as they had competed against professional teams, including the reserve sides of Woolwich Arsenal and Tottenham Hotspur. Southern's problem had been stopping goals and they conceded seventy-eight, the division's highest figure.

As well as playing, Fred believed his new post would involve coaching and recruiting players: an ideal opportunity to play out the remainder of his career, while developing the new skills required to subsequently earn a living out of football. His weekly wages were the maximum £4 then allowed in football and he also collected a £10 signing-on fee. On 2 June 1905, he left Gainsborough for his new role and rented a semi-detached house not far from the Brockley Jack public house in Lewisham Borough.

Fred was in a good mood when he arrived at work the following day, but as he settled down the former Sheffield United forward Jack Almond entered the room and Fred's mood darkened when Almond told him he was Southern United's football coach. Almond's appointment was a big blow and it was clear that Fred's new role of secretary-manager was essentially a desk-based job that even included taking weekly minutes at board meetings. Fred certainly had the skills to do the job. However, the Wednesday man had no wish to be at the beck and call of the directors. He had wrongly assumed that that he would write a few letters and deal with transfer forms before leaving himself time to organise coaching for the players. He also loved the fresh air and an office job would prevent him following his racing passion on the courses throughout south-east England. Fred, though, had no alternative but to do his best as he had signed a contract for the new post. He was cheered by news that he was to be made team captain and in such a role he could expect to be consulted on players and transfer targets.

Over the summer, Fred was rushed off his feet as he sorted out the club's administration systems and, together with Moody and Almond, assembled a squad of professional footballers. They included former Bradford City 'keeper Fred Mearns, who later played for Barnsley in the 1910 FA Cup final. James Whitehouse had been a member of the Aston Villa double-winning side in 1896–97, while centre half Micky Sullivan was a well-travelled professional fresh from a season at Brighton and Hove Albion. Centre forward Thomas McCairns had also previous played for Brighton. Almond recruited Fulham's John Holmes and when West Kirby's John Wood did well in a trial match, Fred Spiksley used his influence to get him a playing contract after which he took him under his wing.

In addition to their SL programme, Southern United joined the United League midweek competition where it was mandatory to play full-strength teams. The local press commented favourably on Southern's ambitions. To add to the growing excitement, the ground was much improved with a covered stand on the enclosed side erected.

However, just before the season started, there was a shock when Major John Sayers was appointed as 'team trainer'. Almond quit in disgust. All the hard work that had been put in appeared to have been wasted. Within half an hour of his arrival, the Royal Military College man had destroyed the happy atmosphere that had been generated among players and staff. The players soon began complaining about Sayers's coaching methods and his dictatorial attitude towards them. Fred later commented on how he was glad to get away from Sayers when he left Southern United.

Southern began their SL fixtures with a 2-2 draw at Leyton where Fred Spiksley was given a wonderful reception when he led his side out. The day was a great success for Wood, who scored twice, the first of which was created for him by Spiksley. The former Wednesday player was on the score sheet in another 2-2 draw the following week in a friendly match at Loftus Road against Shepherd's Bush. He also scored as his side beat Reading reserves 2-0 in an away SL fixture.

There was delight when the draw for the FA Cup second qualifying round meant Chelsea would travel to Southern on 28 October 1905. The Stamford Bridge side had Bill Foulke in goal, but he was ruled out through injury, as was Fred Spiksley. Chelsea won 1-0 but the losers had the satisfaction of being the better side on the day. There was also the added bonus that the match had attracted a crowd of over 7,000.

Chelsea had only been formed in early 1905 when Gus Mears announced he would spend £100,000 on transforming Stamford Bridge, which he bought in 1904, into one of Britain's finest football stadiums. The ground had previously been used for many recreational activities, including circuses and the 1896 Amateur Athletics Association (the three A's) championships, where Arthur Wharton sensationally broke the 100 yards world record. Mears's wealth and ambition meant that although they had yet to kick a ball, Chelsea were elected in the summer of 1905 to the extended Football League. London now had three League clubs in Woolwich Arsenal, Clapton Orient and Chelsea. Slowly but surely, the North's dominance was being challenged. Stamford Bridge was situated in a working class area, but the wealthier parts of the adjoining boroughs of Chelsea and Kensington were within easy walking distance and this soon resulted in the new club attracting a number of showbiz personalities. A spirit of adventure and fun infected those who attended Chelsea's early games.

Finding players was difficult and Mears offered a role to Fred Spiksley in his new set-up by asking him to secretly seek out top young talent and persuade them to sign for Chelsea. It would have initially been a conflict of interests, as Spiksley would have been seeking out players for Southern United at the same time. The role wasn't revealed until Spiksley's *Thomson's Weekly* articles in 1920.

Initially, Mears accepted the England international's advice without demur. When Scottish-born Tommy McDermott was wanted by Dundee, the decision was taken to let him go as Fred Spiksley was convinced that his rival for the inside forward role, Jimmy Windridge, was, as it subsequently proved, a better player. However, he later found that Mears's other business interests made it difficult for Fred to get sufficient time to discuss with the Chelsea owner the merits of future stars. In the summer of 1907, Fred wanted Chelsea to buy Harold Halse from Southend United for £200. When the Londoners failed to carry out the deal, the player was sold to Manchester United where he achieved huge success in a fine side and later played for Aston Villa before finally ending up at Chelsea in 1913.

Earlier, Fred had mentioned two Crystal Palace stars to Chelsea: George Woodger and Charlie Wallace. He had made enquiries and knew both players were available for a combined price of £100. Although the Chelsea board accepted his judgement, his advice was overlooked as it was considered unwise to spend money at a time when they were improving the stadium. Besides, the first team were already doing well. Soon after, however, Chelsea proposed buying the two 'Ws', but by now the fee for each player had risen considerably. In May 1907, Aston Villa purchased Wallace for £500 and he had a great career there. He was still good enough to attract a fee of £1,000 when Oldham Athletic purchased him in 1921. Woodger joined Oldham Athletic and played for England in 1911.

Two weekends after the Chelsea cup-tie, Fred Spiksley scored twice as his side overturned a three-goal deficit to beat West Ham reserves 4-3 at Brown's Ground. On Saturday, 6 January 1906, Fred scored his side's goal in a 3-1 defeat at Portsmouth. It proved to be his final piece of action for Southern United, as he was then sacked from his post. Joining him out of work was trainer John Sayers, a move greeted with pleasure by the players.

Southern United were in fifth place in the SL, but behind the scenes their finances were in disarray and the following Monday it was announced the club had folded, leaving the playing and ground staff without jobs and owing a substantial sum to a number of creditors. The Southern United directors had gambled in thinking big, and without the resources to match their ambitions, the whole affair had been a disaster. Instead of becoming a second Chelsea, Southern United were insolvent and out of business.

Fred Spiksley was out of work, but there was consolation in that he had played six months of football without his knee failing him. Consequently, several managers were keen to offer him a playing role, and in the days following his departure from Southern United he began to consider his options. He also contacted Derby County to recommend that they should sign John Wood, who did well for the Rams over the next fifteen months before signing for Manchester City. Fred would have expected to be paid for finding the East Midlanders a new player.

Just north of London, organised football in Watford started around 1870. In 1906 Watford's player-manager was John Goodall, Fred's former England colleague. With his team struggling, 'Honest John' offered Fred a contract at Watford and he was happy to sign for what proved to be his last playing role.

Watford were out of the FA Cup and struggling in the Southern League with thirteen points from twenty matches. Their new signing replaced Kelly on Saturday, 10 February 1906 against a Southampton side unbeaten in ten matches. Getting Spiksley to play for Watford was welcomed by the *Watford Observer*: 'John Goodall is to come out of retirement to play at inside left in partnership with the former international Fred Spiksley. What memories these two old internationals conjure up! There is still enough football in these men to make a clever and effective wing partnership.'

Watford: Biggar, Aston, Lindsay, Main, McCartney, Richardson, Badenoch, Turner, Eames, Goodall and Spiksley.

Scottish 'keeper Billy Biggar had a tremendous punch and kick, but was prone to a rush of blood. Charlie Aston was well known for his swearing, which displeased the Watford directors because many of the club's followers were female.

Local lad Joe Brooks was a former amateur cycling champion who would later fetch Watford's first ever three-figure sum when he moved to Sheffield United for £275. David McCarthy (or McCartney) was Watford's regular centre half and penalty taker. He later joined Chelsea, thus providing an opportunity for George Fyfe, who signed from Hibernian in the summer of 1905, and the solid centre half would give sterling service for five seasons. Jack Richardson usually played left half but, as a utility player, often filled a variety of positions. George Badenoch, quick and skilful, was Watford's youngest first team player and sadly died in the First World War. Peter Turner was to finish the 1905–06 season as Watford's top scorer. Centre forward Wally Eames had initially played as an amateur before turning professional in 1903 and joining Spurs in May 1906. During the season, Watford recruited Jock Foster from Rotherham to replace Eames and the new man proved to be a prolific goalscorer. His performances led to a record transfer fee to Sunderland. Other Watford players in 1905–06 were William Roland Brown and utility defender Billy Lindsay.

Goodall and Spiksley's inclusion created great interest and despite suffering from flu-like symptoms, Fred felt obliged to play against Southampton when a wiser man would have stayed in bed. A crowd of 7,250 fans were inside the Cassio Ground and were to leave thrilled as Watford won 4-1. Goodall quickly had his team passing the ball along the ground and keeping possession. Spiksley then put his side ahead with a powerful shot, maintaining his record of scoring for every club he played for.

The new signing continued to play impressively, sprinting with the ball at his feet and constantly sending over dangerous crosses. The away side were forced to try to kick the veteran out of the game and he might have scored a second, only to be upended from behind as he tricked his way through to face the Saints 'keeper. Fred refused to take the resulting spot kick, which instead was dispatched by McCartney.

After such a marvellous display, the *Watford Observer* gleefully reported that Goodall and Spiksley had demonstrated how 'the football of today is not in the same class as it was ten years ago. Here were two men long past their prime easily beating the younger generation. News of Spiksley's death has been greatly exaggerated.' Fred was delighted. 'For the first in a long time I felt that warm inner glow of satisfaction in a job well done. Suddenly Watford felt like home.' He noted that pre-match, many wise heads had predicted that Southampton's young side would dominate.

Watford faced Reading away the following weekend and lost 3-1. Fred Spiksley received heavy treatment from the Reading defenders. Afterwards, he examined the big black and blue bruises down his thighs and legs and complained about being more roughly treated in two games for Watford than at any time at Wednesday.

On 24 February 1906 a snowstorm failed to prevent 3,600 fans from watching Watford play Northampton Town at home. Latecomers missed a repeat of Fred's first against Southampton when he scored within a minute. Northampton then scored twice, but Turner equalised just before the interval. On the resumption, Spiksley nodded home from close range to make it 3-2. Eames made it 4-2 and, following a successful Northampton penalty, Spiksley completed his hat-trick in a 5-3 win. The game had been a fast, thrilling one and while Fred was clearly the man-of-the-match, every player had played well. Watford's improving form continued as they beat Brighton 2-1 in the United League, with goals from Eames and Turner. Fred Spiksley and the Brighton right back Chris Buckley provided great opposition for each other and the pair shook each other's hands afterwards.

Two consecutive 0-0 draws, away to West Ham and at home to Fulham, maintained Watford's climb up the table. The latter game was watched by 7,500 spectators, among whom were some only interested in what other supporters had in their pockets. London pickpockets had noted how Watford's crowds had increased. Pick-pocketing was common across all London grounds and now many Watford fans were to experience having their watches and wallets stolen without them realising it. After being starved of the ball in the previous two games, Fred was left disappointed when this was also the case away to QPR.

Watford lost 6-0. The following match, Fred created Watford's goal against Bristol Rovers as Turner scored in a 1-1 draw.

New Brompton then beat Watford 2-0, after which the *Watford Observer* reported that Fred Spiksley had played disappointingly, with two of his corner kicks having gone straight out for goal kicks. The following match, on Good Friday, the outside left was unlucky when two of his shots hit the Luton crossbar in a tense, keenly competitive derby match that ended 1-1. Fred did get on the score sheet away to Portsmouth the following day, but Watford lost 4-2.

On Easter Monday, Fred Spiksley played what proved to be the final competitive game of his career as Watford played very poorly and were beaten 1-0 at home to Brighton. The local newspapers were scathing in their criticism, describing it as a complete fiasco. Fred hadn't tasted victory now in eight games: in his eleven Southern League games he had won twice and lost five. Watford were again facing relegation, although as it transpired, the League was later extended to twenty clubs and so this would have been avoided whatever the club's final position. Spiksley was not selected for the final three matches of the season in which Watford took five points to finish in fourteenth place.

Unsurprisingly, there was no new contract offer and Fred, realising the vast number of games he had played had taken its toll, bit the bullet and retired from playing professional football.

John Goodall remained as Watford manager but, following an unsuccessful season in 1909–10, he was sacked. A notice in the *Athletic News* advertised the post. Fred Spiksley and Watford club captain Harry Kent were the two who applied. Both were interviewed for the post and Watford took up a reference from the Wednesday club secretary, Arthur Dickinson, who wrote, 'I can say with confidence that you will not find yourselves a better judge of a professional football player. If you can get him to give up his on-course horseracing activities you will have secured an excellent football manager.'

This reference did Fred no favours. He was asked at the interview about whether his racing passion might interfere with his managerial responsibilities. Fred replied: 'Well, gentlemen, I would very much like to take up this position. But what I do in my private life is no business of my employers. I am not prepared to forfeit my racing. If you wish me to do so, then, gentlemen, I shall have to say goodbye right now.'

Harry Kent was appointed, but only after initially agreeing to submit his team selection to the Watford officials for approval, something Fred certainly wouldn't have tolerated. Kent managed Watford for sixteen seasons and took them into the Football League.

Whilst it was a disappointing end to his professional playing career, Fred retired after having achieved every major honour in the game. With approximately 350 goals to his name playing at outside left, he was certainly the greatest player in his position from the 1890s and many who saw him play maintained he was the greatest outside left the game had ever seen.

This record was made even more remarkable because Fred didn't play for the glamorous clubs of the time. At his peak, Spiksley would have been first choice for any side and if he *had* played for Aston Villa, West Bromwich Albion or Sunderland, he would have captured more titles and medals. However, playing for Wednesday gave Spiksley the opportunity to develop legendary status, and although opportunities for top honours were severely limited, when they did come along, he took them.

Chapter 21

Treading The Boards with Charlie Chaplin

Touring the music halls with Fred Karno

Fred Spiksley now desperately needed alternative employment. He had been a major football entertainer and so when he saw an advertisement for a footballer to perform on the stage, he jumped at the chance. It would lead to him working for the inimitable circus and pantomime king Fred Karno, and performing with Charlie Chaplin.

Fred Karno was born Frederick John Westcott in Exeter on 26 March 1866. His father's work as a cabinet-maker meant the family moved frequently before settling in Nottingham, where Fred combined school with work in a lace factory, putting his 2 shillings (10p) weekly wage into the family purse. This upbringing stood him in good stead as it taught him the principles of tenacity, honesty and the value of money.

Despite his father arranging a plumber's apprenticeship, Fred absconded one day to watch an acrobatic troupe perform in the big top of a travelling circus. The spellbound youngster then ran away to join a travelling circus and his hard work and sheer dedication to become an accomplished acrobat would eventually pay off when he made his breakthrough on the flying trapeze. This meant he no longer had to undertake less glamorous roles such as handing out leaflets and banging a drum to encourage people to 'roll up and see the greatest show on earth'.

Westcott loved the great outdoors, animals, clowns, grease paint, colour and magical atmosphere of the Big Top. He was intent on being a major star and eventually turned solo in a circus act on the horizontal and double trapeze. This saw him combine being a ringmaster and clown, while also working daily on twenty shows of sketches and slapstick comedy.

Following a highly successful season at the Scotia Music Hall, Glasgow, Fred, now calling himself Karno, toured with his acrobatic troupe on the continent, appearing in major circuses and shows in Cologne, Amsterdam and Brussels. Back home, Fred teamed up with Sewell and Tysall, performing across the South East where their slapstick knockabout routines raised the roof.

In 1894, the trio appeared for a week at Barnard's Music Hall, Portsmouth, on a bill topped by boxer Jem Mace, whose sudden illness one evening led to Fred Karno and comedian Tom Leamore filling in with some improvised comedy based on Karno's old pantomime sketches "Love in Tub". The hilarious sketch went down a storm and Karno repeated it at the Gaiety Music Hall, Birmingham, following which the Karno Sketch Company was born. The company soon become recognised and it was later commonly accepted that: 'Fred Karno was the finest exponent of pantomime in the country.'

A brilliant acrobat, actor, director, manager, fixer and producer, Fred Karno was also a shrewd businessman with an eye for making money. Never seeking personal fame, he planned numerous laughable situations and possessed an almost unique ability to write slapstick comedy, which, with the help of scriptwriters, he turned into great success stories. He is universally accepted as the inventor of the custard pie-in-the-face joke.

In the summer of 1906, Fred Spiksley was delighted to discover a newspaper advertisement seeking professional footballers to take part in a new sketch show called "The Football Match". Fred desperately needed employment and was confident that his flicks and tricks would be just what Fred Karno wanted. Consequently, he set off to Vaughan Road in Camberwell to offer his services.

Karno was delighted to see Fred Spiksley and immediately hired and empowered him to find two other recently retired professional footballers for the show. Fred persuaded Aston Villa and England internationals Charlie Athersmith and Jimmy Crabtree to join him on the Fred Karno bandwagon at a handsome weekly salary of £7 10s (£7.50) each. Rehearsals started on 30 November 1906 and after these went well, all three signed a six-month contract commencing on Christmas Eve.

While glad of the work, Fred had harboured hopes of a more prominent football role as, in November 1906, QPR had advertised for the club's first ever 'football coach and manager'. The struggling West Londoners wanted a top football man to build a team that fans would want to watch, as the Great Western Railway Company had offered QPR the tenancy of a brand new Archibald Leitch-designed football stadium adjacent to Park Royal railway station. Fred's thorough application was seriously considered, but the post went to Jimmy Cowan, the former Aston Villa centre half, who had played for QPR in 1902. Cowan lead his new team to the Southern League title in his first season and did well before ill-health forced him to resign. Fred wondered if he should have asked for less than £7 10s (£7.50) a week to do the job at QPR. Whatever the actual reason, he lost out and was off on his travels with Fred Karno's company instead.

Recognising how popular football had become among the masses, Karno had collaborated with his lead comedian, Fred Kitchen, and opened his new show in Manchester's Palace Theatre on 27 December 1906. A huge panoramic backcloth was commissioned to stretch right round the stage and featured a huge crowd of football spectators. The skill was to bring this to life and was where Karno's genius kicked in. He toured Manchester and recruited 100 extras – a mixture of adults, children and dwarfs – whom he placed precisely so that their faces merged with the faces painted on the canvas. It was almost impossible to distinguish reality from illusion – a technique replicated decades later by Alfred Hitchcock. Artificial hands and arms sewn into the cloth and the addition of two very powerful electric fans created a brilliant effect on stage for the twice-nightly show that also had a matinee four times a week.

When the professional football players were introduced to the audience by the referee at the start, they ran out to tremendous applause. When they displayed their ball juggling skills and tricks, the noise was deafening, especially for Fred Spiksley, who was back in his schoolboy days of showing off to the audience. The football match that was played out thrilled the audience, so much so that at the Glasgow Coliseum performance on 4 March 1907, an occupant of a private box, Alexander Russell, became so excited he fell into the stalls 15ft below, landing on William Forsyth, a clerk, who suffered a broken neck.

The Football Match was one of Fred Karno's most successful shows. There were three scenes: the training quarters, outside the football ground and the football match itself. The undoubted star of the show was Harry Weldon, Billy Meredith's great friend, who played the lead role of "Stiffy" the 'keeper. Weldon's catchphrase was 'S'no use!' and he had a curious indefinable method of getting his audiences to laugh along with him. He also had a peculiar way of delivering his lines with a gurgle, followed by a unique whistle. Stiffy brought Weldon his greatest success.

The Football Match told the story of a titanic struggle in a forthcoming cup-tie between the Midnight Wanderers and the Middleton Pie-Cans. It involved an attempt to bribe Stiffy and much of the realism was supplied by the skilled former professional footballers recruited for just that purpose. In addition to the dialogue, the Stiffy Song was sung throughout the show and the chorus in the first six months was as follows:

But when Stiffy's between the sticks – when Stiffy's between the sticks
He can stop any kind of ball – a football or a brandy ball
And as Frederick Spiksley says when he starts to do his trick
What's the good of trying to score – when Stiffy's between the sticks?

The chorus changed over time, depending upon the professional footballers that were in the show, which included Vivian Woodward of England and Chelsea in 1912.

After opening in Manchester, the show broke all box office records as it moved across the country with the *Leicester Mercury* on 15 January 1907 stating: 'Fred Karno has struck gold, much of this success is down to the remarkable drollery of Harry Weldon.'

With the Fred Karno Company spending up to a week in a city, there was little to do during the daytime. To fill in their time, the performers decided to stage charity football matches, giving the public the opportunity to witness an exhibition match full of ex-professionals. While performing at the Palace Theatre in Manchester in January 1907, the "Fred Karno's Comedy Football Company" and "Puss in Boots Pantomime Company" played on Manchester City's Hyde Road ground. Fred Spiksley, enjoying his second run in the sketch show, played at full back alongside Arthur Wharton and they helped guide the Karno side to a 6-2 victory.

On 9 February 1907, a *Sheffield Independent* football reporter had bumped into Fred at the Division One match between Aston Villa and Sheffield Wednesday, which the away side lost 8-1. The reporter noted: 'Fred Spiksley was looking fit and well, and was well pleased with his lot as a member of the touring Fred Karno Company in a sketch called "The Football Match".'

Fred's contract with Fred Karno ended in May 1907. A month earlier, the post of coach/football manager at Tottenham Hotspur had become available. After nine seasons in North London, John Cameron, who had led Spurs to FA Cup glory in 1901, had sensationally quit his post. Fred immediately applied for the job at White Hart Lane, as did Sandy Tait, the current Spurs captain.

On Monday, 15 April 1907, Fred played outside left at Tottenham for Corinthians FC, whose side contained Tait, in a charity match for the Tottenham Drill Hall Fund. Fred had bumped into Wreford Brown, his captain on the great day when England had beaten Scotland 3-1 in 1898. On hearing that Fred had retired from playing, Wreford Brown had surprisingly asked him if he might become involved in the game. 'He described it as my swansong and I believe my appearance was the only time a professional footballer played for the famous amateur team', said Fred, later. Spurs won 2-1, but the defeated side's goal came from Spiksley. 'A long dropping shot at the end of 25 minutes', reported the *Daily Mirror*. Only 1,000 were present, but after what was his final organised football game, Fred was taken on a lap of honour by Wreford-Brown and was given a standing ovation.

An extremely proud Fred thus departed White Hart Lane confident that with the Spurs fans' backing he stood a chance of the post. In fact, it was unexpectedly given to a man who hadn't even applied for it: Fred Kirkham, a commercial traveller and experienced referee. As a football manager, however, he was to prove unpopular and it was no surprise when he resigned on 27 July 1908.

That same year, Fred reappeared in a number of Karno shows, including at the Newcastle Empire Palace on 2 March, Blackburn Palace on 9 March and Glasgow Palace on 30 March. The shows saw him performing alongside Charlie Chaplin on up to fifty occasions, with the first being at the Shepherds Bush Empire on 24 February 1908, with others including the Blackburn Palace on 9 March 1908 and Glasgow Palace on 30 March 1908. After a successful short audition period in which he made his debut at the New Cross Empire on 10 February 1908, Chaplin was offered a permanent weekly contract at £3 10s (£3.50) on 21 February 1908, joining his older brother Sydney as a Karno employee.

Wearing a slouch hat and big cape, Charlie played the third lead sporting a small black moustache that in time would become one of his trademarks. He was said to have delivered his first lines in the Football Match: 'Aha! Stiffy, my boy, a word in your ear!' However, his presence, little antics and funny movements initially left Karno unconvinced that Chaplin was a star in the making.

When the tour finished on 25 May 1908, Karno subsequently sent Chaplin to accompany Sydney to theatres in Balham and Camden, where he was allocated a minor role in the Mumming Birds sketch. In November 1908, Charlie Chaplin was back playing in the Football Match and by December the following year, his standing had risen so much that he played the lead role of Stiffy at the Willesden Hippodrome on 13 December 1909. Chaplin was on his way to stardom as was taken to America by Fred Karno in 1911. Performing in various sketch shows, starting with "A Night in an English Music Hall" Chaplin's billing became increasingly prominent in the American papers until his name outgrew that of the Karno Company. However, while Chaplin's future was secure, Fred Spiksley's career was becoming an increasing concern.

Chapter 22

Bankrupt

Gambling finally catches up with Fred Spiksley

Fred's money worries intensified when, on 15 August 1908, he appeared at the Sheffield Police Court and was found guilty of 'loitering in the streets for gambling purposes'. He was fined £2 and with little income, this was a big blow. On Monday, 31 August 1908 he was again fined £2 after being arrested at Lincoln City football ground two days previously, where he had been seen by Police Constable Jewels to receive and pay out bets at the Lincoln bicycle sports event. Fred had claimed he hadn't taken any bets from any strangers, but when his sports programme was handed to the Lincoln Police Court chairman, Alderman Harrison, it listed nearly 100 amounts from 1s to 2s 6d (5p to 12.5p). Harrison remarked it was a great pity that English games should be vitiated by 'the pernicious principle of betting'. The case was widely reported.

Just over a month later, on 25 September 1908, the Midland Counties Football League appointed Fred Spiksley to their official referees' list as a replacement for the retiring Fred Bye. Spiksley had earlier been appointed as a linesman but on Saturday, 24 October, he made his refereeing debut as Sheffield United reserves beat Leicester Fosse reserves 2-1. The following weekend he was in charge of the reserve match between Grimsby Town and his former club Leeds City, which was won 3-0 by the away side. Four further reserve team fixtures followed over the following two months: Grimsby v Rotherham Town, Notts County v Barnsley, Notts County v Chesterfield and Sheffield United v Hull, which finished 7-1.

During this period, Fred's reminiscences were published in the *Sheffield Telegraph's* sports paper, the *Green 'Un*. This, and the refereeing, would have provided some income but something more permanent was required. Having completed his apprenticeship, the footballer did have a trade to fall back on, but the number of compositors now required for the printing trade had fallen by half due to the invention of monotype in 1908. At the same time, pay rates had risen from £1 to £2 a week. Yet it seems unlikely that Fred, despite clearly hurtling towards bankruptcy, would have gone back into compositing even if there had been plenty of jobs. After all, he had become accustomed to a lifestyle that left him with plenty of free time for horseracing.

Fred's wages as a footballer had, of course, never been big enough to provide a nest egg for when he finished playing. His wages of £4 a week were certainly good, but were nothing like the sort of money the top footballers of today receive which, if managed properly, could ensure a very good standard of living after football.

With gates constantly increasing, it wasn't surprising that players at the major clubs wanted more money. In December 1907, the Association Football Players' Union (AFPU) was formed with Billy Meredith at its head. The players wanted the maximum wage lifting and also knew how badly any injured footballers were treated by their clubs. In 1910–11 the AFPU did manage to win a wage increase to £5 a week, but the maximum wage was to stay in place for almost another half century. Meanwhile, the 'retain and transfer system' that gave the clubs total control of who the players could play for remained in place for just as long.

On 28 January 1909 a receiving order was made against Fred Spiksley, then of 148 Moorgate, Retford in Lincoln County Court. Fred himself had presented his own bankruptcy application and appeared in court on 5 March 1909. He was described by the official receiver as a printer/compositor and part-time journalist, and his liabilities totalled £81 5s 2d (£81.26), with no assets available to his creditors. The official receiver began the public examination process by enquiring about Fred's current occupations before it was revealed that he had been a professional footballer. He was also asked about his journalism, income and expenditure during his period as a footballer. Fred explained that his debt was a result of his final season with Sheffield Wednesday. Having won the League title in 1903, the footballer had expected to be awarded a second benefit match for his twelve years of loyal service. He hoped to make around £300, more than enough to clear his debts, but a serious knee injury in a pre-season practice match had ended his top-class playing career and had denied him the chance of the benefit game.

He was asked about his house and its contents and he informed the court that his wife, Ellen, held the tenancy and owned all the contents. He claimed that at the time of his accident he had owed around £400 and although he had done his best to reduce this, he now had no income and didn't know how he could pay his debts. When he was asked when he had stopped paying people, Fred didn't reply. He admitted that he had no income and was living on the charity of his mother, father, friends and family. He was asked if he had been reduced to begging. It was a question that nettled. 'I do not beg and I have never begged in my life.'

The receiver attacked again, asking Fred if he stood on street corners with his hat out? Fred retaliated, 'No, I don't'.

'Do you solicit money from your friends?'

'No, I don't.'

When the receiver asked how much he was currently earning, Fred stated he was occasionally given assignments writing football articles for local and national newspapers, which provided him with £75 a year. He was also occasionally paid for scouting for professional football clubs when given a shopping list of a clubs' requirements, he then had to travel right across the country searching out talent. There was a market for good professional footballers, but unearthing a good 'keeper was no good if a client wanted a goalscorer. There was also competition from other scouts, which meant it would come down to deviousness, persuasion and money to persuade the protégé to join a particular club. In 1909, professional football clubs might pay up to £1,000 for a really exceptional player.

At this point, the receiver intervened, saying, 'But they don't pay that amount of money to you though do they?' 'No', said Fred, '"I wish they did!' to which there was an outburst of laughter in the courtroom gallery and the public examination was adjourned. Fred was later declared bankrupt and it wasn't until 10 October 1916 that he was discharged, subject to five years' suspension, when appearing at Lincoln Bankruptcy Court. It was reported 'no dividend had been paid… (and) his assets (were) insufficient to pay the expenses of the bankruptcy'.

Following his retirement as a professional footballer, Fred Spiksley's life had followed a series of ups and, more generally, downs. In 1911 a number of newspapers reported that he had been engaged as a coach to several distinguished English clubs, but failed to shed much light on the subject. It is unlikely that Fred would have been appointed as a senior first team coach since his addiction to gambling meant he was notoriously unreliable.

Fred was in need of a major challenge. Football was spreading across Europe and 1908 Manchester United became the first English club to tour continental Europe with a summer trip to the Austro-Hungarian Empire. In the autumn of 1908, the first men's football tournament was held at the London Olympics and third-placed Netherlands were coached by Fred's former England international colleague, Edgar Chadwick, who went on to manage the Dutch national team on twenty-four occasions.

In 1912, Stockholm was to set to be the venue for the Fifth Olympiad, for which all competitors had to be amateur. Quite understandably, the home nation wanted to do well in all sports, which was going to be difficult in the football competition as Sweden had been hammered 12-1 in 1908 by gold medalists Great Britain. Small local football competitions had only begun after 1894 and following the formation of local federations, the Swedish FA was formed in 1904. Sweden desperately needed a good football coach.

In the summer of 1910, Fred accepted a short contact to coach IFK Norrköping in Sweden, where he took charge of three official games that all ended in victory.

Among the players who participated under Fred's direction was Rudolf Haglund (1889–1961), who played for Norrköping between 1909 and 1921 and was the manager between 1924 and 1935. Another player was Hjalmar Westergren, who was 17 years old when he made his debut. Shortly after Fred Spiksley's visit to Norrköping he became a successful director in the club and was a member of the Swedish Football Association board between 1917 and 1935. Curt Hartzell (1891–1975) was also a gymnast who won an Olympic Gold in 1912 whilst Louis Groth (1891–1972) played three time for the Swedish Football team.

In 1911 the Lazarol factory owner, Mr Anders Lindahl, agreed to provide funding to the Swedish FA for a top class football coach. The appointee would have an initial brief to prepare the Swedish national team for a high profile match against the German Federation on 18 June 1911. Thereafter, he would remain throughout the summer to provide specific help to, among others, clubs in the Middle Swedish League. The Swedish FA approached the FA and Football League and received glowing references on Fred Spiksley's suitability from Frederick Wall, the FA secretary, top class referee John Lewis and Football League president John McKenna.

On Thursday, 18 May 1911, Fred Spiksley said goodbye to his wife Ellen and son Fred junior, now a 13-year-old teenager, and journeyed to Harwich, en route to Gothenburg, where he arrived on Saturday, 20 May 1911, the evening after FA Cup winners Bradford City had slipped to a surprising 1-0 defeat by the Swedish national side.

Also staying in Sweden were Fred's old team, Sheffield Wednesday, who were making their first overseas continental tour with games in Sweden and Denmark. Wednesday had been puzzled to discover that the opening match was on a Sunday. Orgryte, winners of ten Swedish championships between 1896 and 1910, were coached by Chesterfield-born Charles Bunyan, who had played nine games in goal for Derby County but was best known for having conceded an English record twenty-six goals when playing in goal for Hyde United against Preston in the FA Cup. Not that this fiasco had dented Bunyan's self-confidence: he was something of a pompous individual who even had had his own calling cards printed describing himself as *'Professeur de Fotboll'*.

Wednesday proved much too good for Orgryte and, without breaking sweat, easily won 5-0. Despite Swedish enthusiasm for the sport, there was a decided lack of football knowledge on display and Fred wasn't impressed with the long ball game that the local team had adopted. If this was typical of Swedish football then he had a lot of hard work in front of him. At the end of the match, Fred was able to surprise the Wednesday officials and players and the following day he joined up with the Wednesday party and enjoyed a day out with the players.

After paying his hotel bill, Fred departed by rail with his sea chest from Gothenburg on Wednesday, 24 May. He was met in Stockholm by Ruben Gelbord, a Swedish FA board member who owned a local sports shop, who took Fred to his lodgings where he would spend the next four or five months. The Englishman was pleased that his landlady spoke some English. Fred would have to rise early each morning for coaching and teaching football in two primary grass pitch locations: the Rasunda IP and Ostermalm Parks and Stadia. The former was inaugurated in the autumn of 1910 and only closed in 2012. It had been the home of AIK, the 'General Sports Club', for ninety-one years. It had cost 45,000 krona to construct, a huge sum in 1910, and had covered stands and seats for 1,300 spectators. Unfortunately, the swampy ground wasn't really suitable for growing grass and the stadium was considered to be too far away from the city by most people.

On his first day, Fred Spiksley met Swedish FA officials and players, and was given a whistle-stop tour of the city. On top of his coaching work, Fred was expected to visit football clubs and centres across Sweden to watch matches and assess the abilities of the players. What was required was the building of a strong and skilful national side that could compete on equal terms with other nations. Fred needed to identify talented players who were passionate and enthusiastic about football and also willing to listen, work hard and constantly practise to improve their football skills.

Buoyed by a report in *Idrottsbladet*, the leading Swedish sports paper, that he was gentle, friendly and liked by the players, Fred enthusiastically watched numerous matches and players on his travels, setting up football clinics and organising coaching sessions. His number one priority was to teach Sweden's top amateur footballers a completely different way of doing things. Such a task is never easy and understandably, the players were apprehensive as they had never had a professional football coach before.

However, the new coach had a number of things going for him, including his reputation of his exploits in the Football League, FA Cup and international matches. Fred's flair for languages also helped and he quickly began understanding Swedish, including a number of phrases that he employed to address his new players the first time they met. In return, the players immediately liked the new man in charge. Having said that, Fred pulled no punches in telling the players that there would be lots of hard work involved and he urged anyone not up to the challenge to leave. Furthermore, if players turned up so much as a minute late to training, they were sent home.

The new coach began by teaching players how to trap the ball and how to use the chest to cushion it in the air and bring it dead to a player's feet. He then turned to how to shield the ball from an opponent and keep possession, while at all times maintaining complete control with the outside of the boot. When the players had mastered the art of dribbling with the ball, Fred taught them how to kick it and coached them in the main ways to do so: the short crisp pass, the centre or cross-field ball, the corner kick and how to shoot.

He instilled in the Swedes that, after shooting, the most necessary skill was the ability to pass the ball to an unmarked teammate. This was achieved with the short crisp pass hit with pace to the intended recipient using the top of the foot known as the instep. Fred went to great lengths to explain that passing with the inside of either foot was misguided as the inside side muscles were much weaker than those on the outside. The difference was that when a player passed the ball with the inside of his foot, it would slow down before reaching its target, thus allowing opponents the opportunity to intercept the ball.

Fred spent a lot of time helping the players to get the basics right. He taught them how to cross, taking great care to explain the importance of keeping one eye on the ball while looking out of the corner of the other eye to see where best to place the cross for the forwards. He would then make sure they planted their standing foot properly, before swinging their free leg through the ball using the instep for power and accuracy in the cross. He would spend hours rolling footballs into the path of players while constantly repeating, 'One eye on the ball, look to your target, plant your foot, swing your leg through the ball'.

Fred Spiksley believed that exceptional goalscorers were gifted and born with natural ability. It was possible, though, to become a good shot through practice and hard work. It was all a matter of intensive training. Fred handed down his guide to good goal scoring with the following advice:

Lesson 1 – Dribble with the ball from the halfway line, learn to shoot for goal while on the move before being closed down by opponents.
Lesson 2 – Shoot with power and direction by keeping your head over the ball with your standing leg well planted. Swing your free leg through the ball using the top of the foot.
Lesson 3 – For extra power in a long shot at goal, flex the knee joint to accelerate the leg as it extends through the ball to generate increased power and thus achieve the best possible force behind the ball.
Lesson 4 – For accuracy, keep your head over the ball and flex the ankle to steer and control the flight of the ball with confidence towards the goal.
Lesson 5 – A shot at half speed that finds the corner of the net is better than a cannonball that flashes outside the goalpost.

> Lesson 6 – Always keep thinking, weigh up the goalkeeper and his strengths and weaknesses. Shoot to his weaker side. If he struggles to stop ground shots then shoot low. If he's nervous about dealing with high balls under the crossbar, then try a heavy charge.

When Spiksley wrote about shooting skills in 1928, he drew particular attention to the best strikers of the day being 'endowed with the right kind of legs' saying that players such as Steve Bloomer, Bob McColl and Dixie Dean had:

> Perfect legs for driving the ball, and a gift, doubtless unsuspected, of placing the unemployed leg in the right position to give proper effect to their drives. Those who saw Bloomer and McColl playing in the past, or have seen Dean today, will understand perfectly what I mean by 'shooting legs'. Without the right-shaped legs most players will find shooting a rather difficult art. Although there are, of course, exceptions to every rule.

Fred believed that footballers were born and that only 10 per cent of a player's overall ability could be affected by training and the right kind of attitude. He was also a disciple of combination (pass and move) football, wanting short quick passing along the ground to unmarked colleagues. One of his favourite exercises was to line up his forwards on the halfway line and get them to pass the ball along the line as they advanced together before one took a shot. Another was 'piggy in the middle' in which two players in the middle attempted to intercept an errant pass from players attempting to pass to one another. Several of the training drills that Spiksley believed would develop a player's skill can still be witnessed by top professional teams during training sessions and pre-match warm-ups, today. In terms of skill training, there is little doubt that he was way ahead of his time.

Fred had never worked harder in his life, but he really enjoyed what he was doing and could see that he was making a big difference, especially as he could pass on his instructions now that he had quickly mastered the Swedish language.

Most of the Swedish side at the time played for Orgryte, but there were also Gothenburg-based players from IFK Gothenburg, FF Gothenburg and Kopings IS. From Stockholm there were players from AIK, Djurgardens, IFK, Gavle and Mariebergs.

The side selected for the big game against Germany at the Rasunda on 18 June 1911 were as follows:

Oskar Bengtsson (Orgryte), Knut Sandlund (Djurgardens), Jacob Levin (Orgryte), Ragnar Wicksell (Djurgardens), Gotrik Frykman (Djurgardens) (captain), Sixten Oberg (Mariebergs), Herman Myhrberg (Orgryte), Gustaf

Efkberg (Stockholm), Karl Gustafsson (Kopings), Josef Appelgren (Orgryte), Karl Ansen (AIK).

Germany, meanwhile, lined up as follows:

Moller (Kiel), Kipp (Stuttgart), Worpitsky (Victoria Berlin), Dumke (Victoria Berlin), Droz (Prussia Berlin), Hunder (Victoria Berlin), Burger (Munchen 1860), Ugi (Leipzig), Hempel ((Leipzig), Viggers (Victoria Hamburg)

Charles Buchwald from Copenhagen was appointed as match referee and Ruben Gelbord was Sweden's linesman for the game. The Swedish side were selected by a five-man committee consisting of Wilhelm Friberg, Anton Johansson (the 'General of Football'), John Ohlson, Hans Hallen and Edvin Sandborg. It is not known how much influence Fred Spiksley had in the team selection.

Gustafsson was Sweden's leading international goalscorer with nine goals in eight games. However, it was the outside left in the side, Karl Ansen, who was considered the best forward. He was 24 and had played eight international games. Bengtsson was making his eighth appearance for his country, while Sandlund, Oberg and Esbjerg were all debutants.

The game was the first international in Stockholm and was played in front of a crowd of 3,000. The home side went ahead on 28 minutes when Gustafsson was sent clear courtesy of a brilliant ball from Myhrberg, leaving Moller with no chance of saving his shot. One minute later Gustafsson hit a great shot past the German 'keeper and Sweden led 2-0 at half-time.

Buoyed by their success, the home side played some excellent football on the restart but were guilty of missing four gilt-edged chances. This allowed the German team to take the initiative and the away side struck twice in quick succession to level the score. Things then went from bad to worse for Sweden, when Bengtsson was beaten by a deflected shot and Germany led for the first time.

The home side were handed a lifeline on 68 minutes when Gustafsson was upended in the penalty area. Having already scored twice, the Swedish centre forward was the obvious man to take the spot kick. But to the crowd's surprise, the captain of the home side, Gotrik Frykman, saw this as his responsibility and had agreed with Fred Spiksley beforehand that he would take any penalty kicks. Unfortunately for the Swedes, he missed, after which the home side piled forward in search of a deserved equaliser. However – and no doubt readers have heard this story many times since – in the final minute of the game, Germany broke forward to make it 4-2, with Charles Buchwald ignoring offside protests to allow the goal to stand. The Swedes had been the better team and had led for much of the game, but Germany had won!

Fred was understandably upset by the result, when on any other day Sweden would have won comfortably. The Swedish coach also blamed himself for agreeing that Frykman should take the penalty kick. What had really counted against the losing side, though, was their lack of composure when shooting. Practice could help ensure that was less likely to be the case in the future and despite the result, it was clear from their performance that Fred Spiksley's coaching had massively improved the quality of the Swedish side.

According to Swedish FA reports, over the following weeks Fred visited Vasteras and later Karlstad, which is 160 miles west of Stockholm. There he saw IFK Karlstad play short, fast passes to beat Karlskoga IF 9-0, with the latter reported as playing long balloon balls. Fred also worked with the Stockholm AIK players as the *History of AIK*, published 2012, states in the section covering 1911: 'Maybe the very first successful autumn of 1911 was due to the fact that the players in the summer got instructions from the English football coach Fred Spiksley who was moving round Sweden.' AIK won the Swedish championship, which was run as a knockout competition, beating IFK Vasteras, IFK Eskilstuna, IFK Stockholm and then IFK Uppsala 3-2 in the final. Fred appears to have left Sweden at the start of September as there is no mention of him being present at the international in Stockholm on 17 September, which saw Norway crushed 4-1. Whether his contract had ended or he had left early is unknown. His time in Sweden had been a very rewarding one and he had transformed Swedish football by teaching the players how to play the combination game, as well as instilling genuine pride in the players by working together as a team. He had also made many friends, including Ruben Gelbord and Torsten Husen, not forgetting his players, who were all sad to see him leave. Fred returned to Retford in a good mood.

The Olympics in Sweden took place in the summer of 1912 and in the football, the home nation lost to the Netherlands 4-3 and Italy 1-0; there was to be no football glory for the hosts. Great Britain and Denmark eventually made it to the final and the former won 4-2 to take the gold medal. Sweden's failure to make, at least, the semi-finals of the competition led to immediate recriminations with the departing Charles Bunyan heavily blamed for the failure to win a single game.

In 1913 the Swedish Olympic Association agreed to provide finance to employ a coach for the next two years. The Stockholm FA were determined to have Fred Spiksley, but he had already obtained a new one-year post as coach to Munich 1860. If the Swedes wanted him they would either need to buy out his contract or wait. However, when Fred informed his prospective employers that he wanted a three-year contract up to the end of the planned 1916 Olympic Games, the Swedish Olympic Association saw this as unrealistically expensive and it was decided to search for a new coach in a different direction. In the event, the First World War meant the 1916 Berlin Olympic Games were cancelled.

Chapter 23

Germany 1914

A lucky escape from a German prison

Great Britain was the first industrial nation and from the 1870s onwards, Germany followed suit, accomplishing in thirty years what had taken Britain over a hundred. By 1914 Germany was the major competitor to Britain and the US in world trade, banking, insurance and shipping, and now sought to transform itself into a global power. However, its late development meant it had missed out on the 'scramble for Africa' which, between 1870 and 1914, had seen the percentage of the continent directly controlled by the European imperial powers rise from 10 to 90 per cent. This contributed to tensions between the imperial powers and led to a succession of crises. These finally imploded in August 1914, when a complex network of alliances drew the major European nations into military conflict. Looking back over a century later it seems obvious that the First World War was coming, but that wasn't how events were viewed at the time. In the spring of 1914, Burnley, Bradford City, Tottenham Hotspur and Celtic all safely toured Germany.

On 28 June 1914, Franz Ferdinand, the heir to the Austrian throne, was assassinated by Serbian nationalists in the Bosnian capital, Sarajevo. It was a sensational event but few people predicted it would result in war. Yet one month later, Austria declared war on Serbia and by 4 August 1914, France, Germany, England and Russia were all at war.

Thousands of British subjects were left trapped in enemy territory, including the Spiksley family. After completing his contract with the Stockholm FA, Fred had become engaged in 1912 as head coach to Munich 1860, one of eight teams in the Bavarian League. According to Fred 'the club I am engaged with is the most famous gymnastic club – in Germany...we have 4,756 members with the right of entrance being alike to both sexes...they have splendid grounds. Football is going ahead, and sooner or later England will require her very best amateurs to hold their own in matches with this county.' He believed goalkeepers in Germany and England were on a par with each other. The former England international became headhunted for the same post by the ambitious 1FC Nuremberg (FCN), who had just built the 'Zabo' stadium and were to become the most famous football club in Germany, with their record number of national championships only finally matched by Bayern Munich in 1986. Formed on 4 May 1900, the club started out playing rugby before switching to football.

England and Germany had many ties in the late nineteenth century, including the marriage of Queen Victoria to Duke Albert of Saxe-Coburg and Gotha. English schools for sons of the wealthy were common in major German cities. There were also many British merchants and businessmen over there. Football soon became popular and the first clubs appeared in 1880. In 1889 a team of English professional footballers, including Billy Bassett and Edgar Chadwick, beat a combined Berlin XI in Germany on two occasions, by 13-2 and 10-2. In 1900 the Deutscher Fussball Bund (DFB) was formed and in 1901 a combined Berlin side visited England to meet a handful of professional clubs and lost 5-1 to Southampton and 6-2 to Aston Villa.

The first German national championship in 1903 was won by VfB Leipzig, marking the start of northern dominance in German football. Walther Bensemann, however, was determined to change this. In 1893 he had appointed a man named Coopers as captain and coach to FV Karlsruher, as well as a priest named Archibald White as chairman of the newly-formed South German Football Union.

In 1908, Bayern Munich won the Southern Bavaria championship under the direction of a Mr Taylor. In 1910, FV Karlsruher lifted the national trophy with assistance from William Townley, the former Blackburn Rovers player famous for scoring a hat-trick at the 1890 FA Cup final against Wednesday. Townley then joined SpVgg Furth and after success there became coach to Bayern Munich, just as hostilities commenced.

FCN had employed Felix Servas, an ex-Britannia player, and a man named Walker, whose German amounted to 'Beer good!', as coaches before they recruited Fred Spiksley to the position. 1FC Nuremberg had invited professional English teams from England to play them in an attempt to learn and develop a style of play that would elevate them to the top of German football. Heavy defeats had been endured just prior to Spiksley's appointment, with a 5-1 defeat to QPR in 1912, followed by a 7-0 thrashing from Middlesbrough in 1913. Fred had impressed senior officials and 1FCN players upon his arrival in Nuremberg, adopting the same approach that had gained him respect during his time in Sweden. His reputation was to grow further as the next English side to visit the Zabo were Tottenham Hotspur on 6 May 1914.

According to the official history of 1FC Nuremberg, the Tottenham players 'met an almost unbeatable wall in our defence and found in that beautiful "defence" was our goalkeeper Weschenfelder – our obstacle'. The match ended

1-1 and was widely considered as a 'kind of victory' for German football. Fred was doing well. He had published an article in the *Athletic News* titled 'Leaguers Abroad' and parts of it read as follows:

> Germany at the present time is receiving far more education in football than the German FA and the followers of the game thoroughly realise. Already this spring, Glasgow Celtic, Burnley, Bradford City and Tottenham Hotspur have made tours ... attendances and enthusiasm would compare favourably with what we see in England. The benefit derived from the visits of these English teams is far in advance of what could be accomplished in several months' work by a coach, as a collective display of good football is far preferable to an individual demonstration.
>
> From these visits the Continental players receive examples in every art connected with the game – trapping, heading, dribbling, feinting, combination and the quick changing of positions – to say nothing of the strategy of the backs and half-backs. The superiority of the Danes over the other Continental teams was undoubtedly derived from the many English clubs that visited their country. The referee in the Sweden and German match at Stockholm in 1911, who was a Dane, was emphatic in his explanation to me that they owed much to the British professional teams for their success.
>
> Bradford City and Tottenham have just concluded tours which, combined, entailed the carrying out of nineteen games...Tottenham Hotspur's first game was against Hanover on 3 May, when before 8,000 people and after leading by three clear goals at half-time, they won by 6-3. Nurnberg were met on 6 May, and the result, 1-1 was received with great jubilation by the 6,000 visitors, a record crowd for the mid-week match in Nurnberg.

Fred's success was abruptly cut short as a week after war was declared, the *Gainsborough News* special war edition of 11 August 1914 reported: 'No news has yet come to hand of Fred Spiksley, who with his wife and son are presumably still in Germany.'

Upon the outbreak of war, British subjects in Germany became classed as "enemy aliens". The Spiksleys had to report to the local police station and surrender their passports and travelling documents. They had their photographs and fingerprints taken and were told to report every three days. With British diplomatic representatives having departed, the US Embassy assumed protection responsibilities for over 4,000 British nationals.

German mobilisation was rapid and gigantic. War fever was everywhere and Nuremburg citizens took to the streets singing patriotic songs. A German told Fred: 'If the Kaiser says we fight, then we fight.' Fred soon discovered the railway station was reserved for the military.

On 19 August, Fred, together with his wife, son and a young woman who was staying with them, were arrested as they alighted from a tramcar in Nuremberg city centre. The local public had taken to catching spies, real or, more generally, imaginary, and the Spiksleys had been overheard speaking English. After several hours in police detention, they were released when Fred produced an earlier police letter allowing the family to be at liberty.

Four days later things changed for the worse. According to Fred: 'On account of mythical statements in the German papers to the effect that a Bill had been passed by the English Parliament forbidding English firms to employ Germans and dissolving all partnerships with Germans, all foreigners in Germany between 17 and 45 were at once arrested and thrown into prison as criminals.'

Fred and Fred Junior were placed in solitary confinement. They were both bullied and beaten, whilst the only sustenance they received over a period of four days was one piece of uneatable black bread and some water. Overcrowding intensified and sanitary arrangements deteriorated as more foreigners were rounded up. Among Fred's new companions was the local English consul, who had an acute heart condition. When he called a warder, his doctor's request was flatly rejected. Eventually, a lack of space in the cells made it impossible to place any more prisoners in them: a Frenchman arrived and was locked in a cupboard less than 3ft feet square with nowhere to sit. The desperate man could be heard banging on the cupboard where he remained for 21 hours until he was released, and by which time he was half dead.

When interviewed in early September 1914, Fred said he 'had quite made up my mind that I should be kept as a prisoner until the end of the war'. In late October 1914, a vigorous press campaign in Germany demanded retaliation for the alleged internment of all Germans living in England. In fact, general internment in Britain didn't begin until 13 May 1915, after the sinking of the Lusitania inflamed public opinion. On 31 October 1914, Germany issued an ultimatum to Britain that unless all German civilians were released by 5 November, then every Englishman in Germany would be interned. When the order was ignored, on 6 November all British subjects aged 17 to 55 were arrested.

Most of the internees in Germany were then transferred to the civilian detention camp at Ruhleben ('peaceful life' in English), a former racecourse just outside Berlin. Scarcely a section of British society was unrepresented, including football, with Steve Bloomer and John Cameron both incarcerated. Most of the eventual 4,400 prisoners were packed into eleven stables. Each prisoner had a space 10ft square, into which they had to fit themselves and all of their belongings.

Germany, nevertheless, adhered to the Geneva Convention and the detainees at the camp administered their internal affairs. Consequently, over time a minisociety evolved and sport, with football in particular, was to play a pivotal role in the life of camp detainees. League and cup competitions were organised and on 16 November 1914, Oldham Public Schools XI played Tottenham Scratch XI in the final of the first Ruhleben football competition.

Whilst life at Ruhleben was bearable, it still marked the first instance in modern history of the mass internment of aliens. The prisoners had committed no crimes and were condemned without trial to four years' imprisonment. Fred avoided Ruhleben because, to his surprise, a visiting doctor who came to his prison cell and examined him declared that he wasn't fit for military service and must be released.

Meanwhile, Ellen Spiksley had remained free to roam around Nuremburg. Unable to speak German and with no food, money or water, she was fortunate when FCN, keen to help their former coach leave Germany, arranged a meeting with the American consul, who in turn persuaded the local German military commander to see the Englishwoman.

At first the commander insisted that Ellen's husband and son must remain incarcerated and she was informed that the US Ambassador James. W. Gerard had arranged a train to Holland for stranded American subjects. Ellen was told to join the train and when she refused to go without the rest of her family, she was informed that she would be deported. At this point Ellen broke down in tears and, unable to stand seeing a grown woman cry, the hard-hearted commander reconsidered his decision and handed Ellen a signed order releasing her loved ones.

A German count then took Ellen to Fred and Fred Junior, who were astonished when they walked out of prison to find Ellen greeting them before all three were taken to catch the departing train carrying American subjects. However, on arrival they were informed that no English people would be allowed on the train. After being forced to spend the night in a squalid nearby room, Fred attended the nearest police station where he was informed that he could obtain a pass to Lindau, nearly 400 miles further south, on the German border close to neutral Switzerland. A party of thirteen British subjects, including the English consul with whom Fred had shared the police cell in Nuremburg, all caught the train together to Lindau, with fingers crossed that they would be able to journey on to Switzerland.

On their arrival, however, all of the men were informed they could go no further. The consul then intervened to tell the authorities that the police had released the men as they were incapable of military service. It was thus agreed that they would need to undergo a further medical examination to see if this was true! The English consul himself immediately secured the necessary medical certificate confirming he was unfit for hostilities, but not so a fit Fred Spiksley. Was he to remain stuck in Germany? The former footballer was told he would be re-examined by a doctor the following morning and so he immediately hit 'upon a plan to secure the certificate'.

He had suffered from an injured right knee for many years and felt that a liberal supply of very hot water would enable him to dislocate it. He thus rose early the next day and spent two hours applying boiling hot water to the joint. On entering the surgery, the doctor began testing Fred's muscles, which were in great condition. The former England international was still as fit as a fiddle, but when the doctor asked him if he could run, Fred said he could do so only for a short while as otherwise his right knee would dislocate and come out of its socket. When he was requested to demonstrate, Fred did a little run and pretended that his knee had dislocated, but was deliberately putting the knee out of joint. He then stood on his healthy left leg before putting the right knee in and out of the socket several times and on each occasion, the joint cracked so loudly that the doctor immediately agreed that he was unfit to fight.

Fred then joined the rest of party to sail across Lake Constance to Switzerland, and from there the British travelled via Zurich, Bern, Lausanne and Geneva to Lyon, where they were held up for an hour after a trainload of wounded soldiers arrived from Saint Dieu following a fierce battle. Fred spoke to some of the soldiers when they reached Lyon and they told him how several thousand Frenchmen and Germans had lost their lives.

Fred, Ellen and Fred Junior arrived in Paris on the same day that bombs were dropped on the French capital for the first time during the war (30 August 1914). The Spiksleys arrived home from Paris on 2 September and Fred was quickly interviewed about his experiences by a *Sheffield Independent* journalist and the story appeared in the paper on Friday, 4 September 1914.

Chapter 24

America's Missionary

Developing the game in the USA, Mexico and Peru

Arriving back in England, life wasn't easy for the Spiksley family, especially as their belongings were still in Germany. With no money or home, finding work was essential. Fortunately, Fred managed to become a munitions inspector at Vickers, in Sheffield, for 34 shillings a week (£1.70). The job was a fresh challenge for Fred, but he quickly built up a good reputation in what was an important war-time job.

Sheffielders had rallied to the war cause and 900 men had joined the Sheffield City Battalion by 11 September 1914. On 12 May 1915 – just weeks after Sheffield United had beaten Chelsea 3-0 in the 1915 FA Cup final – the battalion left for Staffordshire and, after service on the Suez Canal, they arrived at the Somme on 3 April 1916. On 1 July 1916, 248 Sheffield men were killed when Allied Forces attacked German lines. One of many macabre elements of the war was that several of the armaments used by the Germans were Sheffield made. A total of 5,139 Sheffielders were killed in the First World War, including civilians who experienced Zeppelin raids aimed at Sheffield's industry: bombs dropped on 25 September 1916 killed twenty-eight people and injured nineteen.

The threat from the sky was replicated from under the sea when, in 1915, the Germans declared the seas around the United Kingdom to be a war zone. At around 2.15pm on 7 May 1915, off the southern coast of Ireland, a German U-boat torpedoed, without warning, the British luxury ocean liner *Lusitania*, on a voyage from America to Liverpool. The Germans suspected the boat of carrying ordnance and ammunition from America and the arguments raged throughout the war period as to whether the ship was a legitimate target. The *Lusitania* sank inside eighteen minutes, with only 761 of the 1,959 passengers and crew surviving. With 128 Americans killed, the incident turned public opinion in the USA against Germany and ultimately contributed to the American entry into the war in 1917. By then a number of other passenger ships had also been sunk by German U-boats.

After reading a letter that arrived in the first week of May 1915, Ellen and Fred would have been relieved to have left Germany. The letter came from a friend in Germany, an English woman who had married a German and was free to remain in the country, and described a difficult life without sufficient food to eat. The husband had become embittered against the English, regarding his part within the war, which is not disclosed, as a punishment for marrying an Englishwoman. He was convinced that England started the war and that the English must pay.

Life in England for the Spiksleys was more comfortable, but it wasn't easy. Fred remained bankrupt and money remained tight. In the summer of 1915, Vickers was approached by the War Office to find six volunteers willing to risk travelling to the US to work as ordnance officers and oversee essential military supplies bought by the British Government from American factories. The work would involve checking crates, consignments, weapons and ammunition bound for the Western Front. Following the *Lusitania* tragedy there were few people who wanted the posts. Fred Spiksley, though, desperately needed the money and the pay was attractive, especially as bonuses were on offer if shipment and delivery targets were met. He signed up for the trip and departed with five other Sheffield men on the SS *Oduna* as it sailed from Liverpool's Princess Landing Stage on 7 August 1915.

Fred was one of three married men who made the trip, the others being William Walker and Lewis Hague, both aged 35. The single men were Frank Barker, aged 30, William Henry Smith, 22, and John Barker, 20. When the *Oduna* steamed into Manhattan Harbour against a backcloth of New York skyscrapers, the Statue of Liberty on Ellis Island would have been a sight to behold. All six men arrived with $50 in their pockets, supplied by the War Office. Their lodgings had been arranged by the Washington Steel and Ordinance Company and Fred was to stay with the Murphy family in Newark, New Jersey. Although, it's believed that Fred's job in America was intended to last the duration of the war, this would not be the case and after around a year overseas, he returned home.

Although he didn't particularly enjoy working in the munitions factories, it was a job he was evidently good at and, with the necessity of bringing money in, Spiksley returned to Vickers. It was reported in the *Daily Record* in 1917 that he had been a 'very busy munitions worker for a long time past in Sheffield, and has built up a fresh record'.

Money must have remained tight throughout war time, as it was also reported in the same paper that Fred was having to walk 37 miles a week in order to get to work. At least he could enjoy the fresh air! During his second period at Vickers Fred applied for his discharge from bankruptcy at the Lincoln

County Court. He had been a bankrupt for almost eight years, but had recorded no misdemeanours during this period. However, Fred was left disappointed by the outcome, because although he succeeded in receiving a discharge, the judge suspended this for five years, meaning Fred would remain bankrupt until October 1921.

When an exhausted Germany signed the Armistice with the Allies on 11 November 1918, munitions factories were no longer needed and with millions of soldiers set to be discharged, finding work became harder. The Spiksley family still had no savings and on 22 March 1919, the Sheffield newspapers reported that the former England football international was living back in Moscar, Sheffield. He was devoting his spare time to getting as fit as possible in order to enter 100 yards handicap events with the aim of capturing the prize money on hand for the winner and earning extra income from betting on himself to finish first.

Meanwhile, Fred and Ellen's relationship was floundering. On 25 November 1918 Ellen had opened a letter addressed to him from America. She may already have become suspicious of transatlantic letters arriving for Fred, and her suspicions were to be confirmed. The letter was from Margaret Murphy from Newark, New Jersey, and the contents revealed that a sexual relationship or liaison had been established between Fred and Margaret while he was staying with them in America. Rather than confront her husband, it appears Ellen kept the contents of the letter secret for some considerable time. Regular training may have offered Fred not just an opportunity to win some money, but also a chance to keep out of his wife's way.

Tensions between Fred and Ellen would, however, continue to escalate until just before the start of the 1920–21 season, when their relationship broke down irrevocably. Fred quit the family home and returned to Gainsborough. William put him up and, as on previous occasions, Fred would help William with his under-the-counter bookmaking business. In his spare time, Fred resumed his training up on the hills in Thonock Woods, aiming to stay unnoticed by the long arm of the law and the public who, by warning bookmakers he was in fine condition, would ensure reduced odds on him winning any race he entered.

On 20 November 1920, Fred was setting off early to Manchester when he received a summons to appear in the Sheffield Police Court, where he was required to answer charges of desertion brought by his wife. He travelled to compete in the Manchester veterans' 100 yards sprint handicap and after paying his stake money, collecting his number and discovering his handicap, he went to the betting ring where he backed himself to win. What he didn't disclose was his real name and, relying on no one recognising him, he ran under the assumed name of Frederick Hayward (Fred Junior's middle name) and won, collecting £30 in prize money and a very tidy sum from the bookies. It was a good day.

Three days later wasn't a good day. Charged with 'desertion and failure to look after his wife', the unrepresented Fred unwisely pleaded 'not guilty', after which Ellen's lawyer, Harold Jackson, expressed his sorrow at the plea but promised to bring out some unpleasant home truths. The hearing's first part was occupied with establishing basic details of the couple's relationship, including the fact that husband Fred had left the marital home on 16 August 1920. Since then, he had failed to contribute to his wife's upkeep although he had contributed £12 towards rent.

In the course of Ellen's testimony she explained that she had in her possession the November 1918 letter to Fred, signed by Margaret in Newark, New Jersey, where, coincidentally, Fred was billeted when working as a munitions inspector during the war: Margaret's terms were apparently extremely endearing to Ellen's husband. It turned out that another letter had arrived on 1 October 1920 at 118 Broomspring Road. Clearly Margaret must have been unaware that Fred had departed to Lincolnshire and it was now four years since the pair had seen each other. Nevertheless, this second intercepted letter was, if anything, more passionate and demonstrated that the pair must have been in correspondence with each following Fred's return to England in 1916. Furthermore, it showed he had been lured back across the Atlantic to help establish the first recognisable football league in America: the America Soccer League.

'At last my darling the most wonderful news. I still can't believe it's true, and I shall not believe it until you reach me and I can hold you in my arms. I hope the days will pass quickly; this will be the happiest Christmas.'

Mr Jackson then asked Fred if he was leaving for the US before Christmas, but the reply failed to make any sense when he said he was 'swinging the lead'. Jackson asked if he was bluffing two women and Fred replied, 'Just one'.

Jackson then asked the court chairman to grant an injunction preventing Fred Spiksley from leaving the country until he had been means-tested. It was stated the defendant had left his wife and failed to contribute sufficiently towards her support, even though he was earning a good living as a bookmaker. Fred disputed this by claiming he had sent £12 to his wife.

Under cross-examination, Fred quickly dropped his claim that he didn't know Margaret, stating she was Margaret Murphy. Asked about his finances, Fred admitted working as a bookmaker and to having earned £100 for writing his life story in the Dundee-based *Thomson Weekly News*. He also earned further limited income of a few pounds by being able to use his football knowledge to provide a critique of talented players for professional football clubs looking to sign new players. He admitted to being currently in negotiations with a football club in Mexico City to go there as a coach, and produced a contract to demonstrate he was telling the truth. The same cannot be said when he was asked if he had won £30 in a Manchester running handicap, as he denied doing so.

In his summing-up, the chairman of the bench said it was evident that the defendant had the resources to earn a livelihood and, as such, the duty of the bench was to make an order ensuring that Fred Spiksley provided for his wife. Accordingly, he was found guilty of desertion and there was an order made against him to pay Ellen Spiksley the sum of £2 a week.

In the event, Fred didn't return to North America for Christmas 1920. However, on the day before his fifty-first birthday, he sailed into New York from Liverpool aboard the SS *Carmaria*, to take up his role in establishing quality football in the US, becoming a senior executive for the Pennsylvania Football Association. Football was most prominent in the New York metropolitan area and in Pennsylvania. Formed in 1918, Brooklyn Robins Dry Dock took its name from the workplace it represented: the dock was part of the Todd Pacific Shipyards. The owners hired Fred when he arrived in the US to take charge of the team. It was a successful period as Dry Docks retained the American Cup, a trophy that no longer exists, and captured the National Challenge Cup, a trophy still in use today and which is the equivalent of the FA Cup. Dry Docks beat the Scullions 4-2 in the Challenge Cup final.

Writing for *Spalding's Athletic Annual* in 1921, Spiksley is clearly impressed by what he saw in the US. Indeed, he is often more complimentary of players from his time coaching abroad than he is of English football, believing that with the right training and management, teams in Germany and America would one day be able to match the best English teams. Speaking in 1921 about players in America, he said: 'I could not help but admire the spirit with which these players went about their work. With the men that I have in my eye, I think I could build up a team that would do credit to their country in Olympic Games.' This wasn't an opinion shared by his contemporaries back in England, who at the time believed that the home nations wouldn't be overthrown. Two years after Spiksley's death, England would be embarrassed by the USA in the 1950 World Cup in Brazil.

Fred had several pieces of advice for helping the young American soccer. However, some of it sounds like the same advice handed down to him in 1887 by John Madden, who was establishing his legendary status in Prague at the time:

> Players who wish to become great must do a great deal of thinking, as in no sphere of life did man attain much prominence without such,

and this stands in football... One selfish forward, no matter how good, can spoil the whole team, and I would advocate his services being dispensed with at once... Forwards should shoot often and hard, and particularly when a decent opportunity presents itself. They may make mistakes, but it is better to have tried and failed than to have never tried at all. Always endeavour to bring the ball to the feet and play the ball in the air as little as possible.

Although we don't know as much as we would like about Fred's actions over the next three years or so, we do know that in February 1921 he was coaching Real Club España OD in Mexico City. España were Mexico City's premier football team at the time and would go on to win the Primera Fuerza title that year. Spiksley was photographed with an unidentified Mexican team with a large trophy that may have been the Primera Fuerza.

In the 1970s, Fred Spiksley Junior was interviewed by the local Sheffield press. During the interview he describes how his father was considered football's first missionary, saying how Fred would help support fledgling football associations to set up their infrastructure and teach the local teams how to play the 'English Way'. This mostly involved a passing game with the ball being kept on the floor.

This version of Fred Spiksley's life as a travelling coach does seem to ring true to his time in America, where Spiksley, after initially work in the US, had then travelled to Mexico City to work with numerous teams across the city. Fred would spend a brief time in Peru, making him the first person to coach football across three continents.

Spiksley would return to Mexico from Peru to complete his time in the Americas. In the summer of 1924 he was interviewed by the *Sheffield Telegraph* and the journalist was clearly impressed:

> I never saw him looking better. He has naturally put on weight, but today, now that he is in his 50s, he looks lithe and hardy as ever. Browned by a semi-tropical sun, and carrying not an ounce of superfluous flesh, he looks as though he is still able to put in a good sprint on the cinder path. In fact, some three years ago, shortly before he set out for Mexico, Fred had put out a challenge to beat any man in the country his own age in a sprint race. The challenge was never taken up.

Spiksley speaks highly of the reception he received in Mexico City. He was engaged by the management of the Reformers' Club, run by the white section of the population, composed both of Latins and Anglo-Saxons, among whom the dour Scottish element predominated.

Spiksley's duty was to act as coach for the football section of this great club, which embraces most kinds of outdoor sport. The task was a strange one. Owing to the absence of twilight and the sudden descent of darkness over the earth, all the training had to be done before breakfast. Still, he found his pupils easy to teach, and he quickly welded them into about the strongest side in the country. In fact, the old international states that if some of the team, notably a centre half back, were to make their appearance in English football, they would cause something like a sensation.

After breakfast, Spiksley had time on his hands. He asked one of the club officials to find him a suitable job. Well educated and always notable for strict attention to detail, Fred's thoroughness had not escaped attention and, when the post of head of the Dispatch Department in the Bank of Montreal, an important branch with a staff of 140, became vacant, he was unhesitatingly placed in the position which, by the way, he holds today.

Asked if he proposed returning, the reply was: 'They have asked me to return, and perhaps I may, but I don't quite know.' It was palpable that now he is here, Fred has a hankering to remain.

Spiksley's method of freelancing his services to various football clubs and associations has made it difficult to pinpoint specific achievements and stories that could be included within this book. We do know that by 1924 Fred had coached in Sweden, Germany, Belgium, France, Switzerland, America, Mexico and Peru. This list would be further added to after periods in Germany and Switzerland with Lausanne. He would also spend the 1930/31 season coaching football in Badalona, near Barcelona, including refereeing a match between Barcelona and CE Júpiter.

By 1924, all that was missing from Spiksley's list of coaching achievements was a settled coaching role in English football. It is certain that he had worked with several English clubs on a part time basis, and a 1924 cartoon drawn by Tottenham's Jimmy Seed, the future Sheffield Wednesday player and legendary Charlton Athletic manager, seems to substantiate this claim.

Chapter 25

A Final Flirtation

An underdog Cup run with Fulham, 1924–26

Fred Spiksley's break into coaching in English football arose in 1924 when he was snapped up by a struggling Fulham side, whose new manager Andy Ducat sought success. The former England international had retired from playing in May 1924 and after successful stints with Arsenal and Aston Villa, had played for Fulham between 1921 and 1924. Never cautioned, Ducat also played once for England at cricket.

Ducat had replaced the retiring Phil Kelso as Fulham manager. Playing in Division Two, the Cottagers had narrowly avoided relegation, but heavy debts meant Ducat lacked money to invest in new players. He outlined his philosophy in a series of 'football tips' in *The Mercury* newspaper. To help achieve success, and in a sign of football's growing commercialisation, 'Andy Ducat Patent Boots' were available from the Biggleswade shop of former Luton Town and Fulham player William Albon. Ducat was following in the footsteps of Steve Bloomer, who was the first footballer to have a pair of boots named after him.

The squad Ducat inherited was packed with Scots, including George Aimer, Alec Chaplin, James Torrance and Henry Lafferty. Veteran centre forward George Edmonds had scored the goals which had kept Fulham up. Ducat signed William Prouse at inside right, who scored in the opening League fixture at Bradford City that ended 1-1. When Fulham drew 0-0 at home to Portsmouth on 4 October 1924, they had taken seven points from seven games.

At this time, Fred Spiksley had just returned from his football coaching role in Mexico. It was reported that he was set to coach in Argentina, but within a week of being back in England he had been appointed in a similar capacity at Fulham for a two-year period. His duties included finding promising players and training them along scientific lines.

Fulham were the League's lowest scorers and Spiksley's arrival coincided with them scoring more goals, with six in the following three home matches that yielded two wins and a draw. There was also real pleasure when, on 6 December, Fulham beat Sheffield Wednesday 2-1 at home before a crowd of 18,000. Fulham finished in twelfth place, with only forty-one goals scored in forty-six games.

A Final Flirtation

The 1925–26 season started badly as Fulham lost 3-0 at Sheffield Wednesday. Left half Bert Barrett had come into the side and would go on to make 419 Fulham appearances and play once for England. In December, 'keeper Ernie Beecham, signed from Hertford in the Spartan League, debuted against Blackpool. His subsequent run of 130 consecutive appearances was only halted when he broke his neck.

Eight of the first nine games of the season were lost with only a 1-0 home victory against Stockport County earning any points. Things got slightly better and when Fulham drew 0-0 with Bradford City just before Christmas, they stayed a point above bottom-placed Stockport. Only Clapton Orient had scored fewer goals than Fulham, who had struggled with the new two, rather than three-man, offside rule. The change had been introduced because officials were alarmed by a general goal shortage and the 'experiment' was deemed successful as more goals were scored as a result. In response, the new Arsenal manager Herbert Chapman adopted the W-M formation of two full backs, a centre half, two half backs, two inside forwards, two wingers and a centre forward. The key change was that the centre half became exclusively a stopper rather than – like Charlie Roberts with Manchester United before the First World War – a playmaker. Rather than three half backs there were now two. The inside forwards, or at least one them, also began to drop a little deeper.

The change disappointed Fred Spiksley. In August 1928 he wrote to *Athletic News* stating 'The W formation is an apology for lazy or worn-out inside forwards' and argued 'that it was easier for an attack to be neutralised if the outside forwards were shadowed by the wing halves'. He preferred pre-1925 formations.

On 2 January 1926, Fulham gained revenge for the opening-day defeat by beating Sheffield Wednesday 3-0 at Craven Cottage. Wednesday went on to win the next five matches, with Jimmy Trotter in blistering form: his thirty-seven League goals during the season meant his side won the Second Division title. Fulham's victory against Wednesday proved vital as they ensured that the Londoners finished nineteenth, two points above relegated Stoke City. Fulham beat Bradford City 2-0 at home on the season's final day to avoid relegation into Division Three South.

All of which made it all the more remarkable that Fulham almost reached the semi-finals of the FA Cup. Fulham began by drawing 1-1 at Everton. Playing an open game, Fulham held on until half-time when Dixie Dean netted. However on 70 minutes, Teddy Craig cleverly steered the ball past Harry Hardy to equalise. Everton would have won the match if not for a magnificent late save from 18-year-old Ernie Beecham, who was showered with congratulations afterwards.

A crowd of 20,176 attended the replay. Heavy snow and freezing temperatures made playing conditions difficult, and Fulham were unfortunate when centre half Jock McNab's header hit the post. On 65 minutes, the Cottagers' Bert White scored and although Alex Chaplin later left the field, Fulham held on to win, with Beecham again being the hero following a series of fine saves topped off by a brilliant late stop from Alec Troup. Beecham was chaired off the field by celebrating Fulham fans.

Fulham next faced Liverpool. With Edmonds unfit, Albert Pape led the line. Craven Cottage was packed with 36,381 spectators and after Donald McKinlay failed to clear, Pape put his side ahead on 3 minutes and, even though Dick Forshaw equalised, Frank Penn restored Fulham's lead. Pape made it 3-1 on 56 minutes. When Liverpool pressed, Beecham was in great form and was afterwards again chaired off the field by home fans.

Fulham next played at Notts County where, before a 28,000 crowd, they netted very late on when Bill Prouse, latching on to a perfectly weighted Jack Harris ball, beat Albert Iremonger to set up a quarter final tie with Manchester United, whom Fulham had beaten in the same round in 1908 to reach the last four, at the time their finest FA Cup run.

A Craven Cottage crowd of 28,699 saw Frank McPherson put the northern side ahead in the first minute. There was an immediate equaliser from Pape, whose signature from Manchester United at the start of the season was only made on condition that he could live in Bolton and train during the week with Manchester United. The game was a tight affair, but when right full back Reg Dyer was forced off the field for treatment, Manchester United took advantage and Tom Smith netted to take his side through to a semi-final encounter against Manchester City that they subsequently lost 3-0.

Fulham's brave fight had ended, and after such a poor League season it was no surprise that Ducat tendered his managerial resignation. He continued playing cricket for Surrey and suffered a fatal heart attack while batting for the Surrey Home Guard against Sussex Home Guard in 1942. In the wake of Ducat's departure, Fred Spiksley, whose contract had ended, also left the Cottagers, who were relegated at the end of the 1927–28 season.

Meanwhile, on 16 March 1927, Ellen Spiksley of 118 Broomspring 362 Lane, Sheffield, the wife of Fred Spiksley, swore an oath saying the statements set forth in the petition of Ellen Spiksley were true to the best of her knowledge, information and belief and that there had been no collusion between her and her husband. Fred's address was given as 1 Fussball Club, Bahnhofstrasse 13, Nurnberg, Germany and he was listed as an athletics coach. The statements claimed Fred had deserted his wife for over two years without reasonable cause, 'has frequently committed adultery' and 'that from 1920 up to the present date he has frequently committed adultery with Lena Adams'. Further 'that from around May 1925 to around the month of June 1925 at 27 Third Cross Road, Twickenham in the County of Middlesex, Fred Spiksley has committed adultery with the said Lena Adams'. This period was when Fred was the Fulham coach.

This information was sent to Fred, who was now back in Germany. He was instructed to:

> Take notice that you are required within eight days after service here to enter an application either in person or by your solicitor at the Divorce Registry of the High Court of Justice at Somerset House in the Strand and make answer to the charges in this petition and that in default of doing so the court will proceed to hear the said charges and if proved pronounce judgement in your absence.

The divorce petition was filed in court the following day and on 13 May the case was moved to Leeds Assizes, where it was held before the Honourable Mr Justice Talbot on 22 July 1927. Fred Spiksley wasn't present to defend himself and there would have been little point as he had clearly had a number of affairs and wasn't living with his wife: he wasn't even in the same country as her!

The marriage, which had been solemnised on 5 September 1895, was dissolved 'on reason that since the celebration of the marriage the respondent has been guilty of adultery'. A *decree nisi* was granted and finally made absolute on 13 March 1928. After over thirty-two years of marriage, Ellen and Fred Spiksley were now officially free to go their separate ways. Ellen was to later become an antique furniture dealer and lived out the rest of her life in Sheffield, where she died in December 1965.

Chapter 26

Return to Zabo

Winning the German Championship with 1FC Nuremberg

With millions of casualties on both sides in the First World War, there had appeared to be little chance of Fred being quickly able to return to his pre-war role as coach to Football Club Nurnberg (FCN). However, by 1919 William Townley had returned to his Bayern Munich coaching post and in April 1920, Stuttgart wrote to the Nottingham Forest secretary asking if he could recommend 'a man of the type of James Cowan, John Goodall, Johnnie Holt or Fred Spiksley. The idea that life in Southern Germany would be unpleasant for an Englishman is absolute piffle as indicated by the great popularity of Will Townley ... a high salary and genial surroundings are guaranteed.' Although the Forest secretary ignored the request, it was reported in many papers and Fred wrote unsuccessfully to Stuttgart.

League football in Germany had been suspended during the war. When it resumed, there were regional leagues with the top teams then playing one another in a knockout competition with the winners being awarded the German championship. German football also became a mass spectator sport in the 1920s as many workers had time off, including Saturdays.

FCN's hated local rivals, SpVgg Fürth, won the championship in 1919 but, with the recruitment of Hungarians Petr Szabo and Alfred 'Spezi' Schaffer from MTK Budapest, FCN won the 1919–20 championship without losing a match. Around 30,000 welcomed the team on their return from the final and the championship was won again in 1920–21, 1923–4 and 1924–5. They lost out to Fürth in 1925–26 and many of their best players were coming to the end of their careers, while the changes in the offside law demanded a much quicker style than that previously adopted by the club. Only during the final matches in 1921 and 1922 had a special tactical coach been engaged in the person of former MTK centre half Dori Kurschner. Otherwise, captain Gustav Bark had taken the twice-weekly training seasons when the players played for hours against one another.

After completing his Fulham contract in 1926, Fred Spiksley telegraphed the FCN president Hans Schregele to remind him that at the onset of the First World War, the then president, Leopold Neuberger, had promised he could return as coach once the conflict had ended. Whether he had inside knowledge about the German club's desire to employ a coach, Fred chose the right time as it struck a chord with many club members, who would have remembered him guiding 1FCN to their famous 'kind of victory' against Spurs in 1914. The management committee thus decided to engage him, initially for one year, at a monthly fee of 1,000 German marks.

With all the players being amateur, the training sessions started at 6.30pm. Mondays and Saturdays were allocated to the youth team, Tuesdays and Thursdays to the first team and Fridays to all the other teams. First team matches would take place on Mondays.

In all five pre-season friendlies, FCN beat their opponents and scored thirty-six goals while conceding only five. The day Spiksley arrived he watched a 1FCN reserve team fixture. Youngster Seppl Schmitt caught his eye and although Schmitt was just starting to break into the Nuremberg first team, it's Spiksley who is credited with giving the teenager his first real chance to prove himself. Schmitt was the young blood that was needed if Fred was to turn around the fortunes of an ageing squad. Schmitt would go on to win two German championships, as well as becoming a club legend.

The competitive season started on Monday, 6 September 1926 with a 7-0 home thrashing of FC Bayreuth. FCN were in the Southern League and they finished top of the group with sixteen wins, one draw and just one defeat. They scored sixty-four goals and conceded seventeen. In the last-sixteen match, played at SpVgg Fürth's ground, FCN made short work of Chemnitz and won 5-1 before beating Hamburger SV 2-1 in Hamburg. The semi-final was held at the ASV ground in Nuremberg-Herrnhütte and, with Schorsch Hochsgang playing brilliantly, FCN beat TSV Munchen 4-1.

Meanwhile, in the summer of 1927, Burnley had travelled to the continent to play three friendship games and arrived in Nuremberg to face Fred Spiksley's side on 26 May 1927.

The home side were: Heiner Stuhlfauth, Luitpold Popp, Georg Winter, Emil Koepplinger, Hans Kalb, Hans 'Bumbes' Schmidt, Baptist Reinmann, Georg Hochgesang, Seppl Schmitt, Ludwig Wieder, Heiner Traeg.

Twenty-five thousand fans poured into the revamped Zabo ground when the stadium was opened an hour before kick-off, and before which both sides laid a wreath at a specially-built cenotaph. At the interval the fans were wearing long faces as Burnley held a 1-0 lead. However, Seppl Schmitt notched two in the second period and with goals from Wieder and Hochgesang, the home side triumphed 4-2 and captured the beautiful silver 'Cluberern Cup' that had been donated by Burnley's Georges Richart.

In the other League semi-final, played in Leipzig, SpVgg Fürth, trained by Townley, were beaten 2-1 by Hertha BSC Berlin, who would play the final in their home city at the Grunewald Stadium, which had been built in 1913 to host the subsequently abandoned 1916 Berlin Olympic Games. The stadium was demolished in the 1930s to make way for the new Olympic Stadium that hosted the Berlin Olympics in 1936.

The final on 12 June 1927 was attended by 50,000 people with just 1,200 cheering for FCN.

FCN: Heiner Stuhlfauth, Luitpold Popp, George Winter, Emil Koepplinger, Hans Kalb, (captain) Hans 'Bumbes' Schmidt, Baptist Reinmann, Georg Hochgesang, Seppl Schmitt, Ludwig Wieder, Heiner Traeg.

Hertha Berlin: Goetze, Domscheid, Fischer, Leuschner, Tewes, Mueller, Ruch, Sobeck, Grenzel, Kirsey, Guelle.

Referee: Mr Willi Guyenz (Essen).

The game was notable for being the first German football match to be covered live and in full on national radio. Hanne Sobeck, the Hertha captain, had predicted his side would stand a great chance of winning if the weather was hot and the ground was dry. Unfortunately, the night before the match it rained heavily and continued to do so right up until kick-off, making the playing surface extremely wet.

However, none of this stopped the passionate Hertha Berlin fans from belting out their club songs so that the visiting side could hardly hear their own band of hardy followers. With first teamers Carl Riegel and Anton Kugler injured, Fred Spiksley, who for some unknown reason wasn't present, was forced to field two reserve team players in Koepplinger and Winter.

The noise from the Berlin fans was stilled on 6 minutes when Kalb, who played fifteen times for Germany, netted. Then the FCN captain produced a sterling performance by keeping quiet dangerman Hanne Sobeck, who was renowned for his first touch.

When FCN sought a second goal they were thwarted by the offside tactics of Fischer and Domscheid. These so angered Traeg that when he continually showed his annoyance, it led to the referee admonishing him. Traeg was on dangerous ground as he had already been sent off when playing against Hamburg in the 1922 semi-final – a game that ended with FCN having only seven players on the field.

At half-time in the 1927 final, the score remained 1-0 in FCN's favour. During the break, the sun came out to warm the crowd and those in it supporting Hertha reminded Sobeck of his pre-match comments. However, it was FCN who forced the pace, although they were grateful to Bumbes Schmidt when he cleared a shot that had beaten Stuhlfauth, a brilliant keeper who rivalled Spaniard Ricardo Zamora as the best in the world at the end of the 1920s. Stuhlfauth played when Germany beat Italy for the first time in 1929 and would go on to make twenty-one international appearances.

Jolted at nearly conceding a goal, FCN pushed forward and on 65 minutes a quick throw by Bumbes Schmidt to Ludwig Wieder saw the ball moved on to Heiner Traeg. Looking up, the outside left hit a first-time shot beyond Goetze and into the net to make it 2-0. The scorer then taunted the Hertha hordes by shouting out 'We've won!'

This wasn't quite true, as on 74 minutes the losing side were given an opportunity to reduce the arrears from the penalty spot when Popp fouled Sobeck in the area. Domscheid's shot lacked pace and Stuhlfauth's save was an easy one. The 'keeper was especially popular among FCN fans off the pitch as he ran a wine tavern called Sebaldusklause, which Fred would frequent after training sessions in his desire to relax and get to know his players better. It was here that he met and fell in love with a young waitress, Rose, whom he married in 1929 and subsequently spent the rest of his life with.

Following the penalty save the game was meandering to a close when, on 80 minutes, Traeg took revenge for the kicking he had received throughout the game from Leuschner by booting the Hertha man with his left foot. The winger then abused the referee and was dismissed in what was his last game before retirement. Despite being a man down, FCN comfortably saw out the match to deservedly win 2-0. The *Berlin Tageblatt* newspaper summarised the proceedings accurately by stating, 'Nurnberg's victory was due to greater self-belief and confidence instilled in the team by Fred Spiksley, the coach'.

Despite the newspaper's praise for the successful coach, he had lost enthusiasm for coaching the new German Champions after being slated earlier in the season, along with the players, by the club chairman following the loss of an unimportant game. It was reported in the *Burnley Express and Star* of 1 June 1927 that he had 'lost interest in his work and intends returning home in three weeks time'.

Following his departure, FCN employed Dr K. Michalke and Hans Tauchert, both leaders of sporting exercises rather than football coaches. Until August 1930, when Jeno Konrad was employed, the philosophy of the club remained that great successes could be achieved without a coach and it wasn't until 1935–36 that FCN once again won the championship and cup final.

Fred, aged 59, and Rose Reichel, a spinster twenty years younger, were married on 3 June 1929 at Paddington Register Office. Fred's occupation was listed as an athletics coach, while nothing was listed for Rose, whose father was Johann George Reichel and whose income was listed as by independent means. The couple were resident at the Beaumont Hotel, Princes Square, London, at the time of their marriage.

Chapter 27

The Club by The Coast

Coaching at Badalona FC

In 1903, four years after near neighbours Barcelona FC were formed in 1899, Badalona FC was founded. Now the third largest city in Catalonia, Badalona stands on the left bank of the Besos River and on the Mediterranean Sea. Playing near the beach, Badalona FC soon became known as The Club by the Coast.

In 1929 Badalona FC competed in two league competitions. Before Christmas there was the local Catalan Championship, which was more often than not won by Barcelona. Those clubs finishing in the top three, which had never previously included Badalona, would qualify for Spain's most prestigious knockout competition, the Copa del Rey.

From late December Badalona would then compete in the newly-formed fourth tier of the Spanish National League. This offered the opportunity to work their way up to the recently-established La Liga. Here the familiar Spanish giants that we know today lay the foundations of what was to come and in 1930 Atletico Bilbao had just beaten Barcelona, the first winners, into second place to become the second La Liga Champions. With Barcelona located just 6 miles south, it's easy to see why Badalona's directors became ambitious to achieve greater success with their small club, and in 1930 they decided to invest in a world class coach.

That same year, the local professional basketball team, known initially as Penya Spirit of Badalona, was formed and which ever since has been one of the best sides in Spain. If the football club was to compete for local sports fans' affections, then it would need to rise up the pyramid and play in a higher league. The club were ambitious with enthusiastic owners. They had sought to persuade Bilbao head coach Fred Pentland, who after a mixed career as a player went on to become a highly successful coach on the continent, to join them, but the Englishman chose to stay in the Basque country instead.

Barcelona head coach Jim Bellamy, who had earlier managed in Italy with Brescia, recommended that Badalona FC appoint another English coach in Fred Spiksley, who was then in his sixties. The Gainsborough man, who, of course, spoke Spanish as a result of his time in Mexico in the 1920s, arrived on an overnight train from France at Barcelona train station early on Wednesday, 2 July 1930.

A profile of what the former England international hoped to achieve appeared in the *El Mundo Deportivo* edition of 15 August 1930. The reporter had visited the ground, where football was played within the centre of a running track, to observe Spiksley taking a coaching session with the players.

Club president Mr Vea said that the players were on good salaries and it was hoped to play bigger clubs of international renown. He said of Spiksley 'I really like his training techniques and our players are amazed by him… he has a persuasive smoothness and is energetic at the same time in the way that he organises.' There are comments about players dribbling around imaginary enemies, possibly posts stuck in angles in the ground.

Accompanied by Rosa, Fred, who was at pains to highlight how much the pair enjoyed swimming in the warm Mediterranean Sea, was later interviewed by Olle Bertran for the *El Mundo Deportivo* on 1 December 1930. This was one of four articles in the paper during Spiksley's time in Catalonia. The coach explained that football in Spain was very different as 'Here you play much faster. Good football is played on the ground and in short passes moving forward. Here you dribble with your legs, dribbling should be done with the body naturally and without exaggeration.' Spiksley complained that the players did too much running that tired them out quickly.

He praised Barcelona, who had finished top of the recently-ended Catalan League, but he was disappointed that his new club had finished in third place, with Sadabell finishing in second after the latter won away against his side in a rough encounter. Spiksley was now hoping to do well in the upcoming Spanish Championship season.

In the 1930 Catalan football championship, which consisted of six clubs, Barcelona had won eight, drawn one and lost one of their ten matches. The solitary defeat by one goal to nil on 26 October 1930 was at Badalona, whose success was reported in the papers under the headline 'In a splendid display of enthusiasm the Badalona gave the great surprise by beating the Champions.' This was clearly no fluke as Badalona also drew 0-0 in a home friendly during the season with Real Madrid, whose team included Ricardo Zamora, often regarded as one of the greatest goalkeepers of all time. The annual award for the best 'keeper in La Liga, the Ricardo Zamora Trophy, is named in his honour. Amongst others, Zamora also played for Espanyol, Barcelona and Real Madrid.

In the National League, Badalona managed to beat Sadabell 4-1 at home and ended the season second out of six, behind Valencian side S. Sagunto. In the

Copa Del Rey, Fred's team were given a bye in round one and played Real Betis in round two, beating them 1-0 at home, but losing 2-0 away to go out 2-1 on aggregate. Real Betis, who won promotion from the Second Division at the end of the season, went on to reach the cup final, where they lost out to Pentland's Atletico Bilbao side that also won La Liga.

It was clear that on its day, Badalona under Fred Spiksley was capable of competing with the bigger clubs, but this had come at a cost. One that meant the football club was unable to afford the wages of its players or coach and at the end of the season and with his squad dismantled, Spiksley headed for home on 25 May 1931.

Chapter 28

A Focus on Youth

Passing on the secrets of his success

After leaving Germany, Fred was appointed as coach to Lausanne Sports, in Switzerland. The club were trying to establish themselves and it is difficult to gauge what impact Fred had, but whilst in Switzerland he met Robert Alaway who, as an Eton schoolboy, had first encountered football as a spectator at the 1893 Richmond international between England and Scotland.

Such impact did the game and his new hero – Spiksley – have that in 1905 he founded the amateur Middlesex Wanderers football club, with whom Alaway spent most of his adult life touring the globe. In his 1948 book *Football All Round the World*, he retold the tale of meeting Fred Spiksley two decades earlier, in 1928.

> My introduction to association football was in the company of royalty when I saw my first game – an international on the hallowed Richmond Athletic Ground between England and their historic foes, the Scots. I shall never forget it.
>
> Since then I have seen thousands of football matches in all parts of the world, graced by kings, emperors, princes, presidents and of course millions of the common kind. But an imperishable memory is that glorious spring afternoon of 1893 beneath the quiet trees beside the gentle flowing Thames.
>
> Apart from the spectacle of a real live duke and a princess, the outstanding personalities of this international were the immaculate English wingers – the late W.I. Bassett and Fred Spiksley. What players they were! With every respect to present-day players, these two were undoubtedly greatness personified. To see them both in action in the same game was indeed a schoolboy treat that loses none of its sweetness in old age. Both played a textbook game, with the highlight of the match three brilliant goals scored by Spiksley from the left wing, all within the space of about ten minutes. England won the game 5 goals to 2.

Watching these players as a small boy, I little thought that in after years I should have the great pleasure of knowing these men intimately...

As for Spiksley, it was not until 35 years later that I saw this great figure of a man again; and that was at Lausanne in 1928. The Middlesex Wanderers had gone there to play Lausanne Sports FC, to whom Spiksley was the revered professional coach.

At the after match reception I told Spiksley I had seen him score three goals for England. He had a remarkable memory for the games he played in. Not only did he remember the international but nearly every movement of the game. He went through every one of them again while my eyes popped and my pulse quickened with renewed excitement. I had completely forgotten, but Spiksley reminded me that the referee was J.C. Clegg, the FA chairman, who took no notice that one of the players lost his football boots and turned out in black walking boots.

At the reception, R.A. Stephens, asked Spiksley: 'Do you remember scoring a goal from the junction of the halfway line and the touch line on the Spurs ground?' It happened years and years before but Spiksley remembered it distinctly. Indeed, he produced from his pocket-book a press cutting describing the phenomenon. Then said Stephens: 'I refereed that game. That is why I remember it so well.' And there at the foot of the report was printed: 'Referee: R.A. Stephens.'

The evidence concerning Spiksley's long distance strike at White Hart Lane is that it probably happened during a London Cup match while Fred was playing for Southern United, which means Spiksley still had the timing in his legs to punch through the ball in the way we all remember David Beckham doing at Selhurst Park in 1996. Spiksley would have been about 35 when he scored the goal.

After his one-year contract with Lausanne Sports ended, Fred returned to England and was now well into his fifties.

Despite his long involvement in football, his finances remained unstable and he couldn't afford to retire. In 1929 he arranged with the *London Evening News* to contribute a series of practical hints in *How to Play Football*. It gave him the opportunity to share his forty years' close study of the science and technology of football and the articles were aimed at London teenagers eager to develop their footballing abilities.

As Fred matured as a coach he became increasingly aware of the importance of nurturing talented young players. Writing for *Spalding's Athletic Annual* during his time in America, he was very vocal on how the USFA needed to encourage and develop its talented youth:

> All the legislators in the world will not make players. You must act besides preach. Gentlemen interested must look out for plots of land where these boys can be taken to play. If an important match is in the vicinity, somebody with football at heart should take as many boys as wish to go to see the game. The boys will soon see where the art of the game lies and will not be slow to pick up the main points. What they need is models to work up to.

In 1929, Fred expressed his disappointment at what he saw as the finer points of football having disappeared and at the lack of quality coaches. He felt that many footballers didn't even know the correct part of the foot to kick the ball with – namely the outside – as 'in my humble opinion, it is only the outside of the foot that a football can be properly controlled with'. He argued that muscles on the outside of the foot were stronger than the inside and consequently, the use of the latter slowed down the time it takes for a ball to be passed to a teammate. The same was true for shooting at goal.

He recommended that young players should learn how to kick a tennis ball against the wall, that a left winger should control the ball with his right and vice versa. There were tips on how to trap the ball correctly, keeping your eyes on the ball, back heeling the ball, heading and swerving away from opponents – at which no-one he had witnessed was as good as Vivian Woodward. There was then advice for every different position. The articles were accompanied by photographs of Spiksley demonstrating the various techniques, so that young boys could practise them themselves.

Although Fred didn't always believe that football was constantly improving, there is no doubt that he was never stuck in the past. In the same year as his *Evening News* articles, Fred Spiksley returned to Craven Cottage to record a film for *Pathé News*, who had first covered the FA Cup final in 1901 and then showed the newsreel in cinemas nationally.

Cinema newsreels were silent until 1928, and Fred Spiksley's film was to become one of the earliest surviving films to combine motion picture with sound. The surviving footage is only 84 seconds long and it appears certain that what was recorded was longer as Fred Spiksley, wearing an England cap, jumper and track suit bottoms, can be clearly heard stating 'This time I am going to demonstrate some further aspects of the game'. Despite its brevity, it may well be the first ever football training film and it seems likely it was made to be taken into schools and be shown to youngsters in order to help them practise their skills.

Fred is seen working with Fulham's Bert Barrett and Len Oliver who, as England internationals, are seen wearing their international jerseys, and are shown practising back heeling the ball with Fred stating 'which is a very good trick'. The former Fulham coach, whom the narrator describes as 'the well-known football coach' then demonstrates himself the correct way to back heel the ball, before Barrett and Oliver are filmed running down the wing as they first master and then pass the ball with the inside foot to one another.

The surviving footage of film is one of 85,000 films that *British Pathé* made freely available to the general public in 2014 and it demonstrates that at nearly 60 years of age, Spiksley was still forward thinking and eager to embrace the latest technologies to help nurture future talent. An advert for Spiksley's film in the *Sheffield Independent* on 28 November 1929 describes how Spiksley uses a slow-motion camera to show the 'finer intricacies' of ball control. The video is available online.

When Sheffield became one of Britain's 330 local education authorities in 1902, Wesley College (originally built as the Wesley Proprietary Grammar School in 1840) was amalgamated with Sheffield Grammar School and became King Edward VII School in 1905. The all-boys school had a history of preparing boys for entry to Cambridge and Oxford Universities and the 1930s was the best decade for sport as it had teams competing in all disciplines at inter-school level, with many boys competing for the house teams or playing for the school.

Mr Eric Simms, the history master, was responsible for the football teams at the start of the 1930s. His greatest innovation was to obtain the headmaster, Mr Richard Graham's endorsement to employ a professional football coach between September 1933 and November 1936. Fred Spiksley was chosen.

When the former Wednesday wide man arrived for his first day of coaching, he was an old man of 63, wearing his best suit and a remarkably pristine bowler hat. Simms had great pleasure in introducing the man who had won the FA Cup and after which Fred Spiksley explained his coaching background to the group and how he hoped to develop their ball skills and teamwork in order to collectively improve the team. He placed his jacket carefully on the ground, removed his hat and proceeded to demonstrate the art of ball control using his hat as the ball. It was all a bit of fun, but the boys were immediately thrilled by Fred's skills and smiled broadly.

It was now time for the hard work and soon Fred became a hugely positive influence on the school's football. The high standards he set were responsible for the brilliance of the first and second elevens. One of the First XI was Eric Sivil, who became one of the best full backs to play for the school. Sivil's abiding memory of his coach was his insistence that the team must always keep their discipline and maintain the highest standards of sporting behaviour on the field of play. This reflected Fred's own playing career, during which his only sending-off was later rescinded.

This insistence on high behavioural standards did, however, sometimes conflict with the other message that Fred Spiksley stressed. Eric Sivil was summoned into Richard Graham's office where the head told him that his late tackle on an opponent during the previous game wasn't the way to play football as 'sport was not about winning'. Whereupon Eric replied, 'But Sir, Mr Spiksley had told us that football is all about winning'.

Fred's most successful season with the school was 1933–34, when the First XI, captained by Harold Pearson, won all twenty of their scheduled fixtures against their traditional rivals from both public and grammar schools. The only defeat was against a men's club side. A total of 181 goals was scored, easily a record, With Bob Gray knocking in 63. The win of the season was 3-1 over the Repton Public School on Armistice Day. It was the first time that the school had beaten Repton and they also won the return 5-2.

The remarkable achievements that Fred Spiksley inspired were recognised in a rather unusual way when the Ardath Tobacco Company included the King Edward VII school football team in their football cigarette photograph collection in 1935–36, alongside top football teams of the day such as Sunderland, Arsenal, Everton and the 1935 FA Cup winners Sheffield Wednesday, who beat West Bromwich Albion 4-2 in the final at Wembley.

Meanwhile, the *Sheffield Green Un* sports paper noted Spiksley's success with the youngsters in Sheffield. On 12 September 1936 it reported: 'Fred Spiksley's great passion is his burning desire to coach young footballers. It is a pity that no club in the country has used his knowledge and football experience…England has never had a better outside left than Spiksley.'

Fred maintained his links with King Edward's and a local sports fanatic Mick Gill, who lived near the school as a child, later recalled how one 1946 afternoon two elderly neighbours, Charlie Briggs and Ernest Parry, returned home in great spirits. They had witnessed a sprightly elderly man advising some of the school students as they held a practice football match. His skills and athleticism had astounded everybody. The stranger was Fred Spiksley, aged 76.

In the mid 1930s, Gill, a young teenager, had met the former footballer while walking with his dad and the pair had stopped to chat to two well-dressed men at the Hammer and Pincers pub at Bents Green. Gill's father told him the men were Fred Spiksley and George Mooney, the leader of the Mooney Gang, whose violent rivalry with the Park Gang over control of Sheffield's lucrative 'pitch and toss rings' saw one man murdered in the 1920s, two brothers hanged and many others imprisoned before the gangs were finally smashed by a Home Office-instigated flying squad. Mooney twice went to prison but had retired for good from gang matters by 1936, and for the rest of his life he remained a well-known figure on northern racecourses using a pseudonym in order to work as a bookmaker.

Mooney and Fred thus had a common gambling interest and it was while the latter was pursuing his passion for horse racing that he bumped into his former England colleague Steve Bloomer at Derby Midland Station on Friday 19 November 1937. Bloomer was unwell and a testimonial fund had raised sufficient funds for him to go cruising around Australia and New Zealand. Bloomer was en route to boarding the luxury liner *Otranto* as the first part of the trip when he met Mooney at the station. Bloomer died three weeks after returning home in April 1938. His funeral on the afternoon of Wednesday 20 April 1938 at Derby Cathedral was attended by numerous personalities from the world of football, including Fred Spiksley.

Chapter 29

Scientific Football

Fred's revolutionary coaching philosophy

Fred's coaching strategies placed him decades ahead of virtually every coach and it took the FA and professional football clubs over sixty years to catch up by imitating his plans for academies.

During Fred's time in North, Central and South America in the early 1920s, the game back home in England struggled to develop. Emphasis remained on physical fitness and whilst the game became notably faster, the quality of the football on display, even in the First Division, had deteriorated. Whilst supporters could still have their pulses tested in tense, thrilling matches, a lack of skill and art, that Fred himself had entertained the crowds with during his time as a player, had resulted in a more kick and rush game with the ball spending far too long in the air. This way of playing was to continue even after officials, alarmed by the shortage of goals, changed the offside rule in 1925 so that a forward could only be offside if there were fewer than two, rather than three, defenders between an attacker and the goal.

Fred was disappointed with what he saw on his return to England in 1924. 'I have been having a look at the football of our own country, the country that invented the game. And I must confess that I am a disappointed man. All the old enthusiasm and energy are there, of course, plus a good deal more pace than there used to be, but I have no hesitation in saying that the finer points of the game, as we knew then in the nineties, are gradually disappearing.'

Whilst it would be easy to accuse Fred of looking back at his time as a player and wanting to preserve some sort of superiority and look down on the modern game, this could not have been further from the truth. He wrote in the *Athletic News* how it pained him to be coaching abroad, improving the game in other countries to the point where he believed that they would one day not only be able to compete with England, but would be better.

He acknowledged that the stars of the 1920s such as Alec James (Arsenal) and Andy Wilson (Chelsea) were perfect role models for the young footballer to learn from, but he believed that whilst some people in football would hold up these players as examples of how football had progressed, he believed that they highlighted a lack of broader talent in the game. Not enough players had the ability of the few leading examples and this was leading to a steep inflation on transfer fees.

The FA would't have agreed with Fred's belief that continental football would one day overtake the English game. Nevertheless, there must have been some concern about the quality of the national game, because in 1930, the year when England refused to entertain the idea of taking part in the first World Cup in Uruguay, the governing body launched a training programme, fronted by Arsenal manager Herbert Chapman. It was hoped this would be used across the country to develop players coming through the ranks.

At the heart of the FA's coaching system was better communication of how skills should be performed, and they utilised slow motion film to demonstrate correct techniques. Emphasis was placed on trapping, controlling the ball on the move and, obviously, how to kick the ball correctly. Highlighting these key skills fitted in with Spiksley's complaints of the quality of the game at the time and all that was contained in the FA and Herbert Chapman's project ties in with the work Fred had been doing with various teams abroad.

Although Herbert Chapman rated Spiksley as the greatest outside left, it's unclear how well he knew of the coaching work Spiksley had done, and how he reacted to Fred's *Athletic News* article in August 1928, where Fred publicly unpicked his W formation (see Chapter 25).

Both before and after the First World War, Spiksley had spent over a decade coaching in Sweden, Germany, France, Belgium, Switzerland, America, Mexico and Peru, and although this had enabled him to develop his own coaching philosophy that he wanted to bring back to England, his time away meant that Fred was more of an outsider than he had ever been. The FA and Chapman saw no reason to consult with Fred on their new training programme, but if they had they could have advanced the coaching of English teams by decades. Indeed, the ideas Fred had devised wouldn't be used until the days of Sir Alf Ramsey, and variations and development of Fred's ideas are now used by every professional club across the world.

The problem with the FA's new approach was that it relied upon the belief that if you show someone how to do something then if they constantly copy it then they will inevitably get better. Whilst potentially true, Fred's philosophy went further.

At the start of his coaching career Fred had been a big admirer of the way the Manchester United side, which included Billy Meredith, Charlie Roberts and Sandy Turnbull, under the direction of Ernest Mangnall, had used the 'Forcing Game' to win their first League Championship in 1908 and FA Cup in 1909. Tactically this would be the foundation of how Fred got his teams to play, alongside his unwavering belief that good football was always played along the ground and not in the air. But it was during his time in America and Mexico that Fred developed a series of training drills that he believed would develop the key fundamentals of ball control.

In 1929 he wrote:

> Ball control is the real secret of success in this game. A great many players in all walks of the game do not realise the importance of ball control; at any rate they make little effort to acquire it.
>
> Otherwise the game as a spectacle would, generally speaking, compare more favourably with the old days when only scientific football was encouraged, than it actually does.

This again demonstrates that his criticism of the game came from a belief that football should be better than it was at this time.

In 1924 Spiksley had returned to England. It was intended to be a brief stay as he had accepted another coaching engagement across the Atlantic. However, before heading south again Spiksley had a shot at trying to land his first permanent coaching position back home, and he managed to convince the directors at Fulham to allow him to demonstrate his new methods with the Fulham first team (see again, Chapter 25)

The *Athletic News* reported:

> Spiksley has thought out a system of teaching football. This is based on gaining command of the ball. He has invented a series of ingenious exercises which are, no doubt, valuable to all players. He gave a demonstration of his methods to the Fulham team at Craven Cottage in the presence of several of the directors of the club and Andrew Ducat, the manager. His system appeared to create a favourable impression. We cannot help feeling that Spiksley's plan of teaching would prove beneficial and create not only resource, but confidence among young players.

Fred was hired on the spot and cancelled his return to Central America.

Whilst Fred would have been grateful to Fulham for the opportunity they gave him, he must have been left to wonder what he could have achieved at a bigger club. Fulham spent the majority of the 1920s in financial difficulties, meaning that they could only build a squad of modest abilities. Fred's coaching helped maintain a status quo in the Second Division.

The FA pressed ahead with their new programme. Fred returned to teaching on the continent, continuing with his training methods to great success through to the end of his coaching career.

Spiskley had realised that to develop his number one fundamental in football – 'ball control' – more needed to be done. Whilst match situations cannot be practiced at all times, he needed to devise training drills that did more than just involve repeated trapping and kicking of the ball. Therefore, training exercises had to be invented to apply the mastery of ball control whilst the body was in motion and his solution was what he referred to as 'the scheme of sticks'.

Whilst there is an awkwardness about the *Pathé News* film (see *A Focus on Youth* chapter) that makes his use of sticks look rudimentary to the modern viewer, this was far from the case. Through his 1929 articles Fred describes how the sticks can be used to create any number of challenging games for players to play, all of which focused on controlling the ball on the move and under pressure.

If you place the sticks in a circle another exercise in control is provided, while two players passing to each other through the straight line of sticks test the powers of control even further.

Spiksley commented that, 'Club officials could arrange for their players to put in two or three nights a week at this specialised practice. The results would surprise them.'

Other sources describe how Fred would also angle the sticks into the ground to force players to duck and weave around the obstacles, all the time retaining full control of the ball.

Through modern eyes it's easy to take for granted that the use of sticks and cones to create training drills is a fundamental element of football training. Anyone turning up early to watch Pep Guardiola's Manchester City warming up before a match today will see players performing modern variations of what Spiksley described almost a century ago.

But in 1924 these training methods didn't exist anywhere other than in a coaching session led by Fred Spiksley. Several papers including the *Belfast Telegraph* reported that: 'This is the first attempt to introduce scientific methods of ball control into professional football training.'

Coaching with sticks would not be adopted in football coaching methods until the 1960's when England, after proving Fred right in being humbled by other nations, could once again could rightly claim to be the World Champions, a feat they have yet to go anyway near repeating.

Other exercises focused on developing abilities that Fred thought were needed in a match situation, such as the ability to swerve round players and to be light on your feet so that you could turn at pace. He had no time for what he described as 'leaden footed' players, but he invented coaching methods to eradicate this.

Whilst the FA and Chapman offered ball trapping demonstrations with motionless players, Fred was more concerned about how you trap and manoeuvre the ball in one smooth movement whilst on the run, again thinking about skill and matchday application.

Although it's clear that Spiksley understood the importance of fitness work, he was also more interested in development of the right kind of strength for a football match and showed a greater awareness of what would be called 'Sport Science' today: 'If players would develop the muscles below the hips by leg exercises, instead of paying too much attention to club swinging and punchball practice, they would gain a much firmer grip with the leg to resist a heavy charge.'

To Fred Spiksley fitness was not just about training hard, it was about training in the right way to develop the correct muscles to play the game. And whilst he accepted that some players were born footballers, frequently using Steve Bloomer as an example, he strongly believed that the game could be learnt and skills developed through proper scientific methods. He agreed that there were correct ways to perform skills, but believed that in order to develop players to do these well they needed better guidance than to just do that skill over and over again. Through his training drills he could make noticeable improvements to a player within two weeks and turn an average player into an excellent player within two years.

Despite favourable words in the *Athletic News* and in the Sheffield press who continued to keenly follow Spiksley, his methods weren't adopted by other clubs. Meanwhile, other papers such as London's *John Bull Sunday Paper* found it almost humorous that Fred would make top class players dribble the ball between posts, leading their article with the title 'Fancy This'. However, they did agree that poor ball control was a regular feature of the current game.

It should be said that Spiksley was a coach who had high expectations of his players. He didn't take kindly to lateness or a half-hearted approach to training, and towards the end of his coaching career he was quoted as saying of those that did not train properly: 'when you see them on the pitch, they are the ones who are playing badly.'

Fred's revolutionary ideas didn't stop with his training methods. Remarkably Fred was promoting his idea of setting up what he described as 'Football Nurseries' as far back as 1922 whilst he was in America and looking at ways that the recently formed United States FA (USFA) could accelerate the development of the game over there.

Writing in *Spalding's Athletic Annual* he said: 'All clubs affiliated with the USFA should be compelled to contribute to a fund to encourage school football and the allotment of this money to various centres would then be in the hands of capable and impartial gentlemen.'

Spiksley believed that training players with no club affiliation would mean that the emphasis would all be focused on an individual's development, rather than fulfilling the agendas of the wealthy factory owners that ran the clubs in the USA. The former Sheffield Wednesday player detailed how schoolboys should be provided every opportunity to watch the best players and the need for pitches and facilities for the young players. Typically, he also touted for work, stating 'I think that I could build up a team that would do credit to their country in the Olympic Games.'

In 1933, and probably feeling that he had had his last stint abroad, Fred was to return to his idea of setting up a football academy and he attempted this back in Sheffield. He placed adverts in the local press for young footballers to enrol in his Football Nursery, where he planned to continue with his coaching philosophy. Recruiting the right boys proved challenging, so he reshaped his idea and was successful in convincing King Ted's Grammar School to let him train their school team (see again, A Focus on Youth).

It was not until the 1990s that the FA and top-class clubs caught up with Spiksley. Roy Massey, whose grandfather, of course, played so bravely in the same Sheffield Wednesday that won the FA Cup a hundred years earlier in 1896 explains:

> My job, which started part time with Norwich City in September 1991 and became full time in September 1995, was to find players from aged under 9 to under 12 years and which involved finding the best youngsters in North London before the big clubs saw them. This was a radical move as at the time clubs had Schools of Excellence to which they sought to attract players who were, at least, 13 years old.

In 1997 Howard Wilkinson was appointed by the Football Association to revamp youth development. He introduced the FA's 'Charter of Quality' which revolutionised youth football in England. Youth players were to be inducted into professional club academies rather than youth club football itself. One of the aims of the academies was to produce players for the first team. It's cheaper to produce home grown players, who are also aware of the club's philosophy and culture. Each academy that has been set up does, though, have a slightly different philosophy, aim and objective.

For an academy to stand any chance of success it meant that clubs needed to improve significantly their facilities, especially as Wilkinson proposed that they be able to recruit and develop young players from the age of 8.

Before this ruling, clubs signed boys at 13 and they trained at their local club which had a School of Excellence. Boys who showed potential could be signed on schoolboy forms when they reached the age of 14. Before Howard introduced the academies, coaches and scouts at their various clubs were loathed to look at boys as young as 8 years old. They couldn't see the point of recruiting at such a young age. Initially they still couldn't, as following Howard's announcement there were only five clubs immediately enlightened enough to take on board the FA's recommendation regarding recruiting, coaching and running teams for children who were so young. The clubs were Peterborough, Lincoln City, Nottingham Forest, Notts County and my employers, Norwich City.

It doesn't surprise me to discover that Spiksley was way ahead of his time on coaching and young players, as he truly was a remarkable character' says Massey, whose autobiography is set for release in 2022.

Although remarkable at the time, Fred Spiksley's coaching ideas for players of all ages have stood the test of time. If they had been adopted during his lifetime then the Home Nations may well have remained at the forefront of the game for decades, and England would surely now have more than one World Cup to their name.

Spiksley was, of course, not the only top-class English coach to be forced to seek work abroad, but until relatively recently, his name rarely appeared in any articles about these coaches. Hopefully, that will no longer be the case.

Meanwhile, if anyone has information from overseas newspapers about Spiksley's time coaching abroad then please get in touch. The chapter on Badalona was only possible after we were sent information by a Spanish reader of earlier editions of this book. Finally, the www.spiksley.com site will be placing further coaching information online in 2021.

Chapter 30

One Final Bet

The perfect way to go

Little was reported in the newspapers about Fred in the 1940s. It would certainly be interesting to know how he and his wife, a German national, faired living in London during the Second World War, especially during the Blitz periods when many industrial locations in Britain were heavily bombed.

Fred Spiksley died on Wednesday, 28 July 1948 aged 78. The London Olympics were set to kick off and Britain sweltered in temperatures reaching well into the nineties. The England international told friends he was 'feeling bad', before being overcome by the heat and falling dead in Tattersall's enclosure at Goodwood races on Ladies Day.

Fred's main love was always racing and so it was an appropriate ending, although it meant he missed collecting his winnings from the bet he had placed on Aurelia to win the 3.10pm Goodwood Stakes. Aurelia, who beat Billet and Whiteway in a ding-dong finish to win by a head at odds of 100-8, also had a Gainsborough connection as Aura, the dam of Aurelia, was by Dark Legend out of Ars Davina by Gainsborough.

Alan and Joyce Spicksley were holidaying in Great Yarmouth. Joyce later said, 'I recall seeing a newspaper board outside a shop stating "Former England footballer dies at Goodwood Races". Alan immediately knew it was Fred and went inside to buy the paper and confirm what he already knew.'

Following a post mortem without an inquest, the death was recorded at Chichester in West Sussex on 30 July 1948. The body was cremated and Fred's occupation was recorded as a retired athletics coach. It was reported that he had lived in London in recent years but had suffered indifferent health following a major internal operation. He left behind a widow, Rose, who continued to live in the capital until 1960, when her name disappears from the electoral role, and one son, Fred Junior, who lived until September 1978 and was chief electrician at the Neepsend Electricity Station, Sheffield.

Fred Senior had four remaining relatives in Gainsborough, including his sister-in-law, the urban district councillor Mrs Florence Spicksley, and his brother, William, who according to Joyce Spicksley, was 'owed a considerable sum of money by Fred at the time'. Nevertheless, Fred, who left no will, left to his wife, Rose, assets of £477 12s 3d (£477.61), the equivalent of around £17,000 today.

It was over forty-five years since Fred had played his last top-flight match for Wednesday and more than fifty years since he had performed internationally. Very few people still alive could possibly have seen the winger at his best. Nevertheless, a week later a letter appeared in the *Gainsborough News* from C.G. Jennings of 16 Garnett Street, Cleethorpes, who stated that during his seven years working on the paper he had worked alongside Fred Spiksley when he was an apprentice compositor in the 1880s and 90s. Jennings claimed he had seen every England international match and FA Cup final from 1897 till 1934 and 'that with all due deference to (Stanley) Matthews' wizardry, I shall always maintain Fred Spiksley, in possession of the ball, was the fastest forward I have ever seen, his phenomenal speed, his elusiveness and his shooting gifts made him the great player he became.'

Fred Spiksley's Achievements

Winner of every major trophy and honour available from 1887–1903.

First player to score a hat-trick against Scotland.

More than 300 career goals.

The highest average goal ratio of any winger in the history of English football.

Scorer of the fastest FA Cup final goal of all time: 20 Seconds (unconfirmed).

Hat-trick on England debut v Wales 1893.

First player to score back-to-back hat-tricks in international football.

Scored both goals in the 1896 FA Cup final in a 2-1 victory.

First player in history to receive a three-year contract.

Sheffield Wednesday's third leading goal scorer of all time across all first team fixtures, with 170 goals.

Average of more than a goal a game for his local club, Gainsborough Trinity: 131 goals in 126 matches.

First Wednesday player to score at Hillsborough.

Scorer of the first hat-trick at Hillsborough.

Scorer of the first away hat-trick in the Football League for Sheffield Wednesday.

Professional playing career which lasted two decades.

Scored for every club he played for: Gainsborough Trinity, Sheffield Wednesday, England, Glossop North End, Leeds City, Southern United, Watford and Corinthians FC.

Leeds City's first professional footballer and the man who provided the necessary ambassadorial role in 1905 that helped Leeds gain Football League status in 1905–06.

First professional footballer to coach across three continents, in countries including England, Sweden, America, Mexico, Peru, Germany, Switzerland, France and Spain.

One of Chelsea's first football scouts.

Host of the first talking football training film for young people.

Managed 1FC Nuremburg when they captured the German Championship in 1927 and was the last Englishman to coach a German title winning team.

One of the quickest players ever to play football, playing the game mainly with the outside of both feet, believing this enabled him to pass the ball quicker and more accurately.

Bibliography

'Reminiscences by Fred Spiksley', *Sheffield Football Special*, 1907
'Twenty Years of Professional Football by Fred Spiksley', *Thomson's Weekly*, 1920
'My Ideas About Football: Essentials for Success by Fred Spiksley', *London Evening News*, 1929
All of the above contributed significantly to *Flying Over An Olive Grove* and are known to be written by Fred Spiksley and not ghost written.

Sheffield Football

A History of Sheffield Football: Speed, Science and Bottom, 1857-1899 – Martin Westby
Blades and the Owls: A Pictorial History of the Sheffield Derby Matches – Keith Farnsworth
Football in Sheffield – Percy Young
From Sheffield with Love: Celebrating 150 years of Sheffield FC, The World's Oldest Football Club – Brendan Murphy
One Hundred Years at Hillsborough – Jason Dickinson
Sheffield Football: A History Volume One 1857 – 1961 – Keith Farnsworth
Sheffield United: Champions 1897–98 – Nick Udall
Sheffield Wednesday: A Complete Record 1867 – 1987 – Keith Farnsworth
Sheffield Wednesday: The Complete Record – John Brodie and Jason Dickinson
The Origins of Sheffield Wednesday – Jason Dickinson
The Romance of the Wednesday 1867–1926 – Richard A. Sparling
The Wednesday Boys: A Definitive Who's Who of Sheffield Wednesday Football Club, 1880–2005 – Jason Dickinson and John Brodie
Wednesday! – Keith Farnsworth

Football History

34 Italian Americans in Baseball, Basketball, Boxing, Football, Golf, Hockey, Racing, Soccer, Wrestling – Fausto Batella
50 Years of Football 1884–1934 – Sir Frederick Wall
Spaldings Official Soccer Guide 1920-21 and 1921-22
Arthur Kinnaird: First Lord of Football – Andy Mitchell
Anfield History, Liverpool: The first decade – Brian Belton
Association Football – John Goodall
Association Football – Ernest Needham
Association Football & The Men Who Made It – Alfred Gibson & William Pickford
Bayern: Creating a Global Superclub – Uli Hesse
Beastly Fury: The Strange Birth of British Football – Richard Sanders

Behind The Glory: 100 Years of the PFA – John Harding
England's oldest Football Clubs 1815-1889: A new chronological classification of early football – Martin Westby
Forgotten: Scotland's Former Football League Clubs – Robin Holmes
Founding Fathers: The Men Who Made Sunderland AFC Volume 1 and 2
Goal-Post: Victorian Football Vol 1 & Vol 2 – Paul Brown
Golden Boot: Football's Top Scorers – Mark Metcalf and Tony Matthews
Harold Hardman: From Meredith to Best, A Man of Football – Roy Cavanagh MBE and Carl Abbott
Herbert Chapman on Football – Herbert Chapman
History of Blackburn Rovers F.C 1875-1925 – Charles Francis
Inverting the Pyramid: The History of Football Tactics – Jonathan Wilson
Origins of the Football League: The First Season 1888/89 – Mark Metcalf
Morbo: the story of Spanish Football – Phil Ball
Mister: The Men who gave the World the Game – Rory Smith
Purnell's 1972 Encyclopedia of Association Football
The 1973 Hamlyn Book of World Soccer
The Ball Is Round: A Global History of Football – David Goldblatt
The FA Cup – Mike Collett
The Official Centenary History of the Football League and the Men Who Made It – Simon Inglis
Political Football: The Life and Death of Belfast Celtic – Barry Flynn
Pioneers of the North – Paul Joannou and Alan Candlish
The Dick Kerr's Ladies: The Factory Girls who took on the World – Barbara Jacobs
The People's Game: The History of Football Revisited – James Walvin
The Story of Association Football – J.A.H. Catton [Tityrus]
The Victorian Football Miscellany – Paul Brown
The Villa Way 1874-1944 – John Lerwill
Those Feet: A Sensual History of English Football – David Winner
Through the Turnstiles – Brian Tabner
The Tales of Ambrose Langley – Ambrose Langley
Ernest Needham: Prince of Half Backs – Ernest Needham

Biographies

Chaplin: His Life and Art – David Robinson
Chaplin: Stage by Stage – A.J Marriot
Colossus: The True Story of William Foulke – Graham Phythian
Football Wizard: The Billy Meredith Story – John Harding
Fred Karno: Master of Mirth and Tears – J. P. Gallagher
My Autobiography – Charles Chaplin
Pep Guardiola: The Evolution – Marti Perarnau
Remember Fred Karno?: The Life of a Great Showman – Edwin Alder
Steve Bloomer: The Story of Football's First Superstar – Peter Seddon
The Forgotten Legends: Manchester United Legends of a Bygone Age – C. Boujaqude, I. McCartney, F. Colbert

Club Histories

1 FC Nürnberg: Die Legende Vom Club – Christoph Bausenwein, Bernd Siegler and Harald Kaiser
All Shook Up: Bury's Amazing Cup Story 1900 & 1903 – Mark Metcalf
Bolton Wanderers FC: The Official History 1877–2002 – Simon Marland
Das Club Lexikon 1FCN – Christoph Bausenwein and Bernd Siegler
Der Club: 100 Jahre Fussball – 1. FC Nürnberg – Christoph Bausenwein, Bernd Siegler and Harald Kaiser
Everton FC 1890/91: The First Kings of Anfield – Mark Metcalf
Everton FC: The Men from the Hill Country – Tony Onslow
History of Blackburn Rovers 1875–1925 – Charles Francis
Manchester: The City Years – Gary James
The Clarets Chronicles: The Definitive History of Burnley Football Club 1888–2007 – Ray Simpson
Nottingham Forest – Philip Soar
Sheffield United Football Club: The first 100 Years – Denis Clarebrough
WHU – Tony Hogg

Complete Record Books

Birmingham City – Tony Matthews; *Blackburn Rovers* – Mike Jackson; *Derby County* – Gerald Mortimer; *Fulham* – Dennis Turner; *Glossop FC in the Football League* - Garth Dykes; *Manchester City* – Gary James; *Middlesbrough* – Harry Glasper; *Sheffield United 1889-1999* – D. Clarebrough and Andrew Kirkham; *Sunderland* – Mike Gibson, Rob Mason and Barry Jackson; *Wolverhampton Wanderers* - Tony Matthews

Who's Who Books

Arsenal, Aston Villa, Birmingham City, Everton, Liverpool, Manchester City, Stoke City, Wolverhampton Wanderers, WBA – Tony Matthews; *Derby County* – Gerald Mortimer; *Newcastle United* – Paul Joannou; *Manchester United, Notts County* – Garth Dykes; *Preston North End* – Dean Hayes; *Sunderland* – Garth Dykes and Doug Lamming; *Spurs Alphabet* – Bob Goodwin; *Barnsley FC* – Grenville Firth and David Wood; *English Football Internationalists and Scottish Soccer Internationalists 1872-1986* – D. Lamming

Social History

A History of Sheffield – David Hey
Durham Miners Millenium Book – Dave Temple
Liberty's Dawn: A People's History of the Industrial Revolution – Emma Griffin
Griffin Ruhleben: A Prison Camp Society – J. Davidson Ketchum
Ruhleben Camp Magazine
The Age of Empire: 1875–1914 – Eric Hobsbawm
The Making of the English Working Class – E. P. Thompson
To Ruhleben and Back – Geoffrey Pyke
Who Owns Britain – Kevin Cahill
Yesterday's Britain – Reader's Digest

Websites

Ancestry.com
The British Library
The National Archives
Adrian Bullock: The Sheffield Wednesday Archive
England Football Online

Newspapers

Gainsborough News; London Evening News; Sheffield Daily Telegraph (Inc. The Green-Un) Sheffield Evening Telegraph; Sheffield Independent; The Athletic News; The Cricket and Football Field; Thomson's Weekly Sports, El Mundo Deportivo.

Other Newspapers

Aberdeen Journal; Birmingham Daily Post; Black And White Budget; Daily Record; Derby Daily Telegraph; Dundee Courier; Dundee Evening Post; Edinburgh Evening News; Evening Dispatch; Football Post; Fulham Chronicle; Glasgow Herald; Hull Daily Mail; Illustrated London News; Illustrated Sporting & Dramatic News Kirkcaldy Guardian; Lancashire Evening Post; Leeds Mercury; Leicester Chronicle; Lincolnshire Chronicle; Lincolnshire Echo; Liverpool Mercury; Lloyd's Weekly Newspaper; London Standard; Manchester Courier; Manchester Guardian Morning Post; New York Times: Northern Echo; Northants Evening Telegraph; Nottingham Evening Post; Nottingham Guardian; Pall Mall Gazette; Reynold's Newspaper; Sheffield Star; Stamford Mercury; Sunday Post; Sunderland Daily Echo; Tamworth Herald; The Daily Graphic; The Era; The Express; The Express On Sunday; The Graphic; The Illustrated London News; The Sentinel (Stoke-on-Trent); The Sketch; The Sporting Life; The Times; Windsor Magazine; Western Morning News Wrexham Advertiser Yorkshire Post; York Herald.

Picture Credits

British Pathé, Brett Hudson, National Football Museum, Sheffield Library, Sheffield Wednesday Football Club, 1. FC Nuremberg Museum, Gainsborough Heritage Association, Spiksley Family, Andy George, John Brodie.

Index

Aberamon Athletic, 163
Accrington, 26, 36-9, 41-2, 48, 52, 57, 60
AFPU (Players Union), 187
Alaway, R., 28
Alcock, C., 5, 21, 65-6, 68
Alexander, C.L., 117-8
AIK FC 1902, 192-4
Aimer, G., 208
Allan, B., 47, 51, 56-7, 82, 97, 100
Almond, J., 120, 148, 174
Anderson, K., 131-2, 134
Angus, J., 28
Armitt, Mr (referee), 79-80, 99-100, 160
Arnott, W., 63, 65, 67-70, 81
Arridge, S., 99, 130
Arsenal, 9, 36, 76, 87, 110-11, 148, 152, 154, 156, 173, 175, 208-9, 224, 226-7
Aston Villa, 26, 52-3, 62, 64, 74, 76-7, 80, 84, 86, 88, 92, 94, 97-8, 102, 107, 115-6, 118-20, 137-8, 140, 151, 154, 158, 161-2, 174, 176, 180, 182, 184, 196, 208
Athersmith, C., 116, 119, 129-31, 180

Bach, P., 125
Baddeley, T., 159
Badenoch, G., 177
Baird, H.G.G., 77, 92
Barnes FC, 4, 22
Barnsley FC, 43, 112, 137, 176, 186
Barrett, B., 209, 223
Barrett, F., 154
Barron, J.H., 86-7
Bartley, T., 130
Bassett, B., 60, 61-4, 68-70, 72, 82-3, 85, 88, 91-4, 171, 192, 199, 208, 225, 230
Baugh, D., 104, 110

Beats, B., 104-5, 110-1
Beddingfield, F., 138
Beecham, E., 209-10
Begbie, I., 88
Bennett, W., 120-1, 123, 147-9, 171
Bentley, H., 79
Bentley, J.J., 78, 149, 163
Best, G., 127
Betts, B., 45-6, 51, 53-6, 80
Biggar, B., 177
Blackburn Rovers, 7, 22, 26, 30, 32, 43-4, 53, 60, 74-5, 77, 80, 94, 102, 116, 137, 151, 157, 161, 165, 196
Blackburn Olympic, 7, 22
Blessington, J., 88-90
Bloomer, S., 54-5, 71, 92-3, 107, 129-31, 133-4, 139-40, 171, 192, 199, 208, 225, 230
Bolton Wanderers, 26, 46-8, 53, 60, 79-80, 93, 99-101, 103, 120, 127-8, 131, 136-7, 139, 145-6, 150, 153, 158, 161, 210
Booth, C., 8, 20, 76
Booth, T., 129-30
Boyle, D., 82
Boyle, P., 125
Bradford City, 170, 173-4, 189, 196, 208-9
Bradshaw, T., 30
Brady, A., 28, 49-55, 75, 79, 82-3, 96-9, 104, 108, 110, 116-8, 122-3, 125, 136-7, 141-2
Brandon, B., 44
Brandon, H., 44-5, 51, 57, 77, 79-80, 82, 94, 97-101, 103-4
Brandon, T., 44-6, 51, 56-7, 74, 90, 137
Brash, A., 80, 99-100, 102, 104, 108, 110, 116-8, 120, 123, 142-4, 147-8

Brayshaw, T., 30
Brierley, J.A., 72, 143
Bristol City, 163
Brodie, J., 37
Brooks, J., 177
Brown, A., (Trinity) 60
Brown, B. (SWFC/Bolton), 47, 51-2, 101
Brown, J. (SWFC), 51
Brown, J. (Glossop), 167
Brown, R., 177
Buckley, C., 178
Bunyan, C., 189, 194
Burgess, H., 134
Burnett, J., 86
Burnley, 8, 26, 29, 40, 42, 53, 56-7, 64, 76, 80, 85-6, 96, 115, 139, 141, 170, 195-6, 213-5
Bury, 34, 96-7, 118-9, 137, 139, 142, 148, 150, 154, 161
Butler, J., 60-1

Cain, B., 46, 123
Cain, T., 96, 100-01
Caldicott, C., 10-3, 16-7, 23, 33, 39
Cambridge University, 4, 93-4, 223
Cameron, J., 184, 199
Campbell, J. (Celtic/Aston Villa), 63, 67-8, 116, 131, 133
Campbell, J. (Sunderland), 53, 124
Campbell, W., 117-8
Cassidy, J., 79
Catton, J.A.H., 72, 94, 106, 134, 158
Cawley, T., 43, 45-6
Celtic, 25, 49, 63, 65, 86, 89, 195, 197
Celtic Park, 88, 91, 94, 131-3, 159
Chadderton, W., 87, 99, 114
Chadwick, E., 60, 63, 67-8, 69-70, 72, 80, 82, 85, 88, 90-3, 188, 196
Chaplin, A., 208, 210
Chaplin, Charlie, 181, 185
Chapman, Harry, 146, 151-2, 154, 156-9
Chapman, Herbert, 146, 151-2, 154, 156-9
Chatt, B., 77, 107
Chelsea, 71, 108, 173, 175-7, 184, 201, 222, 236

Chesterfield, 142-5, 167, 172, 186
Chippendale, H., 85-6
Clare, T., 60, 88, 90-1
Clegg, C., 67, 69-70, 143, 221
Clegg, G. (senior), 143
Clegg, W., 143-4
Cliftonville FC, 85, 87, 92
Connolly, P., 36
Corinthians FC, 59, 74, 88, 92, 94, 115, 117, 130, 165, 184, 235
Cotterill, G., 65, 67, 69-70, 93
Cowan, J., 77, 94, 119, 131, 133, 182, 212
Cox, J. (Southampton), 96-7
Cox, Jack (Liverpool), 160
Coyne, S., 28-9
Crabtree, J., 85-7, 92, 119, 134, 181
Craig, T., 209
Crawshaw, T., 46, 80-4, 92, 97-8, 100-01, 104, 108, 110, 112, 117, 124-5, 137-8, 140, 143, 147, 149, 151, 157, 159-60
Crompton, R., 134, 165
Crystal Palace arena, 84, 102-14, 129
Crystal Palace FC, 106, 176

Dalton, B., 86
Dalton, J., 54
Dalton, W., 87
Darwen, 48, 76
Davenport, K., 47
Davis, H., 49, 51-2, 54, 75, 78, 82-4, 85-100, 102, 104, 108-10, 117-8, 125, 142
Davis, H. 'Joe Pluck', 146, 156-9, 161
Daw, E., 145
Dawson, M., 10
Dean, D., 192, 209
Derby County, 26, 42, 47, 54, 60-1, 75, 77, 80, 88, 92, 99, 102, 105, 127, 144, 147, 150, 161, 166, 170, 172, 176, 189
Devey, J., 77, 85-7, 107, 116, 119, 138
Dickinson, A.J., 37, 49-51, 56, 58, 103, 113, 142-4, 163, 165, 179
Doig, F., 53, 94, 98, 125, 131, 160, 167
Doyle, D., 88, 90-1, 131
Drummond, J., 131-3, 159

Dryburgh, W., 120, 125, 136-8, 142, 154
Ducat, A., 88, 90-1, 131
Dumbarton FC, 18-9, 24, 49-50, 80, 111
Duckworth, J., 35, 145
Dunlop, W., 51-2
Dunne, T., 104, 110
Dunning, B., 77
Dyer, R., 210

Eames, E., 177-8
Earp, F., 74, 76-8, 82, 84, 97-8, 101, 103-4, 110, 113, 117, 123-4, 137, 139, 140, 143-4
Edmonds, G., 208, 210
Elliott, A., 29, 32, 34-6, 39, 41, 76
England national team, 13, 18, 23, 35, 37-8, 43, 46-8, 56-8, 59-73, 76, 79-82, 85-94, 104-5, 108, 117, 119, 123, 125, 129-35, 140, 146, 151, 155, 159-60, 164-5, 170, 175-7, 182, 184, 188, 196, 205, 208-9, 218, 220-3, 227, 232-6
Everton, 13, 26, 29, 37, 49, 52, 54, 56, 60, 63, 74, 76, 80-3, 86, 88, 92, 94-5, 97, 99, 102, 108, 116, 118, 122-3, 129, 140, 144, 151, 154, 158, 160-1, 209, 224

Fantham, J., 164
FCN, 196-7, 212-6, 236
Ferrier, B., 80, 82, 104, 112, 116, 137, 144, 158, 160
Finnerham, J., 93
Fitchett, J., 146
Fitzpatrick, J., 92
Forman, F., 130-1
Forshaw, D., 210
Foulke, B., 54, 120-3, 129, 131, 137, 147-8, 154, 156-7, 171, 175
Fox, J, (referee), 117
Fulham, 174, 178, 208-11, 213, 223, 228
Fyfe, G., 177

Gaffikin, G., 86
Gainsborough Trinity, 1-41, 49, 53, 60, 65, 81, 117-8, 144-5, 165, 235
Gascoigne, P., 164

Gay, L.H., 63, 65, 67-8, 88, 90-1
Geary, F., 37, 144
Gemmell, D., 51
Gemmell, J., 45
Gettins, J., 117-8
Gibson, N., 131, 133
Gibson, W.K., 86-7
Giggs, R., 87
Gillies, G., 172
Glasgow FA, 53-4
Glossop North End, 140, 164-8, 169, 235
Goodall, A., 166-7
Goodall, J., 54-6, 60-1, 63-7, 86, 88-91, 93, 129-30, 134, 177-9, 213
Gosling, R.C., 63-4, 67
Grace, W.G., 115, 173
Greaves, J., 71
Griffiths, H., 104, 108-10
Grimsby Town, 15, 23, 30, 40, 42, 45, 145, 149, 153, 186
Gulliland, W., 88, 90

Haddow, D., 88-91
Hall, A., 51, 53
Hall (Trinity), 144
Hall, W., 71
Hallam FC, 4
Halliwell, 43, 46
Halse, H., 176
Hamilton, E., 100
Hamilton I. J., 63, 65, 67-8
Hannah, D., 98
Hardy, H., 209
Harris, J., 210
Harrison, A.H., 63-4, 69
Hedley, G., 148
Heeley FC, 22-3, 42
Hemmingfield, B., 136, 138
Henderson, C., 104-5, 109
Hendry, J., 57
Henrys, A., 41
Hepworth, N., 170-1
Hibernian, 18, 28, 177
Hickinbottom, E., 55

Hillman, J., 56, 99
Hill-Wood, S., 166
Hodgetts, D., 76, 85-7, 119
Holmes, B., 60, 63-4, 66, 68-9, 86-7
Holmes, J., 37, 45, 76-7, 113, 124, 143, 151
Holmes, J. (Southern United), 174
Holt J., 63, 66-9, 71, 85-9, 91, 99, 212
Horncastle Town FC, 8, 74
Howat, D., 36
Howell, R., 53-4, 75, 120, 123
Howlett, C., 8, 23
Hughes, A., 79
Hull City, 74, 160-70, 172-3
Husen, T., 194
Hutchinson, T., 83
Hyslop, T., 94, 129

Ibrox, 68, 70, 89, 155, 162
Iremonger, A., 210
Ireland national team, 59, 62, 65, 85-8, 91-2, 130

Jackson, PA, 90, 93-4
James, A., 226
Jenkyns, C., 130
Johnson, B., 103, 107, 124, 142
Johnston II, 86
Jones, D., 47, 60-1, 79, 100
Jones, E., 60
Jones, J.L., 130

Kalb, H., 213-4
Karno, F., 163, 181-5
Kaye, A., 120, 123, 125, 137, 140, 142
Keay, W., 97
Kelly, J., 63, 68-9, 92
Kelso, P., 208
Kent, H., 179
Kifford, J., 158
Kingscott, A., 35
Kinnaird, A., 5, 66, 70, 113
Kinsey, G., 63-4, 92
Kitchen, G., 163, 183
Kitchen, J., 158
Knighton, M., 165

Lafferty, H., 208
Lambie, W., 88-90, 94
Lang, J., 7, 43
Langley, A., 8, 74, 78-80, 82-3, 97-101, 103-4, 109-11, 117, 124-6, 140, 143-9, 151-2, 158-65
Layton, W., 144, 148, 159, 165
Leake, A., 161
Leamore, T., 182
Lee, G., 148
Leeds City, 169-72, 186, 235
Leicester Fosse, 170, 172, 186
Lerwill, J., 119
Lewis, B., 60
Lewis, J., 127, 146-8, 169, 189
Lilley, H., 38, 53, 54
Lilley, W. J., 54
Lincoln City, 16, 19, 22-4, 28, 30, 32, 35, 39-40, 121, 145, 149, 167-70, 172, 186, 232
Lindley, T., 134
Lindsay, B., 177
Lindsay, J., 63, 67, 69-70
Lipsham, 156-7
Little, T., 56
Liverpool, 48, 74, 81, 84, 116, 120-1, 123-4, 128-9, 136, 138-9, 147, 150, 152, 154, 157, 159-60, 167, 210
Lockwood Brothers FC, 43
Lockwood, Dr., 47, 149, 164
Lodge, L.V., 92-4, 117
London FA, 53
Lusitania, 198
Luton Town, 145, 178, 208
Lyall, J., 153, 158-61

Mace, J., 182
MacDonald, B., 140
Madden, J., 3, 18-25, 27, 49-51, 65, 89, 205
Maley, W., 63, 68-70
Malloch, J., 150-2, 154, 157, 159, 162
Malpass, B., 102, 104
Manchester City, 9, 93, 130, 150, 154, 165, 176, 184, 210, 229

Manchester United/Newton Heath, 28, 42, 49, 57, 75-6, 87, 118, 146, 165, 188, 209-10, 227
Marrison, T., 160
Massey, J., 54, 97-8, 100-1, 104, 109-11, 117-8, 120, 122-5, 140, 143, 145, 147-8, 153, 231
Massey, R., 112, 231
Matthews, S., 234
Maxwell, W.S., 131, 133
McAvoy, J., 149
McCabe, T., 39, 95
McCairns, T., 174
McColl, R., 162. 192
McCombie, A., 152
McCreadie, A., 88-9
McGeachan, J., 100
McGregor, W., 26-7, 53, 64, 70, 73
McInnes, T., 99
McIntyre, P., 154
McKay, W., 28
McKenna, J., 189
McLeod, W., 14
McLintock, T., 56
McLuckie, J., 150
McMahon, A., 63, 67-8, 70, 88-91
McNab, J., 210
McNeil, R., 98
McReynolds, J., 107
Mearns, F., 174
Mears G., 175-6
Meredith, B., 9, 130, 161, 164, 183, 187, 227
Middlesbrough, 16, 49, 60, 71, 81-2, 149, 157-8, 160-1, 196
Millar, H., 142-5, 147-8, 150
Millar, J., 98, 129, 131, 133
Miller, J., 74, 80
Milne, R.G., 86, 92
Milward, A., 60, 129
Mitchell, D., 63, 67-8, 91
Mooney, G., 225
Morgan, C., 172
Morgan, H., 125
Morgan-Owen, M., 130
Morley, E.C., 4

Morren, T., 170-1
Morris, E., 60
Mosforth, B., 43
Munday, H., 144
Murray, D., 167
Murrell, G., 41

Needham, E., 54, 97-8, 100-1, 104, 109-11, 117-8, 120, 122-5, 140, 143, 145, 147-8, 153, 231
Newcastle United, 124, 139, 141, 157, 159, 162
Nicol, T., 56
Norris, F., 75
Nottingham Forest, 48-9, 51, 53, 78, 101, 116, 118-9, 123, 130, 136, 139, 157, 159, 161, 212, 232
Notts County, 26, 34, 41, 48, 51, 54-5, 57-8, 73, 78, 80-1, 100, 105, 120, 140, 150-1, 154-5, 157-8, 162, 186, 210, 232
Nurse, D., 158

Oakley, W., 92-4, 117-8, 129, 131
Oliver, L., 223
Oswald, J., 57
Owen, W., 104-6

Pape, A., 210
Parry, C., 60, 75, 130
Paton, S., 47, 79, 100
Peden, J., 92
Pelly, F., 88, 90-1
Penn, F., 210
Pennington, H., 151, 157
Perkins, B., 151, 154
Perry, C., 60
Perry, T., 129-30
Petrie, B., 83, 97, 99-101, 104, 109, 117-8
Plymouth Argyle, 162
Ponsonby, J., 92
Popp, L., 213-5
Port Vale (Burslem) FC, 27, 36, 40, 48, 105, 144, 149, 167
Powell, J., 76
Prescott, T., 157

Preston North End, 26, 31, 44, 48, 60-1, 77, 80, 102, 119, 151, 172, 189
Price, Mr (referee), 140
Priest, F., 120-1, 147, 157
Prouse, W., 208-10
Pryce, J., 140, 142-3, 145, 148

QPR, 150, 178, 182, 196
Queen's Park, 63, 65, 67, 81, 89, 94

Raikes, G., 92, 93, 94
Rangers FC/Ibrox, 63, 68, 70, 89, 155, 162
Raybould, S., 157, 159
Reader, J., 82-3, 85-7
Redfern, J., 136-7, 143-4, 148
Reynolds, J., 60, 62-3, 66, 69, 71-3, 76-7, 86-8, 90-1
Richards, B., 83, 161
Roberts, C., 209, 227
Roberts IV, R., 60
Robertson, J., 121
Robertson, T. (referee), 133
Robinson, H., 21, 27
Robinson, J., 35, 55, 95, 129-31, 133
Roose, L., 154
Rose, B.C., 104
Ross, J., 77
Rotherham Town FC, 28, 30-1, 34, 54, 177, 186
Rotherham United, 112
Rowan, A., 49, 51-2, 54, 57
Ruddlesdin, H., 137, 143, 147, 159-60, 162
Ruhleben, 198-9
Russell, B., 44, 52

Sandilands, R., 68, 91, 93
Scragg, A. (referee), 123, 138
Schmitt, S., 213-4
Schofield, J., 34, 60-2, 91
Scotland, 5, 14, 18, 25, 27, 37-8, 49-51, 56-9, 61-3, 65-6, 68-73, 81-6, 88-93, 96, 105, 108, 129-35, 150-5, 159-60, 162, 184, 220, 223
Scott, J., 53

Scott, T., 86-7, 92
Sellar, W., 63, 65-8
Settle, J., 158, 160
Sheffield & Hallamshire FA, 53, 169
Sheffield FC, 4
Sheffield United, 38, 40, 42, 46, 53, 57, 63, 75, 81-2, 88, 96-7, 105, 116-7, 119-20, 123, 127, 130-1, 136, 140-1, 143-4, 152-7, 170, 174, 177, 186, 201
Sheffield Wednesday, 4-5, 29-30, 33, 34-58, 74-84, 95-128, 136-68, 174-5, 178-80, 184, 189, 196, 207-9, 223-4, 231, 234-5
Shelton, A., 58
Shillcock, W., 102
Sillars, D., 88-90
Simpson, G., 165
Simpson, V., 154
Small Heath/Birmingham City, 22, 47, 82, 94, 155
Smith, A., 131
Smith, G.O., 59, 88, 90-2, 94, 117, 129, 130-1, 133
Smith, Jim, 45, 51
Smith, Jock, 74
Smith, S., 92, 116, 119
Smith, T. (Gainsborough Trinity), 14, 21, 28-9, 161
Smith, T. (Man Utd), 210
Smellie, B., 63, 69, 70
Sobeck, H., 214-5
Somerville, J., 79, 100
Southampton St Mary's, 9, 96-7, 105, 148, 150, 177-8, 196
Southworth, J., 7, 53, 60, 75, 85, 88, 90
Spouncer, A., 60
Stanborough, M.H., 93, 117
Stanfield, O., 86-7, 92
Stewart, R.K., 86-7
Stoke, 26, 42, 45, 48, 57, 60-1, 77, 88, 91, 94, 96, 105, 116, 121-2, 127, 137, 141, 151, 154, 160, 209, 239, 240
Stubbs, F., 153, 158
Stuhlfauth, H., 213-5
Sudell, W., 26, 31
Sullivan, M., 174

Sunderland, 28-9, 42, 45-6, 49, 52-3, 70, 74-5, 77, 84, 92, 94, 96-8, 116, 123-7, 130-1, 140, 152, 154-5, 158, 160-2, 167, 177, 180, 224, 238-40
Sutcliffe, J., 60-1, 79-80, 93, 100-01

Tannahill, 79, 100
Taylor, E., 134
Taylor, J., 130
Tennant, B., 104, 108-11
Thickett, 122-3, 147-9
Thomas, J., 32, 34, 39, 41
Thomson, G., 44, 51
Tolpuddle, 2
Tonks, J., 102, 104-5, 109-10
Toone, G., 57
Topham, A.G., 117
Torrance, J., 208
Torrans, S., 86, 92
Tottenham Hotspur, 8, 13, 142, 152, 173, 184, 195-7, 199, 207
Townley, W., 33, 196, 212, 214
Traeg, H., 213-5
Trainer, J., 60-2, 130
Troup, A., 181
Turner, E., 92
Turner, P., 177-9

Ulyett, G., 54

Vaughan, J., 60

Waddell, T., 63, 67-8
Wales national team, 46, 48, 56, 59-63, 65, 85-6, 88, 91, 129-30, 235
Wall, F. (Sir), 72, 87, 189
Waller, G., 171
Walkerdine, H., 34-5, 39, 41
Wanderers, The, 102, 106
Watford, 177-9, 235
Watkin, A., 14, 81
Watkins, A.E., 130
Watson, T., 124
WBA, 26, 42, 47-8, 53, 56, 60, 63, 68, 75, 84, 86, 88, 91-2, 96, 102, 107, 116, 119, 127, 129, 136, 151, 154, 158, 161, 170-2, 180, 224, 239
Webster, J., 76
Webb, I., 158
Wedlock, W., 134
West, Mr (referee), 36, 121-2
Wharncliffe, Earl of, 114
Wharton, A., 31, 175, 184
Wheldon, F., 38, 116, 127, 129-32, 134
White, A., 196
Whitehouse, J., 174
Whitehead, J., 60, 85-7
Wieder, L., 213-5
Williams, B., 83, 129, 131
Wilshaw, D., 71
Wilson, A. (Sheffield Wednesday), 150, 152-4, 156-62, 164
Wilson, A. (Chelsea), 226
Wilson, H., 98, 124, 125, 131
Windridge, J., 176
Wolverhampton Wanderers, 26, 56, 60, 63, 71, 74, 78, 82, 96, 99, 102-5, 107-12, 116, 128, 137, 140, 150, 157-9
Wood, H 104-5, 107, 110
Wood, J., 174-6
Woodger, G., 176
Woodward, V., 71, 184, 222
Woolhouse, H., 45-6, 51, 54, 56, 76-9, 83
Wreford-Brown, C., 117, 130-4, 184
Wright, J., 100, 137, 139, 142-7, 150, 152
Wykes, D., 102

Zabo (stadium), 195-6, 212-3, 215
Zamora, R., 215, 218